CHILDHOOD REALITIES
Working and Abused Childern

CHILDHOOD REALITIES

Working and Abused Childern

Editor

Vinod Chandra

KALPAZ

ISBN: 978-93-5128-185-6

Price: ₹ 925/-

First Published 2016

Published by

Kalpaz Publications
C-30, Satyawati Nagar,
Delhi - 110052
E-mail: kalpaz@hotmail.com Ph.: 9212142040

Printed at : G. Print Process, Delhi

Cataloging in Publication Data--DK

Courtesy: D.K. Agencies (P) Ltd. <docinfo@dkagencies.com>

Childhood realities working and abused children / editor, Vinod Chandra.

pages cm

Contributed articles.

Includes bibliographical references.

ISBN 9789351281586

1. Child labor--India. 2. Child abuse--India. I. Chandra, Vinod, editor.

HD6250.I42C45 2016 DDC 331.310954 23

Contents

Darker Side of Abused Children

Preface

The genesis of this volume lies in the picture painted by the *"Study of Child Abuse: India 2007"* conducted by the ministry of women and child development, Government of India which shows an alarming statistics on various form of child abuse prevalent in India. The study was conducted on 12,447 children in thirteen States and consists of huge official data set at national level for the first time in independent India. Although the prevalence of child abuse in India was high, but it was not well-recognized due to over emphasis of practices of child care and protection in Indian families. The degree of child abuse reported in this study was of an eye-opener for policy makers, child rights activists, parliamentarians, academicians and researchers, etc. The study indicates that two out of every three children were physically abused and more than half of the children reported having one or more forms of sexual abuse. Out of total physically abused children 88.6 percent were abused by their parents. There is quite a high degree of emotional abuse and girl child neglect. Every second child reported facing emotional abuse. The study found that more than the strangers, parents and other care providers themselves are involved in the child physical and emotional abuse.

According to Census of India 2011, out of 1.21 billion population in India children's population (0-18 years) is 472 million. Out of this total child population 29 percent constitutes children in the age between 0-5 years while the share of children in the age between 6-12 years is 28 percent, children in the age between 11-15 years is 27 percent and in the age between 16-18 years is 16 percent. The statistics of child abuse in India is very horrible. According to an estimate, 69 % of children of this child population are abused in some or other forms. As per the International Labour Organization's *World Report on Child Labour 2015* and *CRY*'s recent analysis of the Census 2011, one in every 11 children in India is working. The total 5.5 million children are working in India in which 2.4 million are involved in hazardous work. There are at least 18 million children living on the streets in India. In a number of joint studies conducted by UNICEF and the Ministry of Labour, 75% of the children reported ill treatment by their employer and 91.7% children have reported poor facilities at work in Bangalore. In Mumbai 75.4 % reported ill treatment by superiors and 53.2 reported that facilities were poor. According to another estimate around half a million children are in prostitution in India.

During 2009-10, it was observed by the National Commission for Protection of Child Rights (NCPCR) that child abuse has risen to 763 cases which were only in two digits in 2007-08. It does not mean that the incidents of child abuse were less in 2007-08. However, the awareness of rights of child and child abuse was increased and complaints of incidents of girl child rape, trafficking, humiliation, corporal punishment, physical and mental torture were increased. Before the coming of these reports and public exposure of these startling facts about the magnitude and nature of child abuse in India, there was general atmosphere of public of denial of child abuse in Indian society. People were often denying the existence of child abuse and neglect although it was present in all its forms- physical, emotional and sexual. The common disbelief and subsequent denial to cover-up the family's reputation has made child sexual abuse an invisible crime in India from ages. In the name of family discipline, the child abuse in India has been practiced for long in the institutions like joint family system and patriarchy. There was no yardstick to measure and prevent. This is why the child abuse and neglect was minimally documented. When professionals like doctors, teachers, lawyers, judges, police, child care and/or social workers became aware of various forms of reported and unreported child abuse, a pressure group was formed to legally and socially deal with the issue of child abuse and exploitation in India. After a long discussion in the Indian Parliament and outside the Parliament, a bill was approved on 22 March 2012 to protect children below 18 from sexual abuse and to set up special courts for speedy trial of child abuse cases and to provide stringent punishment extending up to life term for offenders. The bill was converted into an Act, first of its kind, popularly known as the *Protection of Children from Sexual Offences Act* (POCSO).

Abused and working children are physically or psychological maltreated by an adult. Innocent and tender children are abused sexually through a variety of means within or outside family. Children working in family farms, small-scale family businesses, industrial units suffer with pain and toil. These children carry deep scars on their psyche which adversely affect the emotional and mental development of children. The harsh reality is that they do not have a normal childhood what other children have. Working and abused children's sufferings shape their childhood differently. The silent trauma in which they pass through has long lasting impact on their personality even when they become adults.

The present volume is an attempt to outline the grave areas of the child abuse and child labour in India. The book was planned in the year 2012-13 and diversity of disciplines came together to present an interdisciplinary perspectives on children's childhood in India. The editor of this volume owns the responsibility for an inordinate delay in bringing out this book who was engaged with so many administrative tasks over the last few years. In making this book possible, I would like to acknowledge the help and support rendered by Professor Vivek Kumar of CSSS, Jawahar Lal Nehru University, New Delhi. I convey my deep gratitude to him for his encouragement and support. I would also like to convey my sincere thanks to all my contributors who have shown their full patience for the publication. Some of the contributors have submitted their first draft in late 2012 and early 2013. Due to delay in publication they have accordingly revised their chapters and resubmitted it for publication. I am extremely thankful to the Gyan Books and Kalpaz Publishers, New Delhi for bringing out this book on our request. Finally, I owe my gratitude to my partner and co-researcher Aparna Tiwari for assisting me in editorial work and to Shri Anshumali Sharma, Chairperson of Child Welfare Committee, Lucknow for his constant motivation to complete this project.

Vinod Chandra
Editor

The Contributors

Atluri Satyanarayana is Professor of Sociology and founder head of the Sociology Department in Allahabad University. He has obtained his research training from Merrut University and taught in Merrut University and R.D. University Jabalpur before joining Allahabad University. He has done empirical research on child labour in Allahabad. He has published extensively in national and international journals and books.

Aparajita Chowdhury is Professor of Home Science in Berhampur University, Orissa. She has published on child labour and domestic labour in national and international journals.

Anshumali Sharma is Director of Childline Lucknow and Chairman of Child Welfare Committee Lucknow.

B.N. Prasad is Professor of Sociology at A N Sinha Institute of Social Sciences, Patna.

Divya Pande is Assistant Professor of English in Nari Post Graduate College of Lucknow University, Lucknow.

Helen R. Sekar is Senior Fellow at V.V. Giri National Labour Institute, Noida, an autonomous body of Ministry of Labour and Employment, Government of India. She is presently the Coordinator of the National Resource Centre on Child Labour (NRCCL). This work entails a mix of primary and secondary research, advocacy, training, planning, monitoring and evaluation. Her initial interest was Labour Administration and Labour Welfare. Dr. Sekar has implemented a number of research, training and Evaluation projects of the IILS, UNICEF, ILO-IPEC, ILO-IPEC-ABSBP and ILO-INDUS-CLP.

Mahaveer Jain was Senior Fellow at V.V. Giri National Labour Institute, Noida and has extensively worked on Child labour.

Rajiv Pandey has worked as scientist in Statistical Branch of Forest Research Institute, Dehradun Uttranchal. He also taught in the H.N. Bahuguna Central University, Garhwal as Associate Professor of Statistics.

Reeta Choudhury is a faculty member in the department of Home Science, S.B. Women's College, Cuttack, Orissa.

Sudip Chakraborty is Associate Professor of Economics in Ananda Chandra College of North Bengal University, Jalpaiguri West Bengal. He has contributed on child labour debate in various journals.

Simrit Kaur is a PhD in Social Work and recipient of many awards, including Maharishee Karve Memorial Prize from the President of India. She has worked extensively on child rights, both nationally and internationally. She has provided technical support at National and state level in policy formulation, planning and implementation of programmes relating to child rights, discriminatory practices against women/girls and Child Protection during Emergencies (CPE). Her expertise is also in undertaking research (qualitative) on gender issues. She has worked with UN and other non-governmental organisations. She is a Gold Medalist from the University of Delhi.

Shivali Sharma is Assistant Professor of Psychology in Institute of Behavioral Sciences Amity University, Lucknow Campus.

Sangeeta Sharma is a Guest Faculty of Political Science in Amity University, Lucknow Campus.

Tushar Singh is Associate Professor of Psychology in Banaras Hindu University, Varanasi.

Vanita Somvanshi is D.Phil in Psychology. She has completed her doctoral study on Social Psychological study of child labour from Allahabad University. She has worked in INDUS child labour project in *bidi* industry in Allahabad district.

Vishesh Kumar Gupta is Associate Professor of Sociology and head of the Post Graduate Department of Sociology in MH PG College Moradabad, Uttar Pradesh.

Vinod Chandra, recipient of Commonwealth Academic Staff Scholarship, has been awarded Ph.D. by the University of Warwick (United Kingdom). He is Associate Professor of Sociology in J.N.P.G. College, Lucknow, affiliated to the Lucknow University, Lucknow, India. In the International Sociology Association he holds the posts of Vice –President (Asia Region) for the period of 2014-18 in the Research Committee on Sociology of Youth (RC: 34). His interest in youth and childhood has involved him in the studies of sociology of children's work and placement of children in the division of labour. He is currently involved in a project to assess the impact of internet and other computer applications on Indian university and college youth.

Working Children's Childhood

1

Child Labour, Culture and Globalisation A Developmental Perspective

Vinod Chandra and Mahaveer Jain

In India, child labour was not an issue till late 1970. Later on with multiple struggles and efforts of governments (Central and the States) and the civic society, it became a labour issue from 1990 onwards, child labour became a part of developmental phenomena at the global level and also in India which linked with child education, child rights, child health, child abuse, child protection, child nutrition, child mortality, child bondedness and human rights due to the constant movement against child labour by several organizations (Jain 2008).

Child labour phenomenon awakened the social scientists in the 1990 to study it. Many studies are available to give deeper insights on child labour [Weiner 1991; Kearney 1997; Sharma *et al.* 2000; Cigno *et al.* 2002; Edmonds 2002; Jain 1996, 2002, 2003, 2004, 2006, 2006(a), 2006(b), 2006 (c) 2007, 2007(a); Lieten, G.K. 2006; Basu and Tzannatos 2003; Castle *et al.* 2002; Edmonds and Pavcnik 2005; Jan 2003; Zutshi 2006; Haider 2008]

In India, there is no systematic research to show the impact of globalisation on children in general and child labour in particular. There are certain empirical evidences that indicate the adverse effect of globalisation on children. Jan (2003), while discussing about the lives of former mill workers in Gujarat stated, "the future of the new generation of children is in jeopardy because their schooling is cut short. The parents can no longer afford to invest in improving the life chances of their children... the labour power of youngsters is a much needed source of income that has to be tapped at an early age". Increasing outsourcing of work to home based production reduced the wage levels as well as the social security systems and incidence of child labour has been increasing in such outsourcing home based productions (Jhabvala, 2003). Swaminathan (1998), based on a study conducted in Bhawnagar, Gujarat (a high income State of India), concluded that economic growth was associate with a significant increase in the number of child workers over the last 15 years. It was noted that children work at simple repetitive manual tasks that do not require long years of training or experience but the work is low paying, involves drudgery and is hazardous. The option of school is lost for most children.

Rayalu (2007) analyse that globalisation is a pronounced form of world capitalism which is working for the interests of globally organised multinational corporations. It is adversely affecting our Human Resources Development.

There are 211 million child labourers in the world. Ninteen per cent of the world's children live in India. There are 360 million (35.3 per cent) children in the age group of 0-14 years and the children in the age group of 5-14 constitute about 253 million (24.6 per cent), out of which 87 million children (34 per cent) are not attending educational institutions in the country. Total number of child labour in the country is 12.7 million, out of which 5.8 million are full time and 6.9 million are part time child labourers (Jain, 2007, 2008, 2008a).

The Government of India is consistently following a proactive policy to tackle the problem of child labour for the last 20 years, and has adopted constitutional, legislative and developmental measures with a view to eliminate child labour. Various initiatives, based on piece-meal approach, such as developing a project-oriented approach, regularization and prohibition of children's work in hazardous nature of work, fixing of hours of work, day and night work, right of the child to work and form unions, etc were taken by the government. This partial and essential approach to eliminate child labour resulted in formulating child labour projects by the State and other organizations under which legislative action and a number of projects to eliminate child labour were initiated. The outcome was the National Child Labour Policy, which covers 250 districts of the country (where child labour is endemic) to eliminate child labour. It covers approximately 0.35 million children out of 12.7 million as per the 2001 Census. If this project continues and we add 100 more districts, the problem of child labour will not still be completely eliminated. On the other side, non-governmental organizations and civic societies have been following a somewhat similar approach and strategy to eliminate child labour (Jain, 2006, 2008a).

Most of those who are working on the issue of child labour eradication are of the opinion that without change in the system, strong political will and poverty removal, nothing could be done on the issue of child labour. It was also felt that although child labour has been accepted as the developmental issue, yet it has been dealt with in isolation. Therefore, we have not achieved the expected results (Jain 2003).

Contrary to this, there are few successful examples on complete abolition of child labour in the country. The State

Government of Andhra Pradesh has achieved considerable success in this direction (Jain 2006, 2007). This has been possible because of their two important initiatives: (i) a new and clear definition of child labour i.e., any child between 5 to 14 years of age, who is out-of-school, is considered a child labourer; and, (ii) emphasis on convergence of services by various government departments and organisations to ensure enrolment of every child in school. These two initiatives generated a positive cultural change in the society towards complete abolition of child labour and became a model for the country (Jain 2008).

This chapter is the part of the study on Convergence of Services towards Prevention and Elimination of Child Labour: A Case Study of Nizamabad District of Andhra Pradesh State in India (Jain and Pande, 2008). The chapter presents the key learning from the field experiences during the study. In the year 1999-2000, there were 197,080 out of school from total population of 587,892 children in the District. It was found during the study that because of special movement by the State government departments to enrol children between 5-14 years of age in the school, there were only 7667 out of school children out of total population of 405,482 children (Sarva Shiksha Abhiyan, Nizamabad) in the district (Jain 2008). The study was aimed at documenting the whole process of enrolling 189,509 out of school children in educational institutions that made various *mandal*s and *gram panchayat*s child labour free. The following are the highlights of the present chapter:

- Positive changes in parents and children, officials at the local, *mandal,* district and community level as well as the impact on culture in general and the society as a whole.

- Movement against exploitation of children in the district and the State.

- Insights to all the under-developing, developing and developed countries on making exploitation of children an agenda for developing a positive culture, peace and future of the world.
- Reasons for the difference in the success rates of enrolment of children in school in different *mandals*.

ABOUT THE AREA

Andhra Pradesh State is fifth largest in area and fourth largest in population in India. There are 23 districts in the State and Nizamabad is one of them. There are 36 *mandals* in Nizamabad district. The total population of the district was 2.3 million and 82 per cent people live in rural areas. The total literacy rate was 53 per cent, out of which 66 per cent were male and 40 per cent were female. The main occupation of the people in the district is agriculture and *beedi* rolling (making of local cigarettes). A large number of migrants from the neighbouring areas migrate to the district to work as agriculture labourers at the time of sowing and harvesting of sugarcane and paddy crops. The majority of *beedi* workers were housewives belonging to backward class communities and schedule castes. Home was generally the workplace for *beedi* rolling. Children along with their parents were usually engaged in agriculture and *beedi* rolling (Jain and Pande, 2008).

In the year 2006-07, the total population of children in the district belonging to 5 to 14 years of age was 405,482 and 7,667 children were out of school. There were 3095 different categories of schools in the district and 1,787 of which were primary level (grades 1 to 5), 656 upper primary level (grades 6 to 8) and 622 high school level (grades 9 and 10). There were also 21 residential and 9 non-residential bridge course schools (objective of these schools was to provide a bridge for child labourers and out of school children to mainstream them in regular schools) (Jain and Pande, 2008).

In the Jakranpalli *Mandal*, there are 29 villages and 15 *gram panchayats*. The total population of the *mandal* was 43,636 out of which 7877 were Scheduled Caste and 3268 were Scheduled Tribe. The total literacy level in the *mandal* was 49 per cent out of which 64 per cent were male and 34 per cent were females. There are 25 primary, 22 upper primary and 11 high school level schools. In the year 2002-03, the total number of children was 9,310 belonging to the age of 5-14 years and 356 children were out of school. As a result of the convergence efforts at the district, *mandal*, and *gram panchayat* level by the Government officials, the *mandal* became child labour free on September 2006 (see Table-1 for details). Table-2 shows the year-wise number of children enrolled in schools for five years.

Table 1: Year wise distribution of child population (5 to 14 years) in school and out of school in the Jakranpalli Mandal

Year	*Total population*	*In school*	*Out of school*
2002-03	9310	8954	356
2003-04	9206	9016	190
2004-05	9136	9041	095
2005-06	9056	8995	061
2006-07 (before *Badi-Bata*)	9591	9568	023
September 2006	9591	9591	Nil

Note: *Badi-Bata* is the locally used term for Special Enrolment Drives Programme, which is being conducted every year in the month of July.

Table 2: Year-wise out of school children, children enrolled during the year and number of children left over

Year	*Out of school children*	*Enrolled*	*Left over*
2002-03	356	202	154
2003-04	190	166	024
2004-05	095	059	036
2005-06	061	058	003
2006-07	023	023	Nil

In Gandhari *Mandal,* there are 80 villages and 19 *gram panchayats.* The total population of the *mandal* was 49,951 out of which 6,430 were Scheduled Caste and 12,259 were Scheduled Tribe. The total literacy level in the *mandal* was 30 per cent out of which 41 per cent were male and 19 per cent were females. There were 76 primary, 12 upper primary, six high school level schools, and one residential bride course school in the *mandal.* At the time of the study, there were 514 out of school children in the *mandal* (see Table-3 for details).

Table 3: Year wise distribution of child population (5 to 14 years) in school and out of school in the Gandhari Mandal

Year	*Total population*	*In school*	*Out of school*
2002-03	12346	9716	2630
2003-04	11748	11629	119
2004-05	9639	9123	516
2005-06	11655	11399	256
2006-07	11610	11096	514

METHODOLOGY

In the year 2000, Veilpoor *Mandal* of Nizamabad District was declared child labour free by enrolling every child of the age group of 5 to 14 in the schools. To understand and analyse the process to make Veilpoor child labour free, a study entitled "Documentation of Strategies Adopted in the Process of Making Child Labour Free *Mandal*: A Case Study of Veilpoor *Mandal* of Nizamabad District of Andhra Pradesh, India" and was published in a form of book (Jain 2006b and 2007a).

1 This paper is the outcome of the opportunity given to the authors for doing the research project on "Convergence of Services towards Prevention and Elimination of Child Labour—A Case Study of Nizamabad District of Andhra Pradesh, India" by the V.V. Giri National Labour Institute. The authors are thankful to the Director of the Institute for providing facilities and encouragement. They are also thankful to Shri Shudhakar Rao, Community Mobilisation Officer, Nizamabad for his support during the field work for the study.

Study on Convergence of Services towards Prevention and Elimination of Child Labour: A Case Study of Nizamabad District of Andhra Pradesh[1] State in India was undertaken to document the sustainability and replicability efforts of the Veilpoor success after six years at the Nizamabad District. Two *mandals* namely Jakranpalli and Gandhari with different child labour statistics were selected for in-depth study. Jakranpally *Mandal* on achieving 100 per cent enrolments in schools was declared child labour free in September, 2006. The other *Mandal* was Gandhari, where 514 children were still out of school—having the highest number of out-of-school children in the district.

The *mandal*-wise list of out-of-school children was taken from the Sarva Shiksha Abhiyan (SSA), Nizamabad to select the two *mandals*. Based on different socio-economic and demographic status of the *mandals*, both the *mandals* were selected in consultation with the District Magistrate and other District level officials of Nizamabad (Sarva Shiksha Abhiyan 2006).

The research investigation was based on primary and secondary data. Primary data were collected by interviewing department heads/government officials of various departments/organisations at district, *mandal* and *gram panchayat* levels and also by interviewing village people. Four *gram panchayats* from Jankranpalli and five from Gandhari *mandals* were randomly selected for the *gram panchayat* level study. Primary data were also collected by attending village, *mandal* and district level meetings, personal observations and by preparing case studies. Secondary data were obtained from government records and available documents from the departments/organisations and also from Internet.

A questionnaire was prepared to collect primary data which included questions such as: status of child labour in the surrounding area, respondent/ department/organisation initiatives and experiences on child labour prevention and elimination, process of convergence of services to enrol every child in school by departments and officials, process of implementation of activities, respondent's perception on convergence of services, respondent's suggestions for making the work effective for prevention and elimination of child labour.

Secondary data covered government orders/ proceedings/circulars, data of in-school and out-of-school children of 5 to 14 years of age from 2002 to 2007, information about school infrastructure from 2002 to 2007, dates and agendas of meetings conducted at district, *mandal* and *gram panchayat* level by the officials, action plan prepared at various levels, strategies adopted, previous reports, and paper clippings.

A list of departments involved in prevention and elimination of child labour through convergence of services at the district level was prepared after thorough review of available documents. Twenty seven different departments were listed out. Total 91 respondents were interviewed at the district, *mandal* and *gram panchayat* level. In addition, 20 focused group discussions with government officials, school teachers, anganwadi workers, self-help-group members and village development committee members were organised to assess the opinion of the people on the process of convergence of services for prevention and elimination of child labour by enrolling every child in school. In all, case studies on 20 children were prepared. Ten were on those children who were earlier child labourers and now going to school and other ten were on those children who were still out of school (children for case studies were selected randomly). Case studies on additional initiatives by dedicated government officials to enrol every child in school and also motivate others to do the same were also prepared.

FINDINGS AND OBSERVATIONS

Convergence of Services with a Focussed Vision of Enrolling every Child in School

The process of convergence of services in district Nizamabad was initiated in the year 1999-2000. Departments/ organizations involved in the process did not receive any extra funds for this activity and they worked as a part of their normal roles, duties and responsibilities. Enrolling every child in school was the vision of all the departments/ organisations in the study area. The issue of child labour eradication was the main agenda of the district administration. It got priority over other agendas of the district. It was observed during the study that 19 departments/organisations at the district level worked on prevention and elimination of child labour through convergence of services by enrolling every child in school. These key departments/organisations were: Education Department, National Child Labour Project Society, Women and Child Welfare Department, Labour and Employment Department, *Panchayati Raj* Department, Social Welfare Departments (Scheduled Caste/Scheduled Tribes/ Backward Classes), Revenue Department and Rural Development Agency. These departments were working together during the survey, identification and rehabilitation of child labourers and out-of-school children. Nehru Yuva Kendra and the departments of Youth Welfare, Adult Education, Police, District Medical and Health, Disabled Welfare, Andhra Pradesh Road Transport Corporation, Public Relation and Municipal Corporation were other supportive organizations. The Sarva Shiksha Abhiyan (SSA) of Education Department has taken the lead with the missionary objective of enrolling every child of the age of 5 to 14 years in schools (G.O.Ms. No. 47, 2001).

Process of Convergence

Clarity of Roles and Responsibilities

Instructions/orders came from the State to the relevant department/ organisation and the District Collector. The District Collector conducted meetings with district level officials, communicated messages/orders to all organisations and discussed about the role of each organisation in effective implementation of the order.

Plan with Definite Time and Schedule

An action plan with fixed time schedule and target at the district level was prepared with the concurrence of all the district level officials. The plan was followed by all the *mandals*. There was fixed time schedule for holding meetings. Meetings were conducted whenever required for taking decisions, preparing plans, taking suggestions and seeking support from each other. However, meetings were held once in a month.

Better Implementation of Plan with Results

Instructions from the District came to the *Mandal* Education Officer (MEO), who circulated them to other departments at the *mandal* level. He also conducted meetings with *mandal* level officials. *Mandal* level plans were prepared with the participation of all the *mandal* level officials. The *Mandal* Education Officer was also responsible for holding meetings with School Head Masters to discuss and communicate the plan of action. School Head Masters further conducted meetings at the school level with teachers, Sarpanches and village people.

Regular Meetings and their Documentation

Orders/instructions from the district were communicated to the Jakranpally *Mandal* and also followed immediately. Meetings were held regularly. A total of 35 meetings were conducted in the *Mandal* from 2002 to 2006 (when the *mandal* was declared child labour free), in which the *Mandal* Education Officer, *Mandal* Revenue Officer and *Mandal* Parishad Development Officer participated. The officials from the Sarva Shiksha Abhiyan at the district level also participated. The main issues discussed in the meetings were: survey and identification of child labourers and out of school children, planning of special enrolment drives, planning of health camps for school children and enrolment of children in the schools.

Specific and Focussed Initiatives

Special enrolment campaigns and drives (locally called *Badi-Bata, Chaduvula Panduga)* to enrol out-of-school children in schools were conducted every year in the month of July for two weeks.

Door-to-door surveys to identify out-of-school children were conducted every year before special enrolment drives.

The data for out-of school children were up-dated before and after special enrolment drives and communicated to all departments.

Residential bridge course (RBC) schools, non-residential bridge course (NRBC) schools, *balya rakshak* (National Child Labour Projects) schools and alternative schools (primary school in the area where there is no other primary school within the radius of 1 km and having minimum 15-20 children) were run for child labourers and out-of-school children.

Table 4: Children enrolled in different types of schools in the district, year 2006-07

Type of school	*Number of schools*	*Number of children*
RBCs	21 (13 for boys, 7 for girls and 1 for disabled children)	1659
NRBCs	9	214
NCLP Schools	36	1672
ALS	52	1637
Mainstream Schools	2977	392,633
Total	**3095**	**397,815**

There was no Residential Bridge Course (RBC) school in the Jakranpally *mandal* at the time of the study. In the year 2002-03, there was one RBC school on the persistent demand of the area. It was opened in the Santosh Nagar where children were engaged in stone crushing. The RBC was closed when these children were mainstreamed. One RBC school for boys with 50 children enrolled was running in Gandhari. There were 21 RBC schools in the district in which 1,658 children were enrolled. Table-4 gives details of children covered by different educational institutions in the district.

District level officials, RBC school in-charge and school teachers were responsible to mainstream the children of RBCs, NRBs, NCLP schools and Alternative Schools in Government schools and the Schools of the District Rural Development Agency. The officials give prior information about this to each other and preparations for admitting the children into government schools are made before the beginning of the academic year.

Scheduled Caste, Scheduled Tribes and Backward Class Welfare Departments were providing hostels facilities to those children of RBCs, NRBs, NCLP schools and Alternative Schools, who had taken admission in the mainstream schools. Officials of Education Department facilitate this work.

Health check up programmes for children were also organised regularly in the Jakranpalli *Mandal*. Health camps were organized twice a year for school children jointly by the SSA, District Medical and Health Officer, District Blind Welfare Society, District Rural Development Agency and Disabled Welfare Department.

Influence of Child Labour Free Veilpoor Mandal

Jakranpalli *Mandal* is situated on the boarder of Veilpoor *mandal*. It was experienced that the complete abolition of child labour in Jakranpalli *Mandal* was the result of influence from the Veilpoor *Mandal*. Veilpoor *Mandal* was recognised at the national and international level as the first *mandal* in the country declared child labour free on 2nd October 2000. The achievement was due to the missionary zeal and visionary approach of Government officials. The officials, who worked in the Veilpoor movement, were also acknowledged by district, state and national bodies. This generated positive flow of energy and became the source of inspiration for others. The *Mandal* Education Officer (MEO) of Jakranpalli was earlier MEO in Veilpoor, who had the spirit and also the experience, which was used to make Jakranpalli *Mandal* child labour free.

Proximity of the *Mandal* to the District Headquarters

Jakranpalli *Mandal* is 25 km from the District Headquarters on a main highway. Because of the proximity of the *Mandal* to the district headquarters, the officials from the district administration undertook frequent visits to the area to supervise the work and give guidance to the concerned *Mandal* officials.

On the other hand, Gandhari *Mandal* is 45 km from the District Headquarters and is one of the very remote areas of the district. District Officials did not make frequent visits to the area to supervise the work.

Culture of Teamwork and Mutual Acknowledgement

It was observed that the officials of the Jakranpalli *Mandal* had good rapport among themselves at inter-departmental and intra-departmental levels due to regular meetings which resulted in empowerment of individuals and departments. The officials were quite informal and free with each other. Messages/instructions were communicated clearly and timely to each other. They acknowledged the participation of officials and initiatives taken by them at departmental/ organizational or individual level. They agreed that the objectives and goals could have never been achieved without each other's cooperation and team work.

On the other hand, there seemed to be less teamwork and mutual cooperation in Gandhari *Mandal*. The reason was lack of supervision and motivation by district officials. The officials were also not interested in the posting in the area due to its remoteness and distance from the district headquarters. Therefore, this *mandal* took time to become child labour free *mandal*.

Culture of Children's Education

There were more educational facilities available in the Jakranpalli *Mandal* compared to Gandhari *Mandal*. There were 58 primary, upper primary and high schools in the *Mandal*. The ratio between primary, upper primary and high school in the *mandal* was about 2:2:1 respectively. On the other hand, there were 95 primary, upper primary and high schools in Gandhari *Mandal*. The ratio between primary, upper primary and high school in the *mandal* was about 13:2:1 respectively.

People in Jakranpalli *Mandal* were aware about the importance of education to their children. A resolution was passed in all the *Gram Panchayats* of the *Mandal* that the work would only be given to those families whose children would be in school. This resolution was basically for migrant labourers. Employers were given the responsibility for implementation of the resolution. The Village Development Committees in the *Mandal* were keeping a constant vigil that all children in the village go to school regularly. *Akshra Abhasam* (Saraswati pooja on the first day of the first class students) was being celebrated at the beginning of the academic session with the participation of the headmaster, teachers, Sarpanchs, parents, local people and children to welcome new children to the school. People of these *mandals* have seen the role of education of children in creating adult employment, manifold increase in wages of adults and respect extended by educated children to their parents.

Culture of Ownership

A feeling of ownership of this mission of sending every child to school was found among officials in the Jakranpalli *Mandal*. The reason was regular visits to schools by the MEO to motivate the concerned officials, supervise the work and give on the spot guidance. This further created good rapport among officials (See Boxes 1 and 2 below).

Box-1

Enrolment of Shyam in school

A boy named Shyam of Santosh Nagar village in Jakranpalli *Mandal* was found grazing cattle by the MEO of Veilpoor *Mandal*. The officer immediately informed the MEO Jakranpalli. The Jakranpalli MEO reached on the spot, talked to the boy and went to his home, gave counselling to his parents, and enrolled him in school.

Box-2

A new beginning for Gangalakshmi

In Kaligote Village (Jakranpalli), a girl named Gangalakshmi got married when she was very little. When she was 12 years of age, one day her in-laws came to take her away. She did not want to go with them; she could not think at that moment how to save herself. She ran towards her school, and cried in front of her school headmaster and told her the whole incident. She also said, "I do not want to stay in my home, I want to study further. Please enrol me in some other school, far from my home. After hearing Gangalakshmi, the headmaster talked to the Community Mobilisation Officer (CMO), Nizamabad. The CMO came to the village. The headmaster, teachers and the CMO went to her home, met with her parents and in-laws and gave counselling. The officials solved her problem. They enrolled her in the Dichpalli Residential School, which was 15 km from her home. She studied there for a year. At the time of the study, she was studying in grade 9 and she was a district level volleyball player.

Culture of Celebrating Successes

As soon as any *gram panchayat* achieved 100 per cent school enrolment, it was declared a "Child Labour Free *Gram Panchayat*" with a celebration with officials from other *gram panchayats, mandal* and district level organisations. At the same time an oath was also taken by all the officials and village people not to support employment of child labour. When entire *mandal* became child labour free in September 2006, it was declared "Child Labour Free *Mandal*" with a celebration. "Child Labour free *Mandal* and child labour free *Gram Panchayat*" posters were posted in important places, such as the *Mandal* Resource Center, school buildings, main entrance of all villages, *gram panchayat* offices, etc.

CONCLUSIONS

The results clearly showed that complete eradication of child labour can be successfully achieved by:

1. A clear and simple definition of child labour that "any child between 5 to 14 years of age, who is out of school, is a child labourer". This definition became the central point of convergence of services and to set the goals at universe level.

2. Convergence of services is only possible when all those who are involved in the process realize that convergence starts from within. A person becomes a change agent with internalization of the process and starts taking child labour eradication as his/her personal responsibility. This leads to motivating others

which extends further to an organizational level. This leads to the institutionalisation of the convergence process. This process result in collective work, stimulating innovation, sharing of experience, working on feedback, sharing positive outcomes with each other and with outsiders, acknowledging and celebrating success, and multiplying and enhancing the approach.

3. The by-product of the process for eradication of child labour benefit adult labourers by getting three to four times higher wages which resulted improvement in their living standard.
4. This convergence model can be replicated to other places in the world. With this approach of convergence and clear definition of child, various other *mandal*s of Nizamabad District are in the process of becoming child labour free by the year 2006-07. There were three *mandal*s where the number of out-of-school children was 25 to 50 and 14 *mandal*s where the number of out-of-school children was in between 50 to 100 (SSA, 2006).
5. This study also reveals that eradication of child labour could be successfully achieved without addressing the issue of poverty. It could be addressed directly with a clear vision of enrolling every child in school.

Presently, there is no uniform and clear definition of the term child labour. There is a need to work together for the eradication of child labour at global level, which would only be possible with a common definition of child labour.

The Jakranpalli *Mandal* model of complete eradication of child labour could work as a nucleus from which the movement can extend to adjoining *mandal*s, districts and States. It would be worthwhile to implement this model at the global level.

REFERENCES

Basu, Kaushik and Tzannatos, Zafiris, 2003. *Child Labour and Development: An Introduction.* The World Bank Economic Review, Vol. 17, No. 2, pp. 145-146.

Basu, Kaushik and Tzannatos, Zafiris, 2003. *The Global Child Labour Problem: What Do We Know and What Can We Do?* The World Bank Economic Review, Vol. 17, No. 2, pp. 147-173.

Castle, R., Chaudhri, D.P. and Nyland, C., 2002. *Child Labour in South Asia: Domestic and International Initiatives including ILO and WTO.* The Indian Journal of Labour Economics, Vol. 45, No. 3, pp. 497-516.

Cigno *et al.* 2002. *Does Globalisation Increase Child Labour*? IZA Discussion Paper No. 470, April. Cited from Zutshi Bupinder (2006).

Cigno, Allesandro, Furio Rosati and Lorenzo Guarcello, 2002. *Does Globalisation Increase Child Labour? World Development,* Volume10, No. 9, pp. 1579-89.

Edmonds Eric V. 2002. *Globalisation and Economic of Child Labour* (A version of this essay was published as "Reduzieil die Globalisiering die Kinderarbiet?" in Neve Ziircher Zeitung, February 23/34. p 29. (Darmonth College). www.dartmonth.edu.

Edmonds, Eric V. and Pavcnik, Nina, 2005. *Child Labour in the Global Economy.* Journal of Economic Perspectives, Vol. 19, No. 1, pp. 199-220.

Education Department Andhra Pradesh. 2003. *Every Child in School—Reaching the Unreached—Our Community.* Government of Andhra Pradesh, Hyderabad, India.

Government Order Ms. No. 47. 2001. *Transfer of Subject "Child Labour" from Women Development. Child and Disabled Welfare Department to School Education Department.* Orders from Chief Secretary's Office to Women Development, Child and Disabled Welfare Department, Government of Andhra Pradesh, Hyderabad, India. 25th January.

Haider, Mostafa, 2008. *Recognising Complexity, Embracing Diversity: Working Children in Bangladesh.* South Asia Research, Vol. 28(1), pp. 49-72.

Humphries, Jane, 2003. *Child Labour: Lessons from the Historical Experience of Today's Industrial Economies.* The World Bank Economic Review, Vol. 17, No. 2, pp. 175-196.

Jain, Mahaveer, 1996. Child labour: A Growing phenomenon in India. Poverty and Employment Situation and Strategies for the Future by Institute of Applied Manpower Research, New Delhi 1996, pp. 295-318. Summary of this paper also published in The *Social Engineer-A Journal of International Perspective on Development* 1996 Vol. 5, No. 1, 58-69.

Jain, Mahaveer, 2002. *Worst Forms of Child Labour: A discussion document.* Presented at the National Trade Union's workshop on Worst Forms of Child Labour jointly organized by AITUC, CITU, HMS and INTUC at Delhi, India.

Jain, Mahaveer, 2003. *Lessons Learnt from Field: A Case Study of Veilpoor Child Labour Free Mandal. Paper* presented in the Workshop on Child Labour organized by YMCA, New Delhi, December 15-16, 2003

Jain, Mahaveer, 2004. *Elimination of Child Labour: A Realistic Preposition.* Paper presented in National Seminar on Globalisation and Child Labour, March 11-12, 2004. Noida: V.V. Giri National Labour Institute, India.

Jain, Mahaveer, 2006. *Globalisation and Labour Market in India: Social Issues, Working Environment and Child Labour.* Paper presented in a seminar on Global Labour Market: Indian Perspective for Norwegian Parliamentarians and also presented at National Workshop on Social – Economic Issues in Child Labour organized by Mahatma Gandhi Labour Institute, Ahmedabad, India from March 16-17, 2007.

Jain, Mahaveer, 2006a. *Insights on Child Labour.* New-Delhi: Manak Publications, India.

Jain, Mahaveer, 2006b. *Complete Abolition of Child Labour: A Possibility.* New Delhi: Manak Publications, India.

Jain, Mahaveer and Sangeeta Saraswat, 2006. *Child Labour from Different Perspectives.* New-Delhi: Manak Publications, India.

Jain, Mahaveer, 2007. *Train-the-Trainer—A Manual on Child Labour.* Noida: V.V. Giri National Labour Institute, India.

Jain, Mahaveer, 2007a. *Bal Shram Ka Sampuran Unmoolan*. New Delhi: Manak Publications, India.

Jain, Mahaveer, 2008. *Convergence towards Prevention and Elimination of Child Labour: Gaps and Challenges*. Presentation at the Workshop on Convergence of Services on Child Labour: Gaps and Challenges organised by International Labour Organisation, New Delhi, India, February 11, 2008.

Jain, Mahaveer, 2008a. *Child Labour in India: An Overview*. Presentation at the Workshop on Child Protection and Education organised by UNICEF India Country Office, New Delhi, India, February 6, 2008.

Jain, Mahaveer and Pande, Suman, 2008. *Convergence of Services towards Prevention and Elimination of Child Labour—A Case Study of Nizamabad District of Andhra Pradesh, India*. Noida: V.V. Giri National Labour Institute. Unpublished.

Jan, Breman, 2003. Coping With Impoverishment. Seminar No. 531. November 2003. A Symposium on Livelihood Struggles of the Informal Workforce. pp. 62-64. Cited in *Globalisation, Development and Child Rights* edited by Kailash Satyarthi and Bupinder Zutshi, published by Shipra Publications.

Jhabwala Renana, 2003. *Liberalisation and Women*. Seminar No. 531, November 2003, A Symposium on livelihood struggles of the informal workforce. pp. 34-40.

Kearney, Neil Bergama, 1997. *Globalisation and child Labour*, General Secretary, International Textile, Garment and Leather Workers' Federation, International Labour Organisation, Geneva.

Levison, Deborah; Hoek, Jasper; Lam, David and Duryea, Suzanne 2007. *Intermittent Child Employment and its Implications for Estimates of Child Labour*. International Labour Review, pp. 217-251.

Lieten, G.K., 2006. *Globalisation and Child Labour*: Possible Consequence. In National Seminar on Globalisation and Child Labour. NOIDA: V.V. Giri National Labour Institute, India.

Rayalu Yugal, 2007. *Impact of Globalisation on the Working Class in India*. Paper published in New Age, November 18-24, 2007. pp. 8-9.

Sarva Shiksha Abhiyan, 2006. *A Document Material for Elimination of Child Labour in the Nizamabad District to Achieve 100 per cent Enrolment.* Department of Education, District Nizamabad, Andhra Pradesh, India.

Satyarthi Kailash and Zutshi Bupinder, 2006. *Globalisation, Development and Child Rights.* New Delhi: Shipra Publications. pp. 1-18.

Sharma, Alakh N., Sharma, Rajeev and Raj, Nikhil, 2000. *The Impact of Social labeling on Child Labour in India's Carpet Industry.* New Delhi: Institute of Human Development. Paper presented at the National Seminar on Globalisation and Child Labour, V.V Giri National Labour Institute, India.

Swaminathan M., 1998. *Economic Growth and the Persistence of Child Labour: Evidence from Indian City.* Indira Gandhi Institute of Development Research. Reprint No. 304.

Weiner, Myron, 1991. *The Child and the State in India: Child Labour and Education Policy in Comparative Perspective.* Oxford University Press, Delhi. pp. XIV, 213.

Zutshi Bupinder (2006). *Globalisation and Child Labour linkages in India: A case study of carpet and the Garment/Apparel Industry.* In Globalisation, Development and Child Rights, (eds) Kailash Satyarthi and Bupinder Zutshi, Shipra Publications.

2

Household Characteristics: A Breeding Conduit to Child Labour

Atluri Satyanarayana and Vanita Somvanshi

The household characteristics of child labourers help in describing, explaining and comprehending the stratum from which child labourers are drawn. As child is part of the larger social context, hence the phenomena of child labour cannot be understood by detaching it from its roots. The contextual background which surrounds the child or in which the child is embedded needs to be taken into cognizance. In their parochial perspective, these characteristics, individually as well as cumulatively, set-up conditions congenial for the birth of child labour. As these are vibrant in facilitating the pervasive existence of child labour in our society, it becomes impetrative to elucidate each of these household characteristics so as to comprehend the phenomena of child labour in totality. Some of the household characteristics, which form the fertile bed for the germination of child labour are - caste and religion of the household, size and type of the household, family assets, parental/traditional occupations, and educational profile of the households. An attempt has been made in this paper to give an account of the status of each of these characteristics at national and regional level as well as according to different work sectors. However, the literature and data covering these various aspects is not exhaustive as this is not the intention of the paper but aim is to annotate their contributions in creating espousing conditions for the birth of the phenomena of child labour. This forms the nucleus of the present paper around which the realistic discussion revolves.

Religion and Caste

Religion and caste are significant factors in explaining variations in the incidence of child labour. Child labourers in India generally belong to two religious communities i.e., Hindus and Muslims, and a very few of them belong to Christian, Jain, and Sikh communities. Among Hindus, child labourers, mainly belong to the cumulatively deprived sections of the society, like Other Backward Castes, Scheduled Castes and Scheduled Tribes (Nangia, 1987; Sahoo, 1990; Tripathi, 1989; UNICEF, 1995). Among Muslims, child labourers mainly belong to lower status groups (Khan and Hasson, 2001).

Caste has a determining role in the incidence of child labour. In the past, organization of Indian society was rather simple. The social structure consisted of various caste groups, which were organized, in hierarchical order. Each caste pursued a certain occupation depending on their position in the hierarchy and any transgression of its occupational boundaries was not socially permitted. It was an ascribed and particularistic society, which ruled out normatively all upward social mobility. This made aspirations and motivations of lower caste people, in the realm of social and economic achievements, inert and static (Singh, Kaura, and Khan, 1980). Thus, social forces, such as low birth status, seal the fates of many children.

Dalit (Scheduled Castes) and *Adivasi* (Scheduled Tribes) communities are amongst the most marginalized sections of the contemporary Indian society. Historically, these communities have suffered from exclusion. Unfortunately, even in the post-independence India, these communities continue to be economically marginalized and still suffer from discriminatory social practices. Individuals with low caste status are far more likely to be employed as low-paid, low-status agriculture labourers earning less than other groups with equal level of education (World Bank, 2001). Therefore, children are likely to be an extremely vulnerable group within such communities.

The extant studies indicate that an overwhelming majority of child labourers come from communities and groups that belong to the lower rungs of the society i.e. Scheduled Castes, Scheduled Tribes, Other Backward Classes and minorities, particularly Muslims (Sahoo, 1990; 1995). According to a study, out of 228 million, 92 million belonged to families below poverty line, of which half the proportion belonged to Scheduled Castes and Tribes (Tripathi, 1989). Nangia (1987) observed that comparatively a higher proportion of Scheduled Caste children work at a younger age for their own and for their families' economic support.

However, there has been change in the organization of the present scenario of the society. The caste restrictions are breaking down under the impact of a democratic polarity and the social group relations are undergoing radical transformation. Thus, people even from the upper castes are joining labour market. Laskar (2000) noted social stratification among Muslim child labourers in lock industry in Aligarh city. Workers comprised of both upper and lower *'biradri'* (caste) - upper caste children join work because of loss of economy and power, while lower class, as a result of historical backwardness. Thus, with changing scenario of the society, child work is no longer restricted only to lower castes but also to the upper castes.

There are spate of studies, which have explored distribution of child labourers according to different religions and castes in different work sectors. For instance, Pati and Swain (1991) found that amongst children working in canteens, garages, and shops in Bhubaneswar, most of them were Hindus (94.4 per cent) followed by Muslims (3.2 per cent) and Christians (2.4 per cent). Behura and Behura (1991) in their study in Bhubaneswar on 165 child labourers working in low-profile restaurants, small hotels, garages, rickshaw pulling, and shoe-polishing, found that most of them (95 per cent) were Hindus and only 5 per cent were Muslims. Out of the total Hindu child workers, proportion of Other Backward Castes was nearly 37 per cent, Scheduled Castes was about 25 per cent and Scheduled Tribes was 21 per cent. Mustafa and Sharma (1996) also found that out of 64 children working as domestic servants in certain localities of Delhi, almost all were Hindus with an exception of one Christian. Sooryamoorthy (1998) observed that nearly two-thirds of children working in Kerala as domestic help or in shops, hotels, or in factories belonged to backward sections of Hindu communities- Scheduled Castes and Tribes, and Other Backward Castes.

The study on child labourers in glass-industry of Ferozabad (Mishra and Pande, 1996) reveals that majority of them were Hindus (87 per cent) and a minor proportion was from Muslim (11 per cent) and other religious communities (2 per cent). Amongst Hindus, the proportion of Scheduled Castes was more (47.8 per cent) than the Backward Castes (33.6 per cent) and upper castes (7.6 per cent). Even, Karunanidhi in 2000 found on the basis of their religious affiliation, i.e. Hindus and Muslims, that the ratio of child labourers employed in the *beedi* industry in North Arcot district of Tamil Nadu was 3:1. Mishra and Pande (1996) too found that about 85 per cent of child labourers in carpet weaving in Mirzapur were Hindus and only 15 per cent were Muslims. Majority of them were from Other

Backward Castes (45.5 per cent) and Scheduled Castes (37.7 per cent). However, proportion of Scheduled Tribes was less than 1 per cent. In the knitting industry of Amritsar, Dhillion and Arora (2001) found that a significant proportion of child labourers belonged to Scheduled Castes and Scheduled Tribes (more than 50 per cent) and a lesser proportion (28 per cent) to upper castes. However, 22 per cent of child labourers did not reveal their caste group affiliations. In diamond industry of Surat, Saradhi (1998) found that nearly 99 per cent of the child labourers were drawn from Hindu communities and that too from upper castes i.e. about 61 per cent.

There are few industries like lock and brassware that are dominated mainly by Muslim and Scheduled Caste children (Burra, 1987). The study by Kumar (2000) also reveals similar findings. Burra (1989); Kumar and Biswas (1992) found that around 75-80 per cent child labourers in the lock industry were Muslims and the remaining were Hindus, especially Scheduled Castes. Khan and Hasoon (2001) too observed the preponderance of Muslim and Scheduled Caste children in the lock industry of Aligarh. Chander's study (2004) on 315 children working in shops, and as self-employed hawkers in Aligarh city, revealed that majority of them were Muslims (70 per cent) followed by Hindus (29 per cent) and other religions like Sikhs, Christians, Jains (less than 1 per cent). Predominance of Muslim child labourers (92.29 per cent) was also found in brassware industry of Moradabad (Kumar, 2000) and they mainly belonged to Backward Castes within Muslim communities. Even the gem polishing industry of Jaipur constitutes of nearly 85 per cent of Muslim child labourers (Kruijtbosch 1996; Indian Institute of Health Management Research, 1992). The study by Lal (1998) also reveals that a higher proportion of child labourers (97.3 per cent) in the gem polishing industry belonged to Muslim communities and only 2.7 per cent were Hindus. Similarly, Manimekalal (2001) found that most of the child labourers in *beedi* rolling, gem polishing, matchstick making, etc. were Scheduled Castes or from Other Backward Communities. Even Burra (1995) reported that amongst children involved in pottery work at Khurja, nearly 70 to 80 per cent of them were Muslims and rest were Hindus, belonging mainly to Scheduled Castes.

Regardless of the place and nature of employment, Thorat (1999) found that the proportion of child labourers (excluding those engaged in household chores) was two-three times higher among Scheduled Castes and Scheduled Tribes than the rest of the population at the national level. As a matter of fact, the share of Dalit and Adivasi children among all the working children (i.e. 41 per cent) was far in excess of their representation (i.e. 31 per cent) in the total child population. A micro study in Andhra Pradesh (Reddy and Rao, 1999) reports highest incidence of child labourers amongst Scheduled Castes followed by Scheduled Tribes, Backward Castes, and other castes. This was also evident in the study by Duraisamy (1997) who concluded that Scheduled Castes\Scheduled Tribe groups contributed more to child labour participation rates in comparison to other social groups. This was evident in almost all the states in India.

Thus, from these studies it can be summarised that most of the child labourers belong to Hindu communities, with the exception of those working in industries like pottery, lock making, brassware industry, and gem polishing, which is dominated mainly by Muslim child labourers. Hindu child labourers preponderantly belong to Scheduled Castes, Scheduled Tribes, and Other Backward Castes, working in tea-stalls, garages, shoe shining, and glass industry. Upper caste child labourers dominate certain industries, where specialized skills are transmitted down the generations within the family, for example, in diamond cutting. However, even among the Muslim child labourers most of them were drawn from Backward Castes and other economically disadvantaged sections. Therefore, it can be reckoned from the aforesaid discussion that child labourers, irrespective of their religious affiliations are drawn basically from the weaker sections of the society like Scheduled Castes, Scheduled Tribes, and Other Backward Castes. Hence, children of cumulatively deprived sections dominate the child labour market.

Family Size and Type

Size of the family has influence on the number of working children. The individual couples while raising their family in their own interest do not care for what would have been better for a society as a whole. As children in poor families are expected to provide security and support to their parents, they start working at an early age. Children are looked upon as an insurance against future hunger. They can be relied upon in difficult times to work and contribute their income to the family (Kumar, 2000). They launch an unfettered procreation scheme, which understandably seems opposed to socially optimum level of fertility (Dasgupta, 1992), thus crest-crumbling the demography of the region.

Review of literature on the size of the household and the proportion of child labourers employed in such households' reveals an ambiguous relationship. Some studies hint at direct relationship between them while others reveal an inverse relationship. National Sample Survey Organization (NSSO, 2000) found that in rural and urban sectors of Uttar Pradesh, 19.32 per cent and 15.34 per cent come from household size of less than 4 members, 32.30 per cent and 32.34 per cent between 4-6 sizes, 30.99 per cent and 28.26 per cent between 6-8, 10.99 per cent and 12.41 per cent between 8-10 and 6.40 per cent and 11.64 per cent above 10 respectively. Nangia (1987) too found strong association between family size and child employment. Children from large families (9 or more members) were more likely to seek wage labour while those from medium-sized families (6 to 8 members) tended to be self-employed and those from smaller families tended to work for the family. In dry-land agriculture in India, Jodha and Singh (1991) found that child labour is an integral part of peasants' adaptive strategies to make fuller use of the production environment in the dry tropics. Vlassoff (1991) concludes after examining the picture of child labour in India, Bangladesh, Nepal, Indonesia, etc., that child labour possibly has a positive effect on fertility as children are regarded as positive assets in the rural areas of developing countries.

Child labourers are usually drawn from those households where the size of the household is larger than the average household size of the state. Kumar (2000) found that the average family size of child workers working in Aligarh lock industry was 6.5 and in Moradabad brassware industry, it was 7.8, which is higher than Uttar Pradesh's average size (5.7 members) per family. In case of carpet weaving too, the average size of the family was more than nine members per household in Bahadohi-Varanasi-Mirzapur belt (Vijayagopalan, 1993; Mishra and Pande, 1996). Karunanidhi (2000) in his study on child workers in the *beedi* industry found that average size of those households where children were pledged to their employers, was higher than the average family size of the state i.e. Tamil Nadu (4.7). The average size of the families of the child labourers working in gem polishing industry was also more than seven (Kruijtbosch 1996; Indian Institute of Health Management Research, 1992; Lal, 1998). In the diamond cutting industry of Surat, the average size of the family of child labourers was six members (Operations Research Group, 1993; Saradhi 1998). However, the average size of the family of child labourers working in glass industry of Ferozabad was in accordance to that of Uttar Pradesh i.e. 5.7 persons per households (Mishra and Pande, 1996).

Children working in number of urban informal sectors are also drawn from households with an average family size around six. For instance, Nath and Majumdar (1991) found that average size of family of children working in restaurants, shops, as domestic help, and as hawkers in Calcutta was 5.9 members per family. Tikoo (2003) too found that mean family size of children working in stitching, chair making, as domestic help, mechanics, hawkers, etc. at Karnal district in Haryana was 6.3 members per family. Chander (2004) found that about 60 per cent of children working in shops and as unpaid family labour, hawkers, and vendors in Aligarh city, had around 6 members per family. Likewise, Sekar (2004) found that family size of majority of children working in slaughterhouse in Delhi was 6.6. Even Tripathi's study (1991) revealed that more than 75 per cent of children working in brick kilns in Phulbani district of Orissa had an average of 6.3 members per family.

However, few studies do point out an inverse relationship between the size of the family and work participation rate of children in these families. Mishra and Pande (1996) reported that as family size increases, proportion of child labourers decreases in carpet weaving industry. Likewise, Dyson (1991) is not convinced that parents in poor countries are guided in their fertility decisions by the economic contribution of children. He feels that the causation, if it exists, goes in the reverse direction, i.e. high fertility means that there are quite a few children in the household. Such contrary findings based on the relationship between the rate of participation of child labour and the size of the household seems to be related to the type of family.

The extant review on the *type of family* reveals that in the past extended family was an institution that exercised restrictive controls over personal advancements. Family was central to being as it prepared its members for all roles that they were expected to play at various stages and in various situations of life. 'Each for all and all for each' was the general norm that governed the family functioning. Parents facilitated cultural values of collectivism, like solidarity, cohesion, and uniformity in the family (Singh, Kaura, and Khan, 1980).

Nevertheless, in the present scenario, the joint family structure is disintegrating and it is no longer capable of providing social and economic security. It is a widely observed phenomenon that the nuclear family is more common as one proceeds down the economic scale. The trend of joint family has declined drastically. In nuclear families, there is more liberty and independence in making personal advancements. In such families, getting hold on family members is much easier than in the joint families. Household heads of nuclear families feel free in asserting their personal decisions and norms in the family. New social context and new ideas are mutually supportive, and they both make it difficult for the family to continue to function as it traditionally did. Difference in income, occupation, and education are not conducive to joint family living, particularly when the family maintains a common purse. This may also happen as a result of nuclear units migrating to other places, for reasons, of non-availability of jobs in original place of residence or inadequacy of housing.

The review on the type of family unfolds that majority of child labourers working in sectors of variegated nature, come from nuclear rather from joint families. For instance, Dhillion and Arora (2001) found that majority of the child labourers working in the knitting industry in Amritsar, belonged to nuclear families (52 per cent) with an average of seven members per family. Likewise, Chander's (2004) study on child labourers in shops, unpaid family labour, and hawkers, in Aligarh city reveals that more than 95 per cent belonged to nuclear families with six members per family. Laskar (2000) too noted that majority of child labourers in Aligarh lock industry came from nuclear or sub-nuclear families rather from joint families. Kumar (1994) also found that most (97.3 per cent) of the respondents working in automobile workshops were from nuclear families. About 60 to 70 per cent of child labourers in Coimbatore belonged to nuclear families (Chenniappan, 1997). Usha and Devi (1997) also found that out of 132 households employed in *beedi* and *agarbatti* industries in Tirunelveli, 68.94 per cent were from nuclear families and 31.06 per cent were from other types of family.

Thus, majority of child labourers come from nuclear rather joint families. One of the probable reasons may be that that in joint families there are many members to provide succour when some crisis erupts, without depending on children's labour. In addition, demographic figures at the national level highlight that the representation of nuclear families in general is more than the joint families (National Family Health Survey- 2, 2000).

As majority of child labourers come from nuclear families, therefore, such households are in general male rather female headed (sub-nuclear families). Vidyasagar (1994) and Daniel (1995) in their separate studies on child labourers working in match industry in Sivakasi concluded that males headed over 70 per cent of the households. Similarly, Kumar (2000) found that 89 per cent of sampled households in Aligarh lock industry and 93 per cent of households in Moradabad brassware industry were male headed. Therefore, it is not only the size of the family but also the nature of family that is important in contributing to the malice of child labour.

Assets

Review of literature on the assets possessed by the households of child labourers reveals that children are regular working members in households owning no resources, such as, that of agricultural labourers, share croppers, *beedi* makers, embroidery workers, etc. These groups form the bulk of landless and agricultural labourers and artisan groups, where questions pertaining to daily livelihood, access to productive assets, and services arise (Jaiswal, 2000). Majority of them owe no or very few assets. Raghuvanshi (2003) found that almost 86 per cent of Dalit households were landless or nearly landless. Those who owned land either owned too little or lacked adequate capital for purchasing resources like seeds, fertilizers, or hiring farm implements. Lack of access or inadequate access to agricultural land and capital leaves them with no option but to force children for manual wage labour.

Inequality of income leads to severe credit constrains. Ray's (2000) report on Indian National Sample Survey data revealed a U-shaped relationship between child labour participation rate and inequality i.e. as inequality increases child labour also increases. The lower 50 per cent of households own only 4 per cent of landholdings. This iniquitous distribution of land, unequal access to productive resources and assets; structurally in-built inequities and a pattern of development intensify and exacerbate these factors. This is the root cause of the prevalence of child labour amongst the poor (Ahmed, 1999). This relationship is not only in developing countries but also in developed countries as well. For example, in Britain, the growing inequality between the 'haves' and 'haves not' had steeped in 1990s. Government policies in Britain proved lucrative to upper and middle class while deepening the disadvantages experienced by the poor. In Britain, more than 2 million children live in households where there is no adult in paid work (Howarth, *et al.* 1999). It provides support to the view of Grootaert and Kanbur (1995) that general economic development, equally distributed between, is the best and the most sustainable way of reducing child labour.

Raja (1993); Vidyasagar (1994); and Daniel (1995) also found that more than 60 per cent of children working in match industry in Sivakasi came from landless households. Sinha (1991) too found that about 56.25 per cent of child labourers in restaurants, tea-stalls, and sweet shops in Calcutta, came from families of landless labourers. Pati and Swain (1991) reported similar finding in Bhubaneswar where more than 75 per cent of children working in various informal sectors were from households with less than one acre of landholding. Aggarwal (2004) reported that majority of child workers in Uttar Pradesh belonged to households with smaller size of landholdings. Vijayagopalan (1993) also concluded that the uneconomical size of landholding in relation to large size of the family forced the households to send their children to seek wage labour in the carpet industry.

Nonetheless, some studies have concluded a significant positive relationship between size of landholdings and child participation rates. Kanbargi and Kulkarni (1991) found that ownership of productive assets of a family serves to directly increase the productive work of children except in farms owning very large landholdings (10 acres and above) or a large number of livestock where hiring of labour for certain activities is required. Landless households had 0.71 per cent of children in directly productive work. Those with less than 2 acres had 1.54 per cent of children in work, 10 or more acres had 1.19 per cent of children in work. Dev (2004) also found that acres of land and livestock in the households have positive and significant relationship with child labour. This indicates that possession of assets, especially, the landholdings may increase the proportion of child participation in work activities. This is probably because children may be working on the family farm and taking care of the livestock, which reduces the need for hiring labour. Thus, irrespective of sectors (i.e. manufacturing, non-manufacturing, or agriculture), child labourers in general, belong to landless or marginal farming households, denoting that majority are dependent on wage labour for their survival (NSSO, 1997).

Parental Occupations

The occupational status of parents has a determining role in child's employment. The type of occupation followed by parents affects the life of the children. The review regarding the parental occupation of child labourers' reveals that a high proportion of children who join work belong to households either with fewer sources or insecure sources of income or those who are still dependent on traditional occupations as their main source of livelihood . Borooah and Iyer (2005) in their study across 16 states in India found that children with parents working as cultivators had a higher likelihood of being enrolled in school than those whose parents were working as labourers. This was also evident in the study by Sahoo (1995) who found that most of the parents of the child workers were daily wage labourers (40 per cent), followed by those who were engaged in wage work as primary and in cultivation as secondary occupation (38 per cent). However, parents of those child labourers who had cultivation as primary occupation and wage labour as secondary occupation, constituted only 22 per cent. Acharya (1982) found that about 70 per cent of child labourers in West Bengal belonged to two lowest agrarian classes, namely poor peasants and agricultural labourers. Gupta and Mitra (1997) also observed that households engaged in petty trade and vending or households dependent on causal employment were the major suppliers of child labourers.

The study of child labourers working in restaurants, factories, shops, domestic help, hawkers etc. in Calcutta (Sinha, 1991) also reveals that majority of the parents were either fishermen (23 per cent) or daily wage labourers (17 per cent) or were retired or were unemployed (17.2 per cent). The study by Pati and Swain (1991) on child labourers working in restaurants, tea stalls, garages, etc. in Bhubaneswar, found that most of the parents of child workers were marginal cultivators (31.2 per cent) and daily wage labourers (29.6 per cent). It also signifies that a smaller proportion of the parents were in service (3.2 per cent) while others (4 per cent) were aged and handicap. Likewise, Chander (2004) found that about 66 per cent of parents of child labourers in Aligarh city were petty shopkeepers and nearly 22 per cent were in private sectors, holding low-status services. Aggarwal (2004) observed similar patterns of parental occupations of the child workers working in both rural and urban sectors in India.

Certain traditional crafts like weaving, pottery making, basket making, and many others are indirectly taught to the child at home. The child begins by occasionally helping the parents but soon participates in the economic activity on a regular basis (Sekar, 1997). These old crafts lend themselves to protracted periods of apprenticeship in which a child is made to accept long hours of work and low pay in the hope of becoming a master (Kanbargi, 1991). This tradition, while might seem unfair to an outsider, is a vital link of providing employment and sustenance to the family (Kamat, 2004).

However, most of these traditional occupations including agricultural activities have become obsolete. These occupations have lost their functional value. They are no longer viable or profitable in carrying out normal survival of the family. Earnings from these occupations are very less as compared to the amount of time, money and energy invested. A dry-land form of farming with traditional cropping patterns can be found over most of central India, particularly the *adivasi* belt. The average productivity in these enterprises is stagnant or declining. Output or income variability is very high and etching out an existence is a major challenge (Chaudhri, 1997). High levels of child labourers tend to exist in areas with limited irrigation facilities and where productive period in dry season is very short (Reddy, 2000).

Moreover, with the rise of modern industrial production, most traditional crafts have disappeared altogether, replaced by skills that form part of large scale production processes. This is because people in order to save time and consume new types of products prefer latter types of goods. Thus, mass production of goods began to eclipse small-scale home-based craftsmanship. Likewise, the advent of modern types of machines for making basic consumer utility items, has badly hit the market of traditional occupations, especially in the rural areas. Items made by machines are attractive, have good finish and are relatively cheaper than those made by the traditional methods. The fast expanding market has made possible the easy availability of mechanized goods, even in remote rural areas. Thus, traditional occupations have lost their value and are no longer considered a reliable source of livelihood for the entire family.

Therefore, the review reveals that most of the parents of the child workers were involved in low, insecure and traditional sources of income. Such occupations along with larger size of the family lead to higher dependency ratio in these families. These families seem to be overcoming such a high dependency ratio through the employment of children in various income generating activities either within family or outside the family.

Educational Profile

Review on educational profile of child workers as well as of the household members indicates that most of them are either illiterates or dropouts before completing primary level of education. A very small proportion of them are able to reach middle or secondary level of education. Number of studies conducted at all India level by different organizations shed light on the educational status of child labourers. UNICEF (1995) carried out a study on 4181 child labourers employed in 16 different factories spread all over India. Of these, 3323 or more than 79 per cent were totally illiterate, 11 per cent had received education till primary level and the remaining dropped out even before. Likewise, NSSO (2000) pointed at literacy rate of 94.9 per cent for primary and 58.8 per cent for upper primary classes. Thus, huge gap between the two classes signifies high rate of dropout.

Similar findings were also reported from different rural-urban settings in India. Kanbargi and Kulkarni (1986) in their study on rural areas (agricultural and non-agricultural sectors) of Karnataka found that 78 per cent of boys in 5-7 years age group attended school. It declined to 40 per cent in 12-14 years age group. This decline was sharp in the case of girls, i.e. 59 per cent girls attended school in 5- 7 years age group and 23 per cent attended in 12-14 years age group. Study by Kurosaki, Ito, Fuwa, Kubo, and Sawada (2006) conducted in 400 households in 32 villages in Andhra Pradesh found that a child who is older and female is more likely to work and less likely to be enrolled in school. This is because parental attitude towards female education is not the same as for male education. Education is often seen as superfluous for girls and unrelated to the tasks they have to perform later as a housewife. This perception of gender roles strongly influences the division of labour between boys and girls.

Sahoo (1995) in two villages of Orissa found that 56 per cent of child workers were illiterate and 44 per cent had education only till fifth class. None went beyond primary level. Likewise, Sharma (2001) found that in rural areas of Patiala district in Punjab, 36.3 per cent of child labourers had no schooling, 38.9 per cent had schooling till primary level and 24.8 per cent till middle level. In urban areas, 67.3 per cent of children were only working rather attending schools or doing household chores. 16.3 per cent combined school and work, and 16.6 per cent combined work and household chores.

Most of the studies conducted in manufacturing units like glass-industry, lock industry, brassware industry, pottery making, *beedi* making, gem polishing industry, garment industry have concluded analogous findings. For instance, Mishra and Pande (1996) found that most of the children working in the glass industry were illiterate (45.4 per cent) or dropped out prior to completion of the primary level of education (34.6 per cent). Nearly 20 per cent continued education along with work. The study on children working in lock industry of Aligarh and brassware industry Moradabad also reveals that most of them were illiterates and only less than 25 per cent had primary level education (Kumar, 2000). Similar trends were also observed in the pottery work (Burra, 1995), carpet weaving (Prembhai, 1984; Vijayagopalan, 1993; Mishra and Pande, 1996), knitting industry (Dhillion and Arora, 2001), and *beedi* industry (Pande, 1996), where majority of children were either illiterates or dropouts before completing their primary level of education.

Even in diamond cutting industry (Surat), 90 per cent of children were dropouts after primary level of education (Operations Research Group, 1993; Saradhi, 1998) and in gem polishing industry (Jaipur), about 40 per cent were illiterates and nearly 60 per cent were dropouts before the completion of primary level of education (Burra, 1995; Lal, 1998). In sectors like restaurants, garages, shops, and vending, the proportion of illiterates varied from 60 per cent in Aligarh city (Chander, 2004) to 65 per cent in Bhubaneswar (Pati and Swain; 1991; Behura and Behura, 1991). The rest of the children were mainly school dropouts at the primary level. Similarly, Tikoo (2003) studied 30 male and 30 female children working in different types of work like stitching, chair making, embroidery, domestic help, mechanics, carpenters, hawkers, etc in slum areas of Karnal district in Haryana. The study found that 25 per cent were illiterate, 68 per cent had education up to primary level and only 7 per cent of male child workers had education up to high school. No female child labour reached high school. Likewise, studies conducted on street child labourers revealed their low educational status. In Bombay, D'Lima and Gosalia (1992) found that nearly 54 per cent of street children were illiterate, 30 per cent had education till primary and secondary level and about 11 per cent were continuing school along with work.

Furthermore, educational profiles of household members also point out that majority of the members are either illiterates or school dropouts. Tripathi (1991) revealed that

83.3 per cent of households were illiterate, 15 per cent were educated till primary level, 1.8 per cent till middle level but none went beyond secondary level. Visaria and Jacob (1995) found that nearly 53-55 per cent of the households of child labourers were illiterate and about 34 per cent households had received secondary or higher education. Likewise, Jodha and Singh (1991) divulged that more than 30 per cent of households were illiterate, 35-68 per cent had education till primary level and 9-12 per cent had education till high school. Even Kumar (2000) in Aligarh lock industry and in Moradabad brassware industry, found that proportion of illiterate household members was 71 per cent and 78.61 per cent respectively and only 29 per cent and 21 per cent respectively were able to reach primary as well as secondary level. Sahoo (1995) too found that more than 83 per cent of household heads were illiterate and about 15 per cent had no education beyond primary level. Lal (1998) also unveiled that 62.9 per cent of households were illiterate, 25.8 per cent had education till primary level, 9.4 per cent till secondary level and only 1.9 per cent went beyond secondary level.

Kurosaki, et al (2006) found that educated parents are more likely to send their children to school rather to work. This is a confirmation of the established regularity throughout the developed world. The existing empirical studies in India have found similar results (Aagarwal, 2004; Basu, Das, and Dutta, 2003; Sakamoto, 2006). This is consistent with the wealth hypothesis (educated parents are usually richer than uneducated parents) and the preference hypothesis (educated parents value education more). Moreover, effect of education is stronger for mother's education than for the father's. Educated mothers prefer sending children to school more than educated fathers. They also found that father's education favours boys more than girls in sending to school while mother's favourable influence is directed equally towards both girls and boys. Similarly, Boorah and Iyer (2005) reported that even when father was literate, maternal literacy had an additional and important role to play in boosting a child's likelihood of being enrolled at school. In particular, the chances of girls being enrolled at school were considerably enhanced when their mothers were literate. Thus, studies have verified the fact that child's education is closely associated with parent's education and aspirations and there exists an intergenerational educational mobility to some extent between the two. However, reality based on the above laid-out data still rests on the fact that household members of child labourers as well as child labourers themselves are in general either illiterates or dropouts after competing primary level of education, denoting no or hairline level of difference in the literacy levels between the two generations.

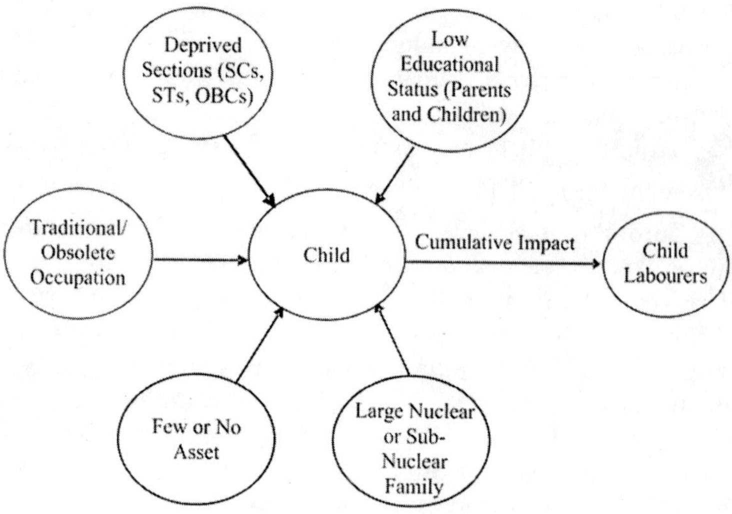

Fig. 1. Cumulative Impact of Debilitating Household Characteristics on Children

Children are usually embedded in primordial relationships. Socialization practices in the family affect the nature and intensity of interactions of the child with the wider society (Lewin, 1960). The larger social context, in which children are implanted, is heterogeneous and deeply ingrained with multiple socio-economic and cultural aspects. The social context of children from upper socio-economic status will invariably differ from children of lower socio-economic status. As child labourers are drawn from poor socio-economic background, they have a distinct pattern of household characteristics that contributes immensely to shove an innocent child into a malicious web of premature adults. It can be gathered from the figure that deprived sections, inclusive of Scheduled Castes, Scheduled Tribes, and Other Backward Castes, with large size of family, either nuclear or sub-nuclear, following obsolete traditional occupations, owning little or no assets, with low level of education, cumulatively impinge upon the child to deprive him/her of his childhood and push him/her into drudgery of work, so as to be bracketed as child labourer or child worker. Thus, these are the breeding conduit to the malice of child labour, which not only give birth but also remain pulsating in sustaining this insufferable practice of child labour.

In a nutshell, the analysis of the household characteristics of the child labourers concludes that child labourers usually come from Hindu communities, mainly belonging to cumulatively deprived sections of society like Scheduled Castes, Scheduled Tribes and Other Backward Castes. They are generally drawn from large sized, nuclear type of households, owning little or no assets. They come mainly from low paid parental occupations, which have irregular, insecure sources of income. Majority of them drop out before completing their primary level of education. Thus, emerging picture of the child labourers is one of pathetic situation and silent sufferers of the prevailing socio-economic conditions in the country.

A Prospective Vision

A child cannot develop into a full-blown human being, unless constructive and congenial environment is assumed for his/her development. Proper care and adequate socialization opportunities enable them to attain optimal human status. As they are vulnerable to innumerable environmental threats their survival and health needs require foremost attention. Their cognitive and emotional development depends to a large extend on the stimulus surroundings, love, affection, human warmth and security. This should be our national resolve for the generation next, especially for children undergoing variable forms of exploitation, like child prostitution and child labour.

These household characteristics lay the bed for germination of child labour. They set up context amiable to the prolongation of child labour. If concerted efforts are targeted at the social, familial, and personal fronts, then we can weed-out the phenomena of child labour from our society. For this, we need to work on assuaging the caste-class discrimination fossilized deeply in the mental make-up of people in our society, since the ages. In Hinduism, existence of *Varna* system based on ancient scriptures, hierarchically divides our society into kings and paupers; privileged and unprivileged; rulers and the ruled. Hence, these stratifications should be negated and a flawless society, characterized with casteless and classless status, wherein metropolis and peripheries co-exist, should be preferred to such irrational arrangements. The children of depressed and oppressed masses should be afforded adequate education and health facilities so as to contribute constructively to the future of our country.

Emancipation of these families from the muddle of poverty can be attained through coordinated efforts of both, government and non-government agencies. There is need to infuse the communities, at the state, district, or village level, with enough optimism and enthusiasm so as to initiate moves for self-employment and income-generation. This bottom-up community participation is essential for economic empowerment in every community in order to abbreviate the reliance on the children for survival of the family. Thus, onus for ameliorating the debilitating situation of these families lies not only on the government and non-government agencies but also on the community to help people cut above their paltry life style.

There is need for a breakthrough in attitudes and perception regarding the concept of *'hum do hamare do'* needs to be popularized among the masses. The pragmatic essence emanating from this catchphrase should be disseminated among the masses. Significant investment in children in the terms of quality education, physical-mental robustness, and overall development can take place only if there are few children. Thus, in the long run quality upbringing should be emphasized more than the quantity. For this, family planning programmes and measures should be widely campaigned and promoted through television, radio, *nukkar-natak* (street plays), pamphlets, etc. This will save the child from becoming prey to the viciousness of child labour.

Education leads to many social benefits, including improvement in standards of hygiene, reduction in infant and child mortality rates, decline in population growth rates, increase in labour productivity, rise in civic consciousness, greater political empowerment and demoralization, and an improved sense of national unity. This potent effect of education will remain latent unless the concept of child-oriented education is munificently practiced. There needs to be flexibility in school timings, recognition of differentials on child aptitudes, and creation of a learning climate in schools that will go a long way in the spread of education. The educational curriculum must be geared to bring the maximum of skill and competence in the child, keeping in view the environment in which he/she is living. Making vocational training a part of the school curriculum would also add life to the dull atmosphere of theoretical knowledge. Moreover, it would enable children later-on to become self-employed or find a decent job after attaining certain skills to earn higher wages and make a better life.

There is an urgent need for attitudinal change, social awareness, and aggressive campaign against the discourage of child labour. Underlying the relevance of childhood and creating sentience about child rights should be regarded as stepping-stones in the direction to sweep the society off the grime of child labour. Though nowadays, at least in urban areas, public awareness regarding the pitiable conditions of working children has sprung up. It has not yet taken the form of mass movement to prevent exploitation of children. Government, media, NGOs should take steps to inform children, parents, employers, and all members of society about the dangers of child labour abuse, the rights of the working children, and the laws and regulations in force in the country. The potentials of mass media and electronic media are used to the maximum to highlight the problem. Non-government organization ought to pressurize the government to implement concrete programmes for the early elimination of child labour. Thus, to abolish child labour, paper begs involvement of people from all walks of life in large measures.

Conclusion

On the basis of household characteristics it can be surmised that child labourers usually come from deprived sections of society like Scheduled Castes, Scheduled Tribes and Other Backward Castes. They are generally drawn from illiterate or less educated large-sized households have irregular, insecure sources of income and owning little or no assets. There are certain derivations which are upshot of this paper. Firstly, there may be host of other household characteristics besides those delineated here that propel child labour; but these household characteristics play a quintessential role in sowing the seeds of child labour. Secondly, these characteristics are not exclusive categories but act in various combinations with one another to give birth to the phenomena of child labour. Thirdly, though each of them have a potent role to play but they are not dynamic enough in themselves to snatch away the innocence of childhood from children and mould them into premature adults. There are certain processes or events taking place within the family (like death of family member, marriage or medical expenses, etc) or outside the family (like obsoleteness of traditional occupations, demoralising school atmosphere, etc.) which impinge upon these household characteristics and succumb them to the depressiveness of the world of child labour. Hence, these characteristics are necessary but not sufficient in explaining the existence of child labour. Thus, in order to understand the phenomena of child labour in totality, these characteristics should be taken into cognizance along with processes or events occurring within or outside the family. This can form the basis for further research, as Part II of the study. .

Nonetheless, we must realize that the obnoxious practice of child labour is deeply entwined in the socio-economic fabric of the society and there is no quick solution to the problem. The eradication of the problem is a long process, more so in a segmented society like ours. However, without loosing heart, we must submit to the lines quoted by Robert Frost in his poem *'Stopping by the Woods on a Snowy Evening'*:

> *"The woods are lovely, dark and deep,*
> But I have promises to keep
> And miles to go, before I sleep
> And miles to go, before I sleep..."

Fertile Conditions for Sprouting of Child Labourers
Large Nuclear or Sub-Nuclear Family
Deprived Sections (SCs; STs; OBCs)
Low Educational Status (Parents and Children)
Traditional/ Obsolete Occupation
Few or No Asset
Child
Child Labourers
Cumulative Impact

REFERENCES

Acharya, P. 1982, July. Child labour. Seminar, 275.

Ahmed, I. 1999. Getting rid of child labour. Economic and political weekly, 33, 27: 1814-1815.

Aggarwal, S.C. 2004. Child labour and household characteristics in selected states. Estimates from NSS 55th round. Economic and political weekly, 34, 2: 173-185.

Basu, K., Das, S. and Dutta, B. 2003. Birth order, gender and wealth as determinants of child labour: An empirical study of the Indian experience. Photocopy.

Behura, N.K. and Behura, B.K. 1991. Incidence of child labour in Orissa: Case studies from Bhubaneswar, in R.N. Pati, ed., Child labour: A socio-legal approach, pp. 119-132. New Delhi: Ashish Publication House.

Borooah, V.K and Iyer, S. 2005. Vidya, veda, and varna: The influence of religion and caste on education in rural India. The journal of development studies, 41, 8: 1369-1404

Burra, N. 1987. A report on child labour in the lock industry of Aligarh, Uttar Pradesh, India. New Delhi: UNICEF.

Burra, N. 1989. Child labour in the brassware industry of Moradabad, Uttar Pradesh, India. New Delhi: ILO/ARTEP

Burra, N. 1995. Born to work: Child labour in India. Delhi: Oxford University Press.

Chander, S. 2004. Child labour in informal sector: A sociological study. New Delhi: Suresh Publications.

Chaudhri, D.P. 1997. Child labour in India in the Asian perspective-1951-1996. Social change. 27, 3-4: 9-33.

Chenniappan, K. 1997. A study on children in Coimbatore hotels, in Children in difficult circumstances- Summaries of research (1985-2000), Delhi: NIPPD.

Daniel, C. 1995. A handout of lecture delivered to the participants of orientation programme for voluntary organization on child labour. Mimeo. Noida, Uttar Pradesh, India: National Labour Institute.

Dasgupta, S. 1992, 12 Aug. Child labour: Dirt being swept under the carpet. Times of India, Bombay.

Dev, S.M. 2004. Female work participation and child labour. Economic and political weekly, 39, 7: 736-44.

Dhillion, S.S., and Arora, A. 2001. Child labour in a prosperous state. In K.P. Kannan, ed., Economics of child labour. New Delhi: Deep and Deep Publication.

Duraisamy, M. 1997. Changes in child labour over space and time in India, 1981-1991. The Indian journal of labour economics, 40, 4: 809.

D'Lima, H. and Gosalia, L. 1992. Street children of Bombay. New Delhi: Child Labour Cell.

Dyson, Tim. 1991. Child labour and fertility: An overview, an assessment and an alternative framework. In R. Kanbargi, ed., Child labour in the Indian subcontinent: Dimensions and implications. New Delhi: Sage Publications.

Grootaert, C. and Kanbur, R. 1995. Child labour-An economic perspective. International labour review, 134, 2: 187 – 203.

Gupta, I., and Mitra, A. 1997. Child labour: A profile of Delhi slums. The Indian journal of labour economics, 40, 4: 841-848.

Howarth, C., Kenway, P., Palmer, G. and Miorelli, R. 1999. Monitoring poverty and social exclusion. York: Joseph Rowntree Foundation.

Indian Institute of Health Management Research. 1992. Child labour in gem polishing industry in Jaipur. New Delhi: Planning Commission.

Jaiswal, P. 2000. Child labour- A sociological study. Delhi: Shipra Publications.

Jodha, N.S. and Singh, R.P. 1991. Child labour and peasant's additive strategies, in R. Kangarbi, ed., Child labour in the Indian sub continent: Dimensions and implications. New Delhi: Sage Publications.

Kamat, 2004. Kamat's potpourri. askkamat@kamat.com.

Kanbargi, R. (ed.). 1991. Child labour in the Indian subcontinent: Dimensions and implications. New Delhi: Sage Publications.

Kanbargi, R. and Kulkarni, P.M. 1991.Child work, schooling and fertility in rural Karnataka, India. In R Kanbargi, ed., Child labour in the Indian subcontinent: Dimensions and implications, pp. 125-163. New Delhi: Sage Publications.

Kanbargi, R. and Kulkarni, P.M. 1986. Child labour, schooling and fertility in rural Karnataka, South India. In J. Stoeckel and A.K. Jain, eds., Fertility in Asia: Assessing the impact of development projects. The Population Council. London: Frances Publishers.

Karunanidhi, G. 2000. The *beedi* industry in North Arcot district, Tamil Nadu. In L. Mishra, ed., Child labour in India, pp. 66-74. Delhi: Oxford University Press.

Khan, N.A., and Hasoon, M. 2001. Child labour in lock industry. In K.P. Kannan, ed., Economics of child labour, pp. 91-99. New Delhi: Deep and Deep Publications.

Kruijtbosch, M. 1996. Child and adult labour in the export-oriented garment and gem polishing industry of India: With case studies from Tiruppur, Bangalore, Jaipur and Trichy, 2nd ed. Utrecht: Indian Committee of the Netherlands.

Kumar, B. and Biswas, G. 1992. A study of problems of working children in brassware industry of Moradabad, Uttar Pradesh. Govind Ballabh Pant Social Sciences Institute, Allahabad, India.

Kumar, B. 2000. Problems of working children. New Delhi: A. P. H. Publishing Corporation.

Kumar, R.M. 1994. Socio- economic conditions of child labour in automobile workshops. M. A. dissertation, Department of Social Work, PSG College of Arts and Science, Coimbatore.

Kurosaki, T., Ito, S., Fuwa, N., Kubo, K. and Sawada, Y. 2006. Child labour and school enrollment in rural India: Whose education matters? The developing economies, 44, 4: 440-464.

Lal, N. 1998. Economics of eliminating child labour in gem stone industries. In R. Anker, S. Barge, S. Rajagopal and M. P. Joseph, eds., Economics of child labour in hazardous industries of India. Baroda: Centre for Operations Research and Training.

Laskar, Baharul Islam 2000. Child Labour in Aligarh Lock Industry. Economic and political weekly, 35, 7: 510-13.

Lewin, K. 1960. Field theory in social science. In D. Cartwright, ed., Group dynamics. New York: Harper.

Manimekalal, N. 2001. Child labour elimination through national child labour project (NCLP)-Some micro level evidences from Tamil Naidu. In K.P. Kannan, ed., Economics of child labour. New Delhi: Deep and Deep Publications.

Mishra, G.P. and Pande, P.N. 1996. Child labour in glass industry. New Delhi: A.P.H. Publishing Corporation.

Mishra, G.P. and Pande, P.N. 1996. Child labour in carpet industry. New Delhi: A.P.H. Publishing Corporation.

Mustafa, M. and Sharma, O. 1996. Child labour in India. New Delhi: Deep and Deep Publications.

Nangia, P. 1987. Child labour: Cause-effect syndrome. New Delhi: Janak Publications.

Nath, P. and Majumdar, P.K. 1991. Working children in Calcutta. In R.N. Pati, ed., Rehabilitation of child labourers in India, pp. 165-170. New Delhi: APH.

National Family Health Survey-2. 2000. Mumbai: Indian Institute of Population Studies and ORC Macro.

NSSO (National Sample Survey Organization). 2000. Child labour and household characteristics in selected states. Estimates from NSS 55th Round. Economic and political weekly, 34, 7: 173-185.

NSSO (National Sample Survey Organization). 1997. Economic activities and school attendance by children of India. Report No. 412. Fifth Quinquennial Survey NSS 50th round 1993-94. New Delhi: National Sample Survey of Statistics, Department of Statistics, Government of India.

Operations Research Group. 1993. Child labour in different industries: Consolidated report, unpublished report. Madras: Operations Research Group.

Pande, R. (ed). 1996. Labour in *beedi* industry in Nizamabad District of Andhra Pradesh. Mimeo. Women's Study Cell, School of Social Sciences, University of Hyderabad, Project Sponsored by Ministry of Labour.

Pati, R.N. and Swain, S.N. 1991. Child labourers in Bhubaneswar city. In R.N. Pati, ed., Child labour: A socio-legal approach. New Delhi: Ashish Publication House.

Prembhai. 1984. Report to the Supreme Court regarding child weavers of Mirzapur-Bhadobi-Varanasi, Varanasi, mimeo, p. 51

Raghuvanshi, L. 2003, Feb. 26. Dreadful pangs of starvation. Northern India Patrika. Allahabad, India.

Raja, D.V.P. 1993. Research study on child labour in match industries in Sivakasi. Madurai: Madurai Institute of Social Sciences.

Ray, R. 2000. Poverty, household size and child welfare in India. Economic and political weekly, 35, 39: 3511 – 3520.

Reddy, B.S. and Rao, K.H. 1999. Causative factors of child labour in Andhra Pradesh: Application of logistic models. IASSI Quarterly, 17, 3.

Reddy, B.S. 2000. IDS Project: Background note on Andhra Pradesh. Osmania University, Hyderabad. Mimeo.

Sahoo, U.C. 1995. Child labour in agrarian society. Jaipur: Rawat Publications.

Sahoo, U.C. 1990. Child labour in Surat textile industry. Social Change, 20, 3: 29-37.

Sakamoto, S. 2006. Parental attitudes toward children and child labour: Evidence from rural India. Hi- stat discussion paper series, no. 136, Hitotsubashi University, Tokyo, http//hi-stat,ier.hit-u.ac.jp/research/discussion/2005/pdf/D05-136.pdf

Saradhi, R.K. 1998. Economics of replacing child labour in diamond industry of Surat. In R. Anker, S. Barge, S. Rajagopal and M. P. Joseph, eds., Economics of child labour in hazardous industries of India. Baroda: Centre for Operations Research and Training.

Sekar, H. 2004. Displacement and its impact on children in informal sector. Paper presented in National Workshop on Development, destitution, and it's impact on child rights- In the context of globalization. March 15-16.

Sekar, H.R 1997. Child labour legislation in India-A study in retrospect and prospect. NOIDA: V.V. Giri National Labour Institute.

Sharma, B. K. 2001. Socio-economic profile of child labour in a developing economy: A case study of Punjab. Mumbai: Himalayan Publishing House.

Singh, M., Kaura, V.P. and Khan, S.A. 1980. Working children in Bombay: A study. New Delhi: NIPCCD.

Sinha, S.K. 1991. Child labour in Calcutta: A Sociological Study. Calcutta: Naya Prakash.

Sooryamoorthy, R. 1998. Child labour in Kerela: Work and working conditions of child labourers in three important cities. Social Action. 48, 1.

Thorat, S.K. 1999. Poverty, caste and child labour in India: The plight of Dalit and Adivasi children. In K.Voll, ed., Against child labour: India and International dimensions and strategies, pp. 154-75. New Delhi: Mosaic Books.

Tikoo, S. 2003. Urban slums and child labour. Social Welfare, 50, 8:15-18.

Tripathi, S.K. 1989. Child labour in India. New Delhi: Discovery Publication House.

Tripathi, S.K. 1991. Exploitation of Child labour in Tribal India. New Delhi: Daya Publishing House.

UNICEF. 1995. Child prostitution- The ultimate abuse. New Delhi: UNICEF: India Country Office.

Usha, S. and Devi, R. 1997. Causes and earning of child labourers in b*eedi* and *agarbatti* industries. The Indian journal of labour economics, 40, 4: 849-858.

Vidyasagar, R. 1994. Report on survey of child labour in the match belt, Tamil Naidu. Mimeo. Department of Social Welfare, Government of Tamil Naidu.

Vijayagopalan, S. 1993. Child labour in carpet industry: A status report. New Delhi: National Council of Applied Economic Research.

Visaria, P. and Jacob, P. 1995. Child labour in India: Results of a methodological survey in Surendranagar and Surat Districts of Gujarat. Ahmadabad: Gujarat Institute of Development Research Publication.

Vlassoff, Michael. 1991. An assessment of studies linking child labour and fertility behaviour in less developed countries. In R. Kanbargi, ed., Child labour in the Indian subcontinent: Dimensions and implications. New Delhi: Sage Publications.

World Bank. 2001. Engendering development through gender equality in rights, resources and voice. New York: Oxford University Press.

3

Plight of Child Labour in Uttar Pradesh : A Preliminary Investigation

B.N. Prasad

Historically, child labour has been an integral part of Indian social system from the very beginning. But it varied in nature and dimension; depending up on prevailing socio-economic structure of the society (Sahoo 1990: 39). In subsistence rural economy, child labour has been part of the social organization in which all members poled their labour to produce for subsistence and survival (Mitra 1980: 10-17). In such a system; work of child not only formed part of labour necessary for reproduction of the system but also value of child labour taken as a part of child's socialization for reproduction of labour power. Child Labour in different historical epoch of India has a chequered history. In ancient India child labour was found in the form of child slavery, which could be bought and sold as commodity . It is revealed from the studies that child slave was very common in ancient Inida. They were engaged in different occupations; mainly agricultural activities (Chaudhary 1982) land led to fragmentation of holdings, as a result a class of landless labourers came in to existence. They used their children as helpers in their economic pursuits.

During Mughal period no serious attempts were made by the kings to eradicate system of child labour. In fact the system had been encouraged. Uneven development of industrialization gave a new turn to overall socio-economic order in the 18th century. Family based economy has been destroyed and large number of people became wage earning labourers. As a result; children were caught in a situation where they had to earn wages for themselves and their families. Work place has been separated from family environment and child has been exposed to unhealthy environment (Ray Chaudhary and Habib 1981: 287). They had to work from morning to late night for a merge earning. The child's ability to grow and develop into mentally and physically sound adult has been severely restricted. Along with industrialization exploitation of child labour has also increased. By the middle of 19th century mechnised large scale production came into existence. State regulations were heavily in the favour of employers. They were free to negotiate with labour. Labour was severely exploited by them for their profits. Many children were employed in cotton, jute mills and coal mines. Some of them were employed even for underground works. With the advent of factory organization, some public attention was drawn towards the existence evils, albeit with strong opposition by the employers (Rai, 2002).

Institutional Initiatives during Colonial Regime

First protective legislation for child labour was enacted in 1881. The Act provided some protection to child labour, e.g. forbidding employment of child below 7 year, limiting working hours to 9 hours per day, making it compulsory that 4 holidays in a month and rest interval should be given to them, along with fencing of dangerous machines. But coverage of the act was quite inadequate as it covered only factory's employees, and did not pay attention to agriculture and unorganized sector; which employ large number of child labour in India. As a result child labour continued as a means of cheap labour.

India Factory Act was enacted in 1891, which was an advance over the Act of 1881. Under the Act- lower age had been extended from 7 to 9 year. Working hour was reduced from 9 to 7 hour per day. Children were not allowed to work at night. However, exploitation of children increased due to inadequate enforcing machinery. The Factory Act 1911 further reduced the working hours of children from 7 to 6 hours and prohibited them to work in certain dangerous process.

Next step in the history of child labour law was Indian Factories (Amendment) Act 1922. Scope of the factory was extended to cover any premises where 20 or more persons were employed and mechanical power was used. Children under 12 year were prohibited to enter into labour market. They were required to have a medical certificate of their age and physical fitness for employment. Working hours were fixed to 6 hour a day with an interval of half an hour to the children employed for more than five and a half hour. Some minor changes in the act were introduced by an amendment in 1923. For the first time mining work had been brought into the fold of labour law. Working hours had been fixed as per the convention of International Labour Organisation. The Mining Act of 1923 fixed the working hours for above ground work at 60 hours a week, and for underground 54 hours a week. Minimum employment age was raised from 12 to 13 year. Indian Factory Act 1931, Tea District Emigrant Labour Act 1933, India Mining (Amendment) Act of 1935, Employment of Children Act 1938 were other significant initiatives to protect child labour. It is important to note that above Laws and initiatives taken to eliminate child labour could not achieve its goal. The labour investigation committee, in its report in 1946 pointed out that the main cause of failure was inadequacy of inspecting staffs to enforce the provisions of the Law.

Government Efforts in Independent India

After Independence; first step in the direction was amendment of factory act in 1948, which increased minimum age to enter into labour market to 14 year. Indian Constitution laid down special protective measures to protect child labour from exploitation. Employment of Children Act 1951 prohibits employment of children between 15 and 17 year at night in Railway and port. In 1961; two important Acts were passed in order to provide large protection to children: Motor Transport Workers Act which prohibits employment of children less than 15 year of age in motor transport undertakings, and Apprentice Act provide for regulating and controlling of trainees. Bidi and Cigar Workers (Conditions of Employment) Act 1966 prohibits employment of children under 14 year.

A report of National Labour Commission published in 1969 observed that child labour persists in varying degree in the unorganized sectors, such as small plantation, restaurant, hotel, cotton ginning and weaving, carpet weaving, stone breaking, bricklaying, handicraft and road building etc. To regulate labour of unorganized sector; Government of Indian passed Contract Labour (Regulation and Abolition) Act in 1970. The Act covers all the establishments and contractors employing 20 or more workers. As there is no specific provision relating to child work, many children can be seen in house construction, roads, etc. under contractors.

Gurupadswamy Committee on child labour submitted its report in 1979. The committee recognized that a distinction has to be made between 'child labour' and 'exploitation' of child labour . Though both are problems but are of different orders. Note should be taken that "labour becomes an absolute evil in the case of child labour when he is required to work beyond his physical capacity, when hours of employment interfere with his wages are not commensurate with the quantum of work done, and when the occupation he is engaged endangers his health and safety, i.e. when he is exploited ." Government has given due consideration to the above recommendations and tired to ensure that children are not subjected work in hazardous conditions, which endangers their physical and mental development. Even if they are employed in non-hazardous occupations, it should be ensured that work is regulated in accordance with Part III of the Child Labour (Prohibition and Regulation) Act of 1986, where it is necessary for the state governments to make rule under Child Labour Act 1986 or under any other legislation so as to protect the interests of child labour. They will be so required to undertake reviews and frame rules as necessary.

The Supreme Court of India, in the case of Bandhua Mukti Morcha, etc. v/s Union of India and Others; has rightly observed that a child of today cannot develop to be a responsible and productive member of tommorow's society unless an environment which is conducive to his social and physical health is assured to him (Mishra 2000: 13). Children signify eternal optimism in the human being and always provide the potential for human development. Neglecting children means loss to the society as a whole. If the children are deprived of their childhood-socially, economically, physically and mentally, the nation gets deprived of potential human resources for social progress, economic empowerment, peace and order, social stability and good citizenry. Thus every form of work whether hazardous or not entails some degree of stress. Hazardous work cripple the health, psyche and personality of a child, while non-hazardous work connotes other form of deprivation, such as denial of access to education and denial of pleasurable activities associated with childhood. Therefore in any case there should be minimum age to enter into labour market. When a person has physical strength, mental and emotional maturity he should enter into workforce.

Conceptual Dimensions

Scholars have varying perceptions about concept of child labour. There are three school of thought related to the issue (Ibid). The first school treats education as the fundamental human right of every child in 5-14 year of age and holds that any child in this age group who is out of school should be treated as working child. It is immaterial whether or not the work is hazardous, as the concept of childhood does not fit into the world of work. They are of the opinion that the distinction between hazardous and non-hazardous is at best artificial and cannot put up with a situation in which millions of children are out of school spending their days at home or doing some work at home without wages or outside home for wages.

According to second school of thought; magnitude of the problem is so enormous that state will find it extremely difficult to create environment and provide infrastructure, logistic support and resources to send all child labours to school, whether formal or non-formal. Therefore they advocate a gradual, sequential and selective approach to the entire issue of out of school children vis-à-vis working children. We should first concentrate on those employed in hazardous occupations, release and rehabilitate them through education, nutrition and skill training and subsequently those children working in non-hazardous processes. According to them; elimination of child labour should be viewed as a long term goal to be achieved progressively rather than at a stroke. They also believe that total elimination of child labour by law is not possible and, therefore advocate a dual approach of prohibition and regulation. This is in sharp contrast with the first school of thought advocating total prohibition.

Third school of thought believes that both civil society and state as the agent of society has failed in- (i) making education a fundamental human right, (ii) creating infrastructure and environment, and providing incentives to ensure access to educational opportunities to all, and (iii) creating positive and conducive school environment that will enable universal retention and participating of children who have enrolled themselves in school and also make it possible for them to achieve at least minimum levels of learning.

Each of the three schools of thoughts has merits and demerits. It is futile to enter into debate of which school take precedence. But the fact remains that access to health, hygiene, sanitation and nutrition for every child in the age group of 0-6 is extremely important to ensure sustained physical growth. Access to primary and elementary education at the age of 5-14 year is an equally important social need. Literate family environment provides quality of preparedness and facilitates access to educational opportunities to the children. But unfortunately most of the families of child labour are illiterate and unable to provide elementary education to their children, largely due to numerous socio-economic constraints. It is in this sense there is a great force in the point of view of first school of thought, i.e. (i) education is a fundamental human rights; (ii) state as the agent of civil society must create infrastructure, provide logistic support and environment for access to free, compulsory, primary education; (iii) state must also simultaneously create opportunities and provide facilities for participation, universal retention, and achievement of minimum level of learning.

According to population census 2001 there are 12 million child labours in India. Magnitude of child labour has increased in absolute terms by about 1 million between 1991 and 2001.

As per census data, trend on the magnitude of child labour is not uniform across the country. There is across the board decline in the incidence of child labour in Southern and Western Indian States, but an increasing trend has been observed in the Eastern and North Indian States between 1991 and 2001. However, there is an increase in the absolute magnitude of child labour between 1991 and 2001 in the states of UP, Bihar, Rajasthan, Punjab, Haryana, Himachal Pradesh and Madhya Pradesh. If we combine the bifurcated states from MP, UP and Bihar, the increase in magnitude is much more than what is seen in the divided states. As for as the percentage share of child labour across the states; Uttar Pradesh account for a larger share of about 15.2 per cent all child workforces in India followed by Andhra Pradesh, with 10.8 per cent. Rajasthan, Madhya Pradesh, Bihar respectively garnered 10, 8.8 and 8 per cent of India's child employment. The share of Uttar Pradesh has shot up from less than 13 per cent during 1991 to 15.2 per cent in 2001, which is a cause of serious concern. (www.ncpcr.gov.in/Reports).

One of the most important government interventions in the field is the flag ship programme called National Child Labour Project (NCLP). The scheme has been started in the year 1988. So far NCLP has covered 400,200 working children. 3.08 lakh children have been mainstreamed into formal education so far. The scheme is running in 250 districts in 14 states. It is in this backdrop a survey of child labour had been conducted in the district of Gonda of Uttar Pradesh with following objectives.

Objectives of the Study

In view of high incidence of child labour in Uttar Pradesh in general and Gonda district in particular, it becomes imperative to examine the factors responsible for the phenomenon. Main objectives of the present study are as follow:

i. To identify those households which supply child labour;

ii. To investigate the reasons as to why those households supply child labour and parents desire to send them school;

iii. To analyse educational, health and working status of child labour.

In view of the above objectives; the following factors have been examined:

1. Socio-economic background of the households of child labour;

2. Socio-economic and working condition of child labour.

Sample Design and Methodology

In order to analyse the mentioned objectives, 900 child labours have been selected on random basis from 3 Nagar Palika areas, 3 Nagar Panchayats and 16 blocks; covering entire district. All the selected child labours and their households have been surveyed on the basis of structured questionnaire schedules. Schedules have been administered at three levels – (i) below 14 years children in the targeted households; (ii) child labours; and (iii) persons above 14 years of the households.

Socio-economic Profile of above 14 year Members of Surveyed Households Distribution by Age-group

In the surveyed households percentage of male has been higher than the female, which is 53.96 and 46.04 respectively. In terms of age-wise distribution of above 14 year family members; percentage of people in the age-group of 15-25 years are the highest, followed by 35-45 and 25-35 years. Members of the mentioned age-groups are highest in Nagar Panchayat, followed by rural areas and Nagar Palika. Family members in the order age-group (45-above 65 years) are less than one-fifth. Above trend shows that people in the active age-group

(15-45 years) is highest in the surveyed households, constitutes more than 81 per cent. They can be creatively engaged to arrest the rising trend of child labour in the district .

Table 1: Distribution of above 14 year members of surveyed households by age (in years)

Location/Age	15-25	25-35	35-45	45-55	55-65	Above 65	Total
Nagar Palika	61 (26.29)	37 (15.95)	84 (36.21)	38 (16.38)	08 (3.45)	04 (1.72)	232 (100)
Nagar Panchayat	58 (37.66)	39 (25.33)	35 (22.73)	14 (9.09)	08 (5.19)	0 (0.00)	154 (100)
Blocks	214 (28.27)	197 (26.02)	202 (26.68)	81 (10.70)	49 (6.47)	14 (1.85)	757 (100)
Grand Total	333 (29.13)	273 (23.88)	327 (28.08)	133 (11.64)	65 (5.69)	18 (1.57)	1143 (100)

Source : Field data.
Note : Figures in brackets show percentages.

Details of Family Size

Surveyed households constitute three dominant religious groups of the district, i.e. Hindu (71.74 per cent), Muslim (28.02 per cent), and Sikh (0.24 per cent). Aggregate data shows that family size of

Table 2: Distribution of surveyed households by family size

Location/ Family size	Below 3	3 to 5	5 to 7	7 to 9	9 above	Total
Nagar Palika	10 (10.99)	35 (38.46)	34 (37.36)	09 (9.89)	03 (3.30)	91 (100)
Nagar Panchayat	05 (9.80)	13 (25.49)	20 (39.22)	08 (15.69)	05 (9.80)	51 (100)
Block	21 (7.72)	73 (26.84)	108 (39.71)	62 (22.79)	08 (2.94)	272 (100)
Grand Total	**36 (8.79)**	**121 (29.23)**	**162 (39.13)**	**79 (19.08)**	**16 (3.86)**	**414 (100)**

Source : Field data.

Note : Figures in brackets show percentages.

5-7 members is the highest, followed by 3-5 persons and 7-9 people. Together they constitute more than 87 per cent. Family size of 5-9 members is highest in rural areas and lowest in Nagar Palika. The trend shows that surveyed households have sizeable number of members. Family size in rural areas is bigger than urban areas, and it increases as we move from Nagar Palika to rural centres. In the absence gainful employment and larger family size; specially in rural and sub-urban areas of the district, children of the families are forced to enter into labour market.

Educational Status

The table below shows that majority of the members; above 104 years, of surveyed households are illiterate. This is followed by educated up to primary level and upper primary. Education up to high school and above is just 8.13 per cent. It is interesting to note that percentage of illiterates is highest in Nagar Palika, followed by rural areas and Nagar Panchayat. Nagar Panchayatis better placed in terms of educational status of the surveyed households, albeit at a lower level. Overall trend show that family environment of

Table 3: Educational status of above 14 year members of surveyed households

Location/ Educat-ional status	*Illiterate*	*Below Primary*	*Primary*	*Upper Primary*	*High School*	*Intermedi ate*	*Diploma*	*Graduate*	*Total*
Nagar Palika	174 (75.00)	0 (0.00)	29 (12.50)	20 (8.62)	07 (3.02)	01 (0.43)	0 (0.00)	01 (0.43)	232 (100)
Nagar Panch-ayat	102 (66.23)	03 (1.95)	17 (11.04)	09 (5.84)	10 (6.49)	08 (5.19)	0 (0.00)	05 (3.25)	154 (100)
Block	564 (74.50)	35 (4.62)	53 (7.00)	44 (5.81)	38 (5.01)	18 (2.38)	03 (0.40)	02 (0.26)	757 (100)
Grand Total	**840 (73.49)**	**38 (3.32)**	**99 (8.66)**	**73 (6.39)**	**55 (4.81)**	**27 (2.36)**	**03 (0.26)**	**08 (0.70)**	**1143 (100)**

Source : Field data.
Note : Figures in brackets show percentages.

the surveyed households does not provide congenial atmosphere and economic support for educational pursuit by their children.

Details of Types of Houses

Aggregate data shows that majority of the surveyed households have their own houses, very few of them are living in rented ones; mostly in Nagar Palika and Nagar Panchayat. In terms of types of houses; *Kaccha* houses are substantially higher than the *pucca* houses, even higher in rural areas. It is interesting to note that percentage of *pucca* houses is much higher at Nagar Panchayat level. This may be due to low land cost as compare to Nagar Palika areas. Overall trend indicates that percentage of *Kaccha* houses increases as one move from urban to rural areas. This shows that majority of the surveyed households are living in a pitiable conditions, where condition of rural poor is even pathetic. Most of these houses are without basic amenities, like safe drinking water, electricity, toilet, sanitation, etc. This might be one of the major reasons for their children to entering into labour market.

Table 4: Type of house of surveyed households

Location/ Types of houses	*Owned*	*Rented*	*Total*	*Pucca*	*Kaccha*	*Total*
Nagar Palika	87 (95.60)	04 (4.40)	91 (100)	41 (45.05)	50 (54.95)	91 (100)
Nagar Panchayat	49 (96.08)	02 (3.52)	51 (100)	27 (52.94)	24 (47.06)	51 (100)
Block	271 (99.63)	01 (0.37)	272 (100)	98 (36.03)	174 (63.97)	272 (100)
Grand Total	**407 (98.31)**	**07 (1.69)**	**414 (100)**	**166 (40.10)**	**248 (69.90)**	**414 (100)**

Source : Field data.
Note : Figures in brackets show percentages.

Occupational Detail

Aggregate data shows that majority of the working members of surveyed households are engaged in domestic works (under-paid or unpaid), followed by non-agriculture and agriculture labour, together constitute more than 90 per cent of their occupational activities. Contribution of agriculture, trade and service is less than 6 per cent. The trend shows the economic condition of surveyed households is quite bad, and it deteriorates as we move from Nagar Palika to rural areas. Almost half of them are engaged in domestic works in rural areas, where percentage of women and children is the highest. Most of them are under-paid or unpaid. Second most important source of income is non-agriculture labour, mostly on casual basis and at a low wage rate. It is in the domain of common knowledge that employment opportunities in the primary and its allied sectors are extremely limited. Employment opportunities in and outside the primary sector and improvement in their economic condition will empower the poorest section of the society; which in turn has definite effect on the problem of child labour in the district.

Educational and Work profile of below 14 year Children and Child Labour Distribution by Age

Aggregate data reflects that children in the age-group of 7-10 years are the highest, followed by 10-13 years, 0-5 years and 5-7 years are 22.57 and 20.73 per cent respectively. Sectoral analysis of data shows that children in the higher age-group (7-13 years) are the highest in the rural areas, followed by Nagar Palika and Nagar Panchayat. The data also reveals that children in the age-group of 7-13 year constitute major proportion; they may be potential child labour which needs urgent attention.

Table 5: Distribution of surveyed households by occupation

Location/ Occupation	*Agriculture*	*Trade*	*Agriculture Labour*	*Non- agriculture Labour*	*Service*	*Domestic works*	*Student*	*Unemployed*	*Old persons*	*Total*
Nagar Palika	01 (0.43)	04 (1.72)	0 (0.00)	122 (52.59)	02 (0.86)	94 (40.52)	0 (0.00)	05 (2.16)	04 (1.72)	232 (100)
Nagar Panchayat	10 (6.49)	06 (3.90)	0 (0.00)	57 (37.01)	03 (1.95)	66 (42.86)	07 (4.55)	05 (3.25)	0 (0.00)	154 (100)
Block	33 (4.36)	01 (0.13)	107 (14.13)	211 (27.87)	08 (1.06)	376 (49.67)	15 (1.98)	01 (0.13)	05 (0.66)	757 (100)
Grand Total	**44 (3.85)**	**11 (0.96)**	**107 (9.36)**	**390 (34.12)**	**13 (1.14)**	**536 (46.89)**	**22 (1.92)**	**11 (0.96)**	**09 (0.79)**	**1143 (100)**

Source : Field data.

Note : Figures in brackets show percentages.

Table 6: Distribution of below 14 year children by age-group

Location/Age	*0-5*	*5-7*	*7-10*	*10-13*	*Total*
Nagar Palika	68 (24.82)	52 (18.98)	72 (26.28)	82 (29.93)	274 (100)
Nagar Panchayat	41 (25.15)	36 (22.08)	38 (23.31)	48 (29.45)	163 (100)
Block	186 (21.38)	183 (21.03)	271 (31.15)	230 (26.44)	870 (100)
Grand Total	**295 (22.57)**	**271 (20.73)**	**381 (29.15)**	**360 (27.54)**	**1307 (100)**

Source : Field data.
Note : Figures in brackets show percentages.

Educational Status

Table below provides information regarding educational status of the surveyed below 14 year children. It is revealing to note that more than 83 per cent children are not enrolled as yet in any school. Those who are enrolled; drop-out rate is extremely high. Drop-out cases from primary to upper-primary is higher in Nagar Palika areas, followed by block level and Nagar Panchayat. It seems that Nagar Panchayat is better placed in this regard. Overall trend shows that majority of the children are out of school; situation in rural areas is even worst. They can be potential child labours, who can be mobilized with incentives to arrest rising trend of child labour in the district.

Table 7: Educational status of below 14 year children

Location/Education	*Not rolled*	*Primary*	*Upper-Primary*	*Total*
Nagar Palika	225 (82.12)	46 (16.79)	03 (1.09)	274 (100)
Nagar Panchayat	129 (79.14)	26 (15.95)	08 (4.91)	163 (100)
Block	732 (84.14)	122 (14.02)	16 (1.84)	870 (100)
Grand Total	**1086 (83.09)**	**194 (14.84)**	**27 (2.06)**	**1307 (100)**

Source : Field data.
Note : Figures in brackets show percentages.

Details of Work Place

Aggregate data reflects that majority of the child labours are engaged in domestic works, followed by agriculture labour and non-agriculture labour. Helpers in shops and working as helpers in households industries are little more than 6 per cent. As we move from Nagar Palika to rural areas child labours as domestic workers increases, but in the case of non-agricultural labourers the trend is reverse. Substantial number of child labours are engaged as agricultural labourers in rural areas; either himself or as helpers. Child labour as helper in shops are also high in Nagar Panchayat and Nagar Palika areas. Variation in nature of works of child labours is largely due to availability of kind of works in the specific areas. But overall trend shows that majority of the child labours are engaged in domestic works; which is largely under paid or unpaid. Same is true for other kind of works as well. They can be motivated to join the schools with incentives and little persuasions.

Table 8: Distribution of work place of child labour

Location/ Work place	*Agri-culture Labour*	*Non-agri-culture Labour*	*Domestic work*	*Help in house-hold industry*	*Helper in shops*	*Total*
Nagar Palika	0 (0.00)	37 (19.38)	126 (65.97)	0 (0.00)	28 (14.66)	191 (100)
Nagar Panchayat	05 (4.76)	07 (6.67)	73 (69.52)	0 (0.00)	20 (19.04)	105 (100)
Block	133 (22.02)	40 (6.62)	421 (69.70)	02 (0.33)	08 (1.32)	604 (100)
Grand Total	**138 (15.33)**	**84 (9.33)**	**620 (68.88)**	**02 (0.22)**	**56 (6.22)**	**900 (100)**

Source : Field data.
Note : Figures in brackets show percentages.

Distribution by Span of Working

Work span of majority of the surveyed child labours is 1-6 months, followed by 1 year, 2 years and above 2 years.

Shorter span of working (1-12 months) is higher in Nagar Palika areas, followed by Nagar Panchayat and rural areas. Longer span of working (1- above 2 years) is higher in rural areas, followed by Nagar Panchayat and Nagar Palika. The trend shows that economic condition of surveyed households is extremely pathetic in rural areas, which forces their children to enter into labour market at a very tender age. Another revealing fact is that almost 42 per cent surveyed children have entered into labour market very recently (1-12 months). It is easier to mobilize those children into the schools.

Table 9: Distribution of child labour by span of working

Location/ Working span	*1-6 Month*	*7-12 Month*	*1 Year*	*2 Year*	*Above 2 Year*	*Total*
Nagar Palika	116 (60.73)	15 (7.85)	26 (13.61)	18 (9.42)	16 (8.38)	191 (100)
Nagar Panchayat	39 (37.14)	0 (0.00)	31 (29.52)	26 (24.76)	09 (8.57)	105 (100)
Block	196 (32.45)	07 (1.16)	195 (32.28)	125 (20.70)	81 (13.41)	604 (100)
Grand Total	**351 (39.00)**	**22 (2.44)**	**252 (28.00)**	**169 (18.78)**	**106 (11.78)**	**900 (100)**

Source : Field data.
Note : Figures in brackets show percentages.

Daily Working Hours

Little more than 61 per cent surveyed child labours work for a shorter duration, i.e. 1-3 hours a day, followed by 3-6 hours abd 6-9 hours. As we move from urban to rural areas shorter duration of working (1-3 hours) decreases and longer duration (3-9 hours) increases. There are few children who are working for 9-12 hours a day; mostly in the Nagar Palika areas. Children who are working for longer duration in rural and Nagar Panchayat areas are largely engaged in agriculture and non-agriculture activities. The trend reveals that majority of the child labours are working for just 1-3 hours daily; they are mostly engaged in domestic works and are unpaid or very little paid. They can be taken to schools with motivation, persuasion and some incentives; even after their working hours.

Table 10: Distribution of child labour by daily hours of work

Location/ Daily Working hours	*1-3 Hour*	*3-6 Hour*	*6-9 Hour*	*9-12 Hour*	*Total*
Nagar Palika	134 (70.16)	26 (13.61)	27 (14.14)	04 (2.09)	191 (100)
Nagar Panchayat	64 (60.95)	24 (22.86)	16 (15.24)	01 (0.95)	105 (100)
Block	354 (58.61)	202 (33.44)	47 (17.78)	01 (0.17)	604 (100)
Grand Total	**552 (61.33)**	**252 (28.00)**	**90 (10.00)**	**06 (0.67)**	**900 (100)**

Source : Field data.
Note : Figures in brackets show percentages.

Monthly Income

More than two-third surveyed child labours earn Rs. 50-200 per month, followed by Rs.200-500 and Rs. 500-1000. Less than 2 per cent earns more than Rs. 1000 a month. Meagre earning is prominent in rural areas, and it decreases towards urban centres. This shows that child labours of urban areas are better paid as compare to their counter parts in rural areas. Overall trend reveals that almost 68 per cent children earn Rs.50-200 per month, and almost 90 per cent earns Rs.50-500 a month. This may be a substantial amount for labouring poor for their survival, but an affordable amount for the government to achieve the wider goal of eradication of child labour. They can be motivated with suitable incentives to join school; more so because their parents are willing to send their children to school, as shown in the table below .

Table 11: Distribution of child labour by monthly income (in Rs)

Location/ Monthly Income	*50-200*	*200-500*	*500-1000*	*1000-1500*	*1500 Above*	*Total*
Nagar Palika	111 (58.12)	59 (30.89)	16 (8.38)	02 (1.05)	03 (1.57)	191 (100)
Nagar Panchayat	70 (66.67)	18 (17.14)	16 (15.24)	0 (0.00)	01 (0.95)	105 (100)
Block	427 (70.70)	122 (20.20)	49 (8.11)	04 (0.66)	02 (0.33)	604 (100)
Grand Total	**608 (67.56)**	**199 (22.11)**	**81 (9.00)**	**06 (0.67)**	**06 (0.67)**	**900 (100)**

Source : Field data.
Note : Figures in brackets show percentages.

Parent's Desire and Suitable Time

Majority of the parent's of child labours are willing to send their children to schools. This percentage is highest in Nagar Panchayat areas, followed by rural areas and Nagar Palika. Most preferable time is morning, followed by noon and evening. Morning is the most preferable time in rural areas, but at Nagar Palika level noon is the most sought after timing, largely because children can do part time work in the morning time; especially as domestic help. In the Nagar Panchayat areas parents' are willing to send to their children at any time. Regarding health problems of their children; majority of the surveyed parents replied in negation at all the three levels. Over all data shows that almost 80 per cent parents are willing to send their children to schools and 61.36 per cent prefers morning time. Almost 97 per cent children do not have any health problem. Right approach with little incentives can bring substantial number of children to schools and arrest rising trend of child labour in the district.

Table 12: Parents' desire to send child labour to school and preferable time

Location/ Desire, Time and Health problems	*Desire*			*Preferable time*				*Health Problem*		
	Yes	*No*	*Total*	*Morning*	*Noon*	*Evening*	*Total*	*Yes*	*No*	*Total*
Nagar Palika	62 (68.13)	29 (31.87)	91 (100)	0 (0.00)	28 (96.55)	01 (3.45)	29 (100)	04 (4.94)	87 (95.60)	91 (100)
Nagar Panchayat	51 (100.00)	0 (0.00)	51 (100)	0 (0.00)	0 (0.00)	0 (0.00)	0 (0.00)	01 (1.96)	50 (98.04)	51 (100)
Block	216 (79.41)	56 (20.59)	272 (100)	54 (91.53)	04 (6.78)	01 (1.69)	59 (100)	10 (3.68)	262 (96.32)	272 (100)
Grand Total	**329 (79.47)**	**85 (20.53)**	**414 (100)**	**54 (61.36)**	**32 (36.36)**	**02 (2.27)**	**88 (100)**	**15 (3.62)**	**399 (96.38)**	**414 (100)**

Source : Field data.
Note : Figures in brackets show percentages.

Summary and Conclusion

Present study reveals that there is inverse relationship between economic status and number of working children. Economic distress of the poor people creates basic urge to send their children to the labour market so that family income may be substantiated by their earnings. In the sample households almost 70 per cent live in *Kaccha* houses; percentage of which increases as we move from urban to rural areas. Most of these houses are without basic amenities, like safe drinking water, toilet, sanitation and electricity. It is also revealing to note that almost half of the surveyed households are engaged in domestic works in rural areas, where contribution of women and children is the highest. Most of them are under-paid or unpaid; and is a part of disguised unemployment. Percentage of non-agriculture labours is the highest in Nagar Palika areas, and it decreases as one move from urban to rural areas. They are better paid as compare to domestic helps; but most of them work on casual basis and at a low wage. Educational status of the surveyed households is extremely discouraging across the board. More than 73 per cent of them are illiterate. It is a proven fact that education is the most important means for upward mobility, but family environment of the child labours does not provide congenial atmosphere and necessary support for academic pursuit. It is important to note that people in the active age-group (15-45 years) is the highest in the surveyed households, constitutes more than 81 per cent. They can be creatively engaged to arrest the rising trend of child labours in the district.

The survey reveals that children in the age-group of 7-13 years constitute major proportion; they may be potential child labours. This is more so because more than 83 per cent surveyed children are not enrolled in any school. Situation in rural areas is even worst. More than two-third child labours are engaged in domestic works; which is largely unpaid or under-paid. Shorter span of working (1-12 months) is higher in urban areas and longer span (1-above 2 years) is higher in rural areas. The trends shows that economic condition of surveyed households is vey pathetic; especially in rural areas, which forces their children to enter into labour market at a tender age. The study further reflects that more than two-third child labours earn Rs.50-200 per month and almost 90 per cent of them earn Rs.50-500 month. Meagre earning is prominent in rural areas, and it decreases towards urban centres. Whatever meagre earning of child labours but is a substantial amount for labouring poor for their survival. This is an affordable amount, as compensation, for the government to achieve wider goal of eradication of child labour, more so because their parents are willing to send them to schools. Almost 80 per cent parents are willing to send their children to schools, the desire increases as we move from urban to rural areas. Morning is most preferable school time in the rural areas but noon is preferred in urban centres, mainly because children can do part time work in the morning time; as domestic help. It is also found that almost 97 per cent children do not have any health problem. The main conclusion that emerges out of the forgoing analysis is that right approach with little incentives and persuasions can bring substantial number of children to schools and arrest rising trend of child labour in the state of Uttar Pradesh.

REFERENCES

Chaudhary, R., Tapan and Irfan Habib (1981). The Cambridge Economic History of India, 1(3).

Chaudhary, Radhkrishna (1982). Economic History of Ancient India, New Delhi: Sage.

Gurupadswamy Committee Report (1979). Report of the Committee on Child Labour. Ministry of Labour, Government of India, December.

Magnitude of Child Labour in India: An Analysis of Official Sources of Data (Draft). PDF. Accessed on 15 March 2012: http://www.ncpcr.gov.in/Reports.

Mishra, L. (2000). Child Labour in India. New Delhi: Oxford University Press.

Mitra, N. (1980). "The Slave Children of Mandsour". Sunday, 8 (19), December.

Rai, C.P. (2002). Child Labour A Reality. Vol. 1. New Delhi: Anmol Publications.

Report of the Royal Commission on Labour in India (1931). Government of India, Central Publication Branch.

Report of the Labour Investigation Committee (1969). Ministry of Labour, Employment and Rehabilitation, Government of India.

Sahoo, U. C. (1990). "Child Labour in Surat Textile Industry", Social Change, 20 (3), September.

The paper is a part of larger study "Survey of Child Labour in Gonda District of Uttar Pradesh", carried out by the author at Giri Institute of Development Studies, Lucknow.

4

Childhood under Threat: Situational Analysis of Children at work in HIV/AIDS affected Families

Helen R. Sekar

HIV/AIDS is not only a public health issue but also one of the most serious socio-economic and developmental concerns. HIV/AIDS epidemic constitutes one of the most dreadful challenges to the development and social progress of many countries in the world. By eroding decades of developmental efforts the epidemic has a damaging impact on the economic development by weakening and killing adults in the prime of their lives as workers thereby annihilating the workforce and corroding productivity. It affects the most productive segment of the labour force. It imposes suffering on individuals and their families. When the adult members are affected by HIV/AIDS, the children in the family become vulnerable thereby aggravating the problem of child labour. When the adults affected by the epidemic discriminated and stigmatized at work place and their earnings of the adults get reduced children are expected to bear the brunt and supplement the family income or become the sole breadwinners. Though HIV/AIDS remains a serious health problem, reducing resistance to diseases among the HIV-infected and leading to long illness and eventual death, it is more than a health issue as it also represents a problem of social and economic development. The long illness does not merely deprive an HIV/AIDS affected person of productive engagement, it also drains the resources of the many other people who have to take care of HIV/AIDS victims, with potentially catastrophic consequences for the economy and the society.

Children who are forced to live on the social and economic margins of society have even less access to information, skills, services and support than children of upper socio-economic categories. If they are already living with HIV, they suffer even worse stigma and discrimination and have virtually no access to care or drugs when they fall ill. Injecting drug use is one of the many addictions among single child migrants, run away children, street children and child labour. There are more and more 'occasional' injectors, and experimentation is frequent and widespread among ragpickers. Most of them do not consider themselves to be regular users of injecting drugs (Sekar, 2004).

To understand the extent to which HIV/AIDS is a major cause for children joining the workforce, it is important to examine how this disease affects families socially and economically. In Indian context, the family is still perceived as a social unit whose members share among themselves the socio-cultural and economic variables that make them a coherent body. As part of this, families serve as a social safety net against external threats. In times of disaster such as flood, earthquake, Tsunami or riots, it is the family members who provide security; in times of illness and death, it is the family that provides care and support. In many places even where governments, NGOs and interest groups provide some kind of support, it is ultimately the family that supplements it. In cases where families fail, Community-Based Organizations and/or NGOs step in to complement the traditional recourses. These organizations require the support of the family and without family support many of these would not function.

The Indian economy remains, by and large, labour intensive. This in turn has meant that labour supply is a critical factor in economic activities. Since prevalence of HIV/AIDS is highest among those in the productive age group, family labour may be reduced thereby increasing the level and rate of poverty. A family in which a parent is chronically ill with HIV/AIDS spends progressively less time in economic activities or engaged in other productive work. Hence, family food production falls and cash income dwindles. This means that many families have to struggle to survive forcing more and more children to work outside the family and in environments that are hazardous and harmful to their health, development and very lives.

Young parents are those who tend to be most affected by HIV/AIDS mortality and morbidity. Consequently, the pandemic creates severe hardship among children where the household breadwinners die or are unable to work because of protracted illness. The death of breadwinners or the inability to work due to illness creates severe hardships for children. Children experience greater poverty as a result of the loss due to AIDS of adult household members who would otherwise be the breadwinners. These losses affect all children in a household and, where infection rates are high, entire communities. Without adequate care and support, children experience deteriorating health, nutrition, education, affection, security and protection. They suffer emotionally from rejection, discrimination, fear, loneliness and depression (ESARC, 1996).

The death of parents has far-reaching implications for the children left behind. The prevailing economic hardships leave the orphans increasingly vulnerable to child labour in order to survive. HIV/AIDS orphans lack parental care and guidance. They are frequently forced by circumstances to drop out of school, moreover, which also denies them the guidance of teachers. This increases their vulnerability to malnutrition, illness, abuse, child labour and sexual exploitation (UNAIDS, 2002).

HIV/AIDS has a negative impact on economic growth. As the pandemic advances, the economic impact grows. The fiscal cost of HIV/AIDS is also significant. Government expenditures to control HIV transmission, to cover increasing medical bills, drugs, training and recruitment of staff etc. (TACAIDS, 2002). This, of course, entailed the diversion of scarce resources from other economic and social demands. Illness and care siphon time and labour away from other vital work. HIV/AIDS undermines private sector development by removing skilled labour, increasing expenditures and reducing revenues. Rural orphaned children have a 20 per cent high rate of non-school attendance than non-orphaned children (Schubert, B. 2003).

A survey of working children conducted in the year 1999 in Uganda noted that orphaned children especially girls were married off by guardians if the household was too stressed (Tumushabe, J., 2003). A study in Nairobi, Kenya found that over one third of orphaned children ended up as street children, commercial sex workers, casual labour, or married as girl children (Njoroge, M., Ngugi E. and Waweru, A., 1998). Epidemiological studies in major urban areas of eastern and southern Africa have shown that 17 to 22 per cent of the girls in the age group of 15-19 years have been HIV infected compared to 3 to 7 per cent of the boys in the same age group highlighting the vulnerability of girl children to sexual harassment and exploitation (UNICEF UNAIDS, WHO, 2002)

When parents are ill or prematurely die, many children especially girls drop out of school to augment the family income, and the number of children-headed households has been steadily rising. Though only a small proportion of the total households are child-headed their very existence is a new phenomenon in Africa and represents an important challenge for policy makers. Child-headed households exist because no relatives are left to care for these children, or the surviving relatives are too burdened to adequately care for the children they have inherited. Many children who become household heads have little option but to seek work to support themselves and their siblings (NMCF, 2001)

The HIV/AIDS epidemic has contributed steadily to the rising number of orphans in the whole world. People dying from AIDS tend to be in their prime years and are often parents. They leave behind children in societies already weakened by underdevelopment, poverty and the HIV/AIDS epidemic itself (Mukoyogo, M. C. and Williams, G., 1991). Death of father has been associated with loss of income, as he is often bread winner, inheritable property meanwhile is often grabbed by adult relatives upon the death of parents (World Bank 1997). Orphaned children are disadvantaged in numerous and often devastating ways. In addition to the trauma of witnessing the sickness and death of one or both parents, they are stigmatized and discriminated by society because of the HIV/AIDS status of their family members. Plunged into economic crisis and insecurity by the loss of their parents and struggling without services or support systems in impoverished communities, children especially girls are left extremely vulnerable to sexual exploitation and abuse, putting them at high risk of HIV infection (Foster and Williamson, 2000). Studies show that the critical determinant is the nature of the family relationships between the orphan and the decision making adult in the family or household. Much of the gap between schooling of orphans and non-orphans is explained by greater likelihood that HIV orphans will live with more distant relatives or unrelated care givers (Paxon, C. and Aleidinger, J., 2003) Orphan children suffer a measure of neglect and deprivation. When they are looked after by the extended family, it is common to find HIV orphans stunted and malnourished. These orphans face a relentless struggle for survival and lack protection against exploitation, abuse, and discrimination (UNICEF, 2003). There is a high correlation between HIV/ AIDS, orphanhood and child labour.

Many orphan children are left with no way to satisfy their basic needs and this is the root cause of child labour (Kaliyati, J. et al 2002). HIV/ AIDS may encourage a new form of social pathology in children orphaned by HIV/AIDS parents. Their vulnerability to child labour may be exacerbated by factors such as the collapse of the family, and other social support systems, dependence on the pension of poor grand parents and lack of opportunity enhancing policies for AIDS orphaned (Ncube, W., 1998). Fewer relatives are willing to take in orphans. In fact they are treated as second class family members. They tend to be discriminated against in everything from schooling to allocation of food. They are sometimes abused and forced to work (UNAIDS/ UNICEF 1999).

This paper discusses the findings of a study conducted in Delhi with the view to understand the growing impact of HIV/AIDs in forcing children into work by examining the impact of HIV/AIDs on children in terms of schooling and entering the labour market and to understand the increasing burden of domestic work and household chores on children due to HIV/AIDs affected members in the family. The study covered a total of 124 households with a total population of 627 constituting 345 male and 282 female.

HIV/AIDs has an adverse impact on demographic structure by taking the lives of parents thereby orphaning millions and changing the very structure of households. Age-wise distribution of sample population in the revealed that children below 14 years constitute 50.2 per cent of total population constituting 57 per cent males and 43 per cent females. The population structure also indicates that only 4 per cent of the population is above 50 years of age and less than 2 per cent are above 60 years of age. The gender-wise distribution of population below 14 years reveals that in all age groups the proportion of female children constitute less than that of male children.

Education of children becomes a casualty when one or more members of the family are infected by HIV/AIDs. Of the total children who were below 14 years and in the school-going age nearly 10 per cent of the children have never been enrolled in school and remained illiterate. These children could not be enrolled in school because of the poor financial condition of their parents after getting infected by HIV/AIDs. In order to supplement family income, the children who are out-of-school are sent for wage work in addition to the domestic chores that they are expected to do. Of the total children in this age group who have reported to be literates, nearly 90 per cent of the children have studied only up to primary level of education. However, 7 per cent of the children have dropped out of school due to a variety of reasons. The predominant reason was stated as financial problem (31 per cent). The need to supplement the family income by going to work was stated as the second major reason (23 per cent) for having dropped out of school. Those who have stated illness of one of the parents and migration to a new destination as reasons for dropping out of school constituted 15.4 per cent each. Similarly, those who have stated physical disability and need to take care of the sick at home as reason for dropping out of school constituted eight per cent each. Of the total children who were enrolled and attending school, most of the female children have been marked for long absenteeism.

Inability to pay the school fees was reported as a predominant reason for children discontinuing their education. The drop-outs were sent to work to bring home some earnings in order to supplement the family income. According to some of the households surveyed, they were not happy with the way their children were imparted education by the teachers as despite attending school regularly the children could hardly read or write anything. The necessity to take care of the HIV infected parents or the family members who fall sick very often, has also emerged as one of the reasons for children discontinuing their education.

The above discussion shows that children were kept out or pulled out of school either to take care of the sick in the family or to supplement the family income by becoming child labour due to decline in the family income or the earnings of the parents. It was also reported, during the field work that children could not be sent to school very many days because the mother was too sick to cook anything for the children. There were also cases reported where children especially girls were asked to discontinue their education to take care of younger siblings who frequently fell ill having been affected by HIV so that the parents could go for wage earning. In many cases, children have already lost one of their parents because of HIV. With the earnings of the single parent, who is also a HIV positive, which is insufficient due to repeated absence from workplace due to frequent sickness, the education of many children becomes a casualty.

Distancing of their families by close relatives who have supported them before have also deprived them of the support for their education. Though nearly one-fifth of the households surveyed felt that children can go to school and go for wage-earning after the school hours an overwhelming proportion of the remaining households felt that children cannot combine education and the work. Many children had expressed that they along with their mother who is HIV positive have been thrown out of their paternal grandparents' house after the death of their fathers due to HIV. This has also resulted in their dropping out of school.

The adults infected by HIV/AIDS are unable to go for wage earning due to frequent illness. When the economic condition of the family gets deteriorated, forced by the impoverished conditions children are sent to work for wage-earning. The quantum and intensity of the child labour problem in the HIV affected families is revealed by the fact that 34 per cent of the total children in the age group of 5 to 14 years are child labourers. Half of the households felt children drop-out of school and become child labour due to the HIV status of the family. Varied reasons were given by the households with regard to reasons for sending their children to work. For a predominant proportion (61 per cent) of the households surveyed it was for replenishing family income and also those children can gain work experience for earning better wages.

One-third of children reported that they have to drop out of school and join the workforce due to poverty and another similar proportion of children stated that they are at work because their family members are affected by HIV and they have to supplement the family income. For the remaining children, it is the death of their one or both the parents that compelled them to become child labour. Child Labour in the HIV affected families by and large are working either in home-based manufacturing sector or in service sector. A substantial proportion of children (78 per cent) are employed in service sector and three-fourth of those who are employed in service sector are working in road-side restaurants and tea shops and the remaining are child domestics.

A predominant proportion of the child labour commuted to their workplace by walk. While a majority of children in the age group of 5 to 14 years in the HIV affected families worked for more than 6 to 8 hours everyday at their workplace, nearly 15 per cent worked for 9 to 11 hours to supplement the family income. For over one-tenth of girl children, the working hours extended beyond 12 hours everyday. The children surveyed expressed that if they do not go to work their parents who are HIV+ may have to go to work despite their illness. A predominant proportion (80 per cent) of children expressed that they are very anxious and stressed out due to the HIV status of their family member especially parents and they try to work hard continuously to distract them from getting into depression. A few children (2 per cent) expressed that because of the HIV+ status of their parents they live with an unknown feeling of guilt. A small proportion (12 per cent) of child labour express that they share their anxieties and perplexities with their friends or representatives of different NGOs who visit their houses.

In addition to the wage work, children also carried out domestic chores at home mainly taking care of the sick family members, washing clothes, sweeping, mopping, dusting, fetching water, etc. With the time spent doing wage work and domestic work, children get very less time for leisure, recreation and other activities. Inadequate wages, overburdened with work and harassment are some of the problems they face at workplace and majority of them reported that they were shouted at even for committing very small mistakes of work by the employers or the one who supervises their work. Many children reported that they do not get to eat their meals on a particular time even if they are hungry at that time of the day.

Children suffer from various health problems mainly due to their irregularity of in-take of meals and malnourishment combined with the unhygienic working and living conditions. Their Nutritional insecurity is also due to low intake of fruits, vegetables, milk, milk products, eggs and other non-vegetarian items. One-third of working children reported that they fall ill quite frequently. Over a majority of children reported to be suffering frequently from stomach problem which may be due to non-availability of potable drinking water both at home and at work place. This is also evident from the fact that nearly one-third of children suffered from Jaundice and other liver related diseases and another one-third suffered from frequent bout of cold and cough and other respiratory diseases. While nearly one-fourth of children complaint of frequent headaches, over one-fifth of children suffered from pain in the joints. The remaining working children reported eye strain, backache, body pain, skin disease, dysentery, ulcer and typhoid fever.

The family members of the child labour are also deeply concerned about a variety of problems such as ill-treatment by employers, non-payment of wages or low wages, need to work at night, exposure to different types of abuse, physical strain, ill-health, etc. and it was also reported by some of the households that many a times children face combination of these problems. Very often, those who are infected by HIV/AIDS hide their HIV+ status from close relatives even from family members with the fear that they may be discriminated and be treated badly and their children may be neglected. Nearly 55 per cent of the households expressed that they are discriminated because of the HIV status of the families. Some of the women reported that when their relatives get to know about the positive status of their infant children they were reluctant to hold them in their hands and were afraid to even touch them. They shared a variety of reasons for being discriminated by others. According to 75 per cent of the households, it is due to their lack of awareness about HIV/AIDS.

Nearly 80 per cent of the total households feel that the future of the children in the families of HIV+ is gloomy and 43 per cent felt that knowing the HIV status of family may lead the children to get frustrated with life and get involved in anti-social activities.The respondents of various households interviewed reported that the combination of adverse psychological situation at home and exploitative situation at workplace result in children getting into depression though the level of depression varies. It was reported by 22 per cent of the households that children use drugs to reduce their anxiety. Nearly 13 per cent of the total households expressed that the child labour display suicidal tendency.They also expressed their opinion that if there is adequate safety net in the form of social security for the families and if children are provided educational facilities after enrolling them in boarding school, children of the HIV infected families can continue their education without being exposed to the frequent sickness and depressed mental condition of the family members who are HIV+ and are struggling with life.

The HIV/AIDS affected in infected individual and families face the social consequences of discrimination and ostracism from friendship groups and relatives. Lack of family support, ridicule and stigmatizing behaviour of the community, denial to means of livelihood are factors reported to affect the overall development of the children in these families adversely. Almost all the respondents have reported that on finding out about their HIV-positive status, they were initially shocked and wanted to hide this fact from their family and neighbours. Disclosure was a real problem as with most of them as it was followed by social stigma, social discrimination and harassment by different people and organizations which led to isolation and insecurity of the individuals infected by HIV/AIDS and the families they belong to. Many of them did not want to share the kind of discrimination and problems they have faced ever since they get to know about the HIV status.

Fear of social ostracism forced some women to hide their HIV status from family members in their natal as well as marital homes. For many of those who have disclosed their HIV status gender played a key role in the nexus between HIV-related stigma, moral judgment, shame, and blame. The marital home for many women played the biggest role in women's discrimination. Give women's lower standing and powerlessness in the social hierarchy, HIV-positive women were more stigmatized and treated as "bad and characterless person". As it widely believed that only immoral people can get the infection, the women with HIV/AIDS bear the brunt of the blame and also thrown out of the house. One woman reported that much more than the shock and stigma, she was hurt most when her child was taken away from her denying her of being a mother to her child despite her struggle to keep him with her at any cost.

It was reported that, while women were blamed and accused for their spouses' infection and condition, rebuked of being of loose character, and cursed for being alive despite their working hard to support the family, HIV-positive men were not blamed for being immoral as long as they are earning for the family. Even when men are not earning they are cared for as mothers have a soft spot for their sons. Some cases were reported where after the death of parents, despite their reasonably good earnings, the elder brothers refused to accommodate them and turned them away. In such cases friends were reported to be their solace and support. Thus HIV-positive men always had someone or other whom they can depend upon.

During the field survey, many of the respondents family members particularly the women reported that denied of their property rights they have been evicted from their marital homes and residences after the death of their spouse due to HIV/AIDS unless she is an earning member of the house and contributing to the family income substantially or when she is required to look after the positive HIV-positive male member of the family, in which case her presence would be tolerated. In most cases women were found themselves shelterless after the death of their husband. HIV-positive woman cannot disclose her HIV status to her natal family if there are other brothers or sister in the husband's family to be married off and she has to bear the ill-treatment and discrimination silently. There is no medical care initiated for her though the HIV-positive male member can always get his treatment by going outside into another town too, but HIV-positive woman is confined to the house and made to do the household work despite her need for medical care.

Parental home is no different for the women infected with HIV/AIDS and very often they are reduced to an object of sympathy and made to realize that they are a burden on the family. If their economic condition allows they may offer her support. Some of them support her willingly while some do it grudgingly as they are not really bound to do support her. She is not the priority for anyone. Poor economic condition in most homes makes the task for the natal family difficult. If she is able and economically of some use she is exploited and many a times it is only the woman's economic status or her earning capacity that determines their access to support from their brothers, sisters-in-law and other members of the extended family.

Many a HIV-positive women, when they move out and stay in their natal house, voluntarily separate their utensils, cook food and wash clothes separately with the intention of not wanting to be a burden on their brothers' family or cause any harm to them and remain grateful for the shelter provided. Even when they stay separately with their children, despite their being aware that physical contact alone cannot lead to transmission of the disease, in the case of their children, they are worried and want to be cautious. Therefore, they make it a point not to share their bed, food and clothes with their children. With the arrival of the women infected with HIV/AIDS back to their natal-home, family members live in persistent fear. In most cases, even if a HIV-positive relative is living with them, they try to maintain barriers by raising a wall or making them to live in a different floor or in a room in the terrace. Their children are not allowed to play with the children of the women infected with HIV/AIDS. Unable to bear such humiliating treatment both at the marital and natal homes some prefer to battle it alone without even getting access to emotional support. The families leave her to her fate.

The members of the households who were HIV+ were preoccupied with thoughts of death and dying and reported to be living under stress for months together which was found to have effects on the immune system. Sustained survival stress had resulted in immune system inhibition which had eventually caused erosion of immune function. Many of them reported that they have been having poor appetite, disturbed sleep patterns etc. Such diminished appetite and disrupted digestion resulted in their weight loss because of malnutrition. Repeated disturbance of sleep patterns in many of them has lead to suppressed immune function. As reported by the care-givers, their overall vitality got reduced which has resulted in their decreased immune function because of which they frequently fall ill and could not attend to or provide for their children's education.

Growing up with mother after the death of Father due to HIV, children are constantly affected by the mental status of their mother who lives with profound sense of hopelessness and loss of direction, purpose, and self-esteem. Thrown out of their paternal grand-parents place and living with maternal grand-parents or uncles they lack trusted support. Children feel that their mother lack self-assertiveness and has very poor coping ability in times of crisis. With very limited capacity for self-care when sick, children stay out of school or had to drop out of school to take care of their ailing parents. The stigma attached to the infection consequently gives rise to shame, a feeling of self-disgust and hatred. Not only they are victims of social ostracism at the community level, but often they are discriminated against by their immediate family. They try to isolate themselves more and more and cut themselves off from social events, outings and other normal activities. The self hatred turns their life into a mere existence for the sake of their children. But they are apprehensive that eventually the future of their children may also get bleak because of their own positive status.

HIV and AIDS has severe implications on children and becomes one of the reasons for neglect and influx of children into different forms of labour. When one or both the parents are infected by HIV/AIDS, they are unable to consistently meet the needs of their child or children. They find it difficult to provide their children appropriate supervision needed, age-appropriate care such as the necessary food, shelter, education or medical treatment. The on-going pattern of inadequate care could be readily observed and also demonstrated through poor hygiene, poor weight gain, inadequate medical care etc. Such neglect can have a significant impact on a child's emotional and physical development and the effects of which can last into adulthood. It impacts on all aspects of a child's health and development including their learning, self-esteem, ability to form attachments and social skills. Neglect in school-going children, ultimately results in frequent absences from school and drop out of school subsequently to join the labour force. To cope-up with the tension of unfulfilled dreams, ill-treatment and harassment at workplace, they try to take tobacco, assuming that it would take away all their worries. When their parents are not able to attend to their children's emotional needs, at an extreme stage children get into the habit of taking alcohol or other drugs in order to cope up with their emotions. Thus, in the absence of the support of their friends and the family, children in these families face social isolation and are at risk of having their health or development neglected for a number of reasons such as homelessness, unemployment and poverty.

Children orphaned by AIDS face widespread stigma and discrimination that impedes their access to health care, education, and other support services. Orphaned girls, especially, tend to become vulnerable to be pushed into sex trade due to their disadvantaged socio-cultural status. Most of the children reported that they suffered stigmatisation and discrimination resulting in social isolation. Most of the children worked in hazardous environments, and were exposed to a variety of health problems including headaches, fatigue, painful joints, coughing, stomach pains, diarrhoea, sneezing, backache and waist ache. Since private health services were very expensive, they recourse to self-medication combined with traditional therapies. On many occasions of illness no care or treatment was sought by them.

Very few of these children advanced beyond primary, dropping out of school to work was more common a factor than failure to pass exams. The situation was worse for orphans. Almost every child said that, if given an opportunity they would return to school. Awareness was low among younger children aged 5 to 11 years. Neither they were aware of the principal cause of HIV/AIDS nor of the symptoms of the disease.

Children are forced to drop out of school either because their parents are dead or too ill to earn money for school fees and other amenities. These children are forced to enter the labour market, however reluctantly, to take care of themselves and their young siblings. When a parent is infected with HIV/AIDS and suffers prolonged ill health, children in the family are affected both emotionally and physically. Children are forced to assume adult roles out of necessity and they become breadwinners of the family or care providers for ill or dying parents. Taking up adult responsibilities at very early ages can seriously jeopardize their health, safety, education, morals, dignity and self-respect. The work done by children is often unpaid or poorly paid and physically and emotionally difficult.

HIV/AIDS has far-reaching repercussions for the poor. Although people at all income levels are vulnerable to HIV/AIDS, the poor bear the brunt of the suffering. Given their limited economic means, costs of care for the sick may be crippling. The poor also have less access to basic health care. In such a situation children are likely to be sent out to work rather than to school. Young, inexperienced and unfamiliar with the ways of the mature world, the school dropouts are compelled to join the army of informal workers who engage in a wide variety of petty businesses. Some of these are hazardous activities including, in their worst forms, occupations such as child prostitution. The latter children are often subjected to sexual abuse and most are prone to early pregnancies – all of which contributes to severe and lasting psychological, social and physical damage, impairing the children's development into responsible adults. Those who engage in prostitution find themselves unable to protect themselves against HIV. As a result, they may end up not only infected with HIV but may also bear children who themselves risk HIV infection. This situation perpetuates the problem of HIV/AIDS orphans and threatens to further increase the incidence of child labour.

Women in general and girls in particular, are biologically and socially more vulnerable to HIV/AIDS – they are disproportionately infected and affected by the pandemic. This jeopardizes any gains in health, nutrition and education for girls that may have been achieved. At the family level, the girl child is more vulnerable to child labour than the boy. Traditionally, girls are supposed to help their mothers with household work, denying the girl child enough time for recreation and school work. In severely adverse conditions, as when the parents cannot afford to pay school fees, the girl child is normally the first to be denied access to family school funds. In situations where parents become incapacitated, the girl child assumes the responsibility of taking care of the sick parent(s) and her siblings. In this case, the children become breadwinners themselves, coping with the economic burden of handling the family.

Many children who become household heads have little option but to seek work to support themselves and their siblings. Orphaned children, including children in households with a parent ill with HIV/AIDS or related illness, may find their education cut short and future economic opportunities compromised. Children from family where one or more adults are HIV infected are more likely to be withdrawn from school than children in non-infected households because, these families cannot afford to retain them in school, need the children to help supplement household income or need their help in taking care of sick relatives.

Thus, AIDS is not only a phenomenon relating to biological concerns but also of socio-economic and political. Given its wide prevalence across age groups, different income groups and geographical regions, it is no longer restricted to specific geographical areas or individuals but can affect and infect fetus, children, adolescents, adults and the very old. The young people, who are the most vibrant human resource and development, are more vulnerable to HIV as compared to the old. They are at the centre of the academic which can be attributed not only to unemployment and poverty but also of the social norms, taboos, attitudes, behaviour, ideologies and inexperience.

Recommendations

Given the extent of discrimination against HIV infected person, it is important ensure that no one should be tested for HIV without his/her consent and permission. Moreover they should be told the results, so that they can take appropriate action to take care of their health if they are infected, and protect their sexual partners from getting infected. If the test shows that they are not infected, then, knowing the results will enable them to protect themselves in the future.

In the districts having high prevalence, Mobile and Migrant populations, women, youth and workforce, NCLP should enhance the coverage of its interventions with a clear focus. Explicit efforts should be made to identify and locate children from HIV/AIDS infected/affected families who are at work, for providing nutritional, educational, recreational and vocational skill development support through the Special Schools. Special training should be given to the teachers of the Special Schools for counseling these children.

The issue of child labour need to be fully integrated into the policy framework of the National AIDS Control Organisations (NACO) and should define immediate action in that direction. The major issues include ineffective targeting of services, inflexible service delivery system, social structure impediments, lack of inter-sectoral and inter-departmental coordination and quality sacrifice for quantity. Though States AIDS Prevention and Control Societies (SACS) play a key role addressing the problem of child labour in the HIV affected families demands the involvement of not only SACS but also the Departments of Labour, Education, Health, Social Welfare, Police, Rural Development, Social Justice and Empowerment, Revenue and SC/ST/BC Welfare. It also needs the involvement of various social partners and stakeholders including Trade Unions, Employers' Organisations, *Panchayati Raj* Institutions and NGOs. The integration of services of these departments will enable addressing the problem of child labour in the HIV affected families easier and more effective.

One of the major policy concerns could be how to identify and target the child labour in the HIV affected families to benefit from the NCLP project. The existing social infrastructure should be geared to locate children who are at work in these families. In order to ensure that benefits of the NCLP reach these children and their families the beneficiary selection must be done carefully using criteria which are both specific and sensitive.

Child labour prevention squads should be formed in all the Districts with representatives of NGOs and Medical Practitioners and this squad can facilitate admission of child labour in the HIV affected families in the NCLP Special Schools or in the educational centres of the Sarva Shiksha Abhiyan (SSA). The child labour families are not able to benefit from some of the development programmes because of the requirement of the beneficiaries to provide certificates of some kind from the local leaders or officials and many social security and welfare programs carry this risk. Efforts to circumvent these barriers have not succeeded. Since the Scheduled Caste and Scheduled Tribe students normally come from interior localities and from low income groups, they need residential facilities close to the educational institutions. Department of Tribal Affairs can extend the facilities of Ashram school scheme could be one of the ways of taking school facilities closer to the children particularly the tribal children. The Scholarships which explicitly meant to deliver education to the poor can be extended to these children.

The State Government should ensure that the adult members of the impoverished HIV affected families of child labour are given priority in the poverty alleviation and self-employment programmes. Revenue Department can facilitate by giving various documents needed by them to avail public distribution, housing facilities, etc. Women in these families should be encouraged to form self-help groups and given priority in the self-employment schemes after imparting appropriate skill training. SC/ST/BC Welfare Department can provide Scholarship and hostel facilities to the children belong to these social groups who have been mainstreamed into the formal schools. The services and facilities of the children homes under Social Defence department should be extended to the child labour who are destitutes, orphans and the children of disabled parents or single parent.

Since a large number of children are malnourished, the problem of malnutrition among children in the HIV/AID infected families can be tackled through a multi-pronged strategy consisting of direct interventions in the spheres of food security, nutrition, sanitation, safe drinking water, poverty alleviation, etc. A well co-ordinated and comprehensive support services should be provided to ensure that the children's developmental milestones are met and that they are cared for adequately. Successful policies and practices in different countries can also be examined for replication, guidance and possible inclusion in the policy. Plan of action to implement such a policy should be established with a timeframe and lines of responsibility.

BIBLIOGRAPHY

Books and Reports

A Rapid Assessment on the Cases of the Lusaka, Copper Belt and Eastern Province, ILO, August, 2002.

Africa's Orphaned Generation (2003) Division of Communication, UNICEF, New York.

Aggarwal, R. (1999) Street Children, Shipra Publications, New Delhi.

AIDS Epidemic Update, UNAIDS/WHO, December, 2005.

Ayieko, M., (1997) From Single Parent to Child Head Households: The Case of Children Orphaned by AIDS in Kisumu and Siaya District in Kenya, Study Paper No. 7, UNDP, New York.

Bhan, S. (1991) Child Abuse: An Annotated Bibliography, Institute of Peace Research and Action, New Delhi.

Bimal, K. (2000) Problems of Working Children, APH Publishing Co., New Delhi

Browne, K. and Davis, C. (1989) Early Prediction and Prevention of Child Abuse, John Wiley and Sons, New York.

Case, A., Paxon, C. and Aleidinger, J. (2003) Orphans in Africa: Center for Health and Wellbeing, Research Programme in Development Studies, Princeton University, New Jersey.

Chesterfield, R. K., Enge, I. and Martinez, P. (2001) Girls' Education and Crisis, USAID, Washington, DC.

Child Labour Survey: Country Report (1999) ILO/CSO, Lusaka, Zambia.

Child Labour Survey: Living Conditions Monitoring Survey Report (1996) ILO/CSO.

Childhood Under Threat, The State of World's Children (2005) UNICEF.

Children on the Brink: A Joint Report on Orphan Estimates and the Programme Strategies (2002) UNICEF, UNAIDS, USAID, Washington DC.

Children Orphaned by AIDS: Frontline Responses from Eastern and Southern Africa (1999) UNAIDS/UNICEF, New York.

Choudhary, U. (2004) HIV/AIDS and Child Labour: Intersecting Risks – May, 2004 (mimeo).

Combating HIV/AIDS: The Ministry of Health and Family Welfare, (2000-2001) NACO.

Confronting AIDS: Public Priorities in a Global Epidemic (1997) World Bank, Oxford University Press, New York.

Corby, B. (1987) Working With Child Abuse, Open University Press, Philadelphia.

CSO (1997) Living conditions monitoring survey report, 1996, Lusaka.

Gangrade, K.D. (1979) Children at Work, Elias Mendelievich, ILO, Geneva.

Gomango, S.P. (2001) Child Labour: A Precarious Future, Author Press, New Delhi.

Govt. of India (1991) Working Children in India: An Analysis of the (1991) Census Data, Registrar General, New Delhi.

HIV Sentinel Surveillance and HIV Estimation, 2006, NACO, 2007.

HIV/AIDS and Child Labour: A State of Art Review with Recommendation for Action, Synthesis Report (2003) ILO-IPEC.

HIV/AIDS Epidemiological Surveillance and Estimate Report (2005) NACO.

ILO/CSO (1999) Zambia Child Labour Survey: Country report, Lusaka.

International Encyclopedia of psychology, Volume 1.

International Encyclopedia of psychology, Volume 2.

International Labour Organization, 4 route des Morillons, CN-1211, March, 2003, Geneva, Switzerland.

Julius, M. and Chileshe, C., ILO-IPEC Tripartite Workshop Report on the Impact of HIV/AIDS on Child Labour in Sub-Saharan Africa, 6th – 8th May, 2003, Lusaka, Zambia.

Kadiyala, S. and Barnett, T. (2004) AIDS in India: Decision in the Making, Economic and Political Weekly, 8-14 May, 2004.

Kelly, M. J. (2000) The Encounter Between HIV/AIDS and the Education, UNESCO, Harare.

Lemba, M. (2002) Rapid Assessment of Street Children in Lusaka, Project Concern International.

Living Conditions Monitoring Survey Report (1996) Central Statistical Organization, 1997, Lusaka.

Mahbub-ul-Haq (2005) Human Development in South Asia 2004, Human Development Centre, Oxford University Press, New Delhi.

Mhatre, S. L. (1995) Child Labour Legislation in South Asia, 1881-1995: A Documentation and Analysis, UNICEF, Kathmandu.

Mishra, L. (2000) Child Labour in India: Oxford University Press, New Delhi.

Monthly updates on AIDS, NACO, 31 August, 2006.

Morgan and Clifford T. *et al.* (1986) Introduction to Psychology, McGraw Hill Book Company, New York.

Mushingeh, A.C.S. et al, HIV/AIDS and Child Labour in Zambia: A Rapid assessment on the case of the Lusaka, Copperbelt and Eastern Provinces, August 2002.

NACO, the Ministry of Health and Family Welfare, Combating HIV/AIDS 2000-2001.

Naerland, V. (1993) AIDS: Leaning to be More Helpful, Kampala, Redd Barna.

Naidu, S. (1984). Child Labour and Health: Problems and Prospects, Mumbai, Tata Institute of Social Science, Mumbai.

Nangia, P. (1987) Child Labour: Cause-Effect Syndrome, Janak Publishers, New Delhi.

Ncube, W. (1998) The African Cultural Fingerprints: The Changing Concept of Childhood in Ncube, W. (ed.) Law, Culture, Tradition and Children's Rights in Eastern and Southern Africa, Brookfield, US, Aldershot, Singapore and Sydney, Ashgate Publishing Company.

Nelson Mandela Children's Fund Report: A Study into the situation and special needs of children in Child-Headed Households, Johannesburg, June 2001.

Pandey, R. (1993) Street Children of Kanpur: A Situational Analysis, V. V. Giri National Labour Institute, NOIDA.

Panicker, R. and Nangia, P. (1992) Working and Street Children of Delhi, National Labour Institute, NOIDA.

Panicker, R. and Desai, K. (1992) Working and Street Children of Delhi: A Situational Analysis, V. V. Giri National Labour Institute, NOIDA.

Paxon, A. C. and Aleidinger, J. (2003) Orphans in Africa: Center for Health and Wellbeing, Research Programme in Development Studies, Princeton University, New Jersey.

Poulter, C. (1997) A Psychological and Physical Needs Profile of Families Living with HIV/AIDS in Lusaka, Zambia, Research Brief No. 2 UNICEF, Lusaka.

Pradhan, B.K. and Sundar, R. (2006) Gender, Impact of HIV and AIDS in India, NACO, NCEAR and UNDP.

Rapid Assessment of Street Children, ILO-CSO: Zambia (1999) Child Labour Survey and CSO: Living Conditions Monitoring Survey Report, 1996.

Rau, B. (2002) Combating Child Labour and HIV/AIDS in Sub-Saharan Africa, IPEC Paper No. 1, International Labour Organization, Geneva, Switzerland.

Reddy, N. (1992) Street Children of Banglore: A Situational Analysis, V. V. Giri National Labour Institute, NOIDA.

Regional Human Development Report: HIV/AIDS and Development in South Asia (2003) UNDP.

Regional Human Development Report: HIV/AIDS and Development in South Asia, UNDP, 2003.

Report on the Global HIV/AIDS Epidemic (2002) UNAIDS, Geneva.

Report on the Mid Term Review of the Strive Project (2003) USAID/CRS-STRIVE, Harare.

Rosenhen, L.D. and Seligman, M. (ed.) (1989) Abnormal Psychology, 2nd Edition, WW Norton and Company, New York.

Rwegoshora, H., Amma, H. and Mbeo, F. (1997) A Country Study towards a Best Practice Guide on Sustainable Action against Child Labour for Policy-Makers: The case of Tanzania, ILO, Dares Salaam.

SAFAIDS/CFU (1966) Orphans on farms: Who cares? An exploratory study into fostering orphaned children on commercial farms in Zimbabwe, Southern Africa AIDS Information Dissemination Service/Commercial Farmers Union, Harare, Zimbabwe.

Schubert, B. (2003) Social Welfare Interventions for AIDS affected in households in Zambia, GTZ, Lusaka, Zambia.

Sekar, H. R. (1993) Girl Child Labour in the Match Industry of Sivakasi: No Light in Their Lives, Child Labour Cell, V. V. Giri National Labour Institute, NOIDA.

Sekar, H. R. and Mohammad, N. (2001) Child Labour in Home Based Lock Industries of Aligarh, V. V. Giri National Labour Institute, NOIDA.

Singh, R. S., Raj, N. and Sekar, H. R. (2003) Hard Labour at a Tender Age. Child Labour in the Home-based Industries in the Wake of Legislation, V. V. Giri National labour Institute, NOIDA.

TACAIDS (2002) National Multi-sectoral Strategy on HIV/AIDS: Tanzania, Dares Salaam.

The Worst Form of Child Labour Convention (1999), SPARC International, Society for the Protection of the Rights of the Child.

Tumshabe, J. (2003) Situational Analysis of AIDS-induced Child Labour in Uganda and Experience of Community Empowerment to manage the crisis, Paper presented at the ILO/IPEC Technical Workshop on HIV/AIDS on Child Labour, Lusaka, Zambia.

UNAIDS (2002) Report on the Global HIV/AIDS Epidemic, UNAIDS, Geneva.

UNAIDS/UNFPA/UNIFEM (2004) Women and HIV/AIDS: Confronting the Crisis, a Joint Report.

UNAIDS/UNICEF (1999) Children Orphaned by AIDS: Frontline Responses from Eastern and Southern Africa, UNICEF, New York.

UNDP (2003) Regional Human Development Report: HIV/AIDS and Development in South Asia.

UNICEF (2003) Africa's Orphaned Generation, UNICEF Division of Communication, New York.

UNICEF (2005) Childhood Under Threat: The State of World's Children.

UNICEF, UNAIDS, USAID (2002) Children on the brink: A joint report on orphan estimates and programme strategies, the Synergy Project, USAID, Washington DC.

Unpublished Documents/Presentations from HIV/AIDS Project Centre at V.V. Giri National Labour Institute.

USAID/CRS-STRIVE (2003) Report on the Mid Term Review of the Strive Project, Harare, CRS.

Vidyasagar, R. and Kumarababu, G. (2000) Child Labour in the Match Industry of Sivakasi, V. V. Giri National Labour Institute, NOIDA.

Women and HIV/AIDS (2004) Confronting the Crisis: A Joint Report, UNAIDS/UNFPA/UNIFEM.

World Bank (1997) Confronting AIDS: Public Priorities in a Global Epidemic, Oxford University Press, New York.

Journals

Akim, J. Mturi and Nzimande, N., HIV/AIDS and Child Labour in South Africa: A Case Study of KwaZulu-Natal, ILO/IPEC–School of Development Studies, University of Natal, South Africa, March, 2003, Paper No. 4.

Anarfi, J. K., Vulnerability to Sexually Transmitted Diseases: Street Children in Accra, in Vulnerability of HIV/AIDS Infection and Effects on AIDS in Africa and Asia/India, Ntozi et al, 1997, pp. 281-306, supplement to Health Transition Review, 7 (Canberra, Australian National University).

Bachman, M. and Booysen, F., Health and Economic Impact of HIV/AIDS on South African Households: A Cohort Study, BMC Public Health, 2003, Vol. 3, No. 14.

Bicego, G., Rutstein, S. and Ableidinger, J., Dimensions of the Emerging Orphan Crisis in Sub-Saharan Africa, in Social Science and Medicine, 2003, Vol. 56, No. 6.

Cornelia, B. 1984, Multiple Personality and Child Abuse: An Overview, Psychiatric Clinics of North America, 7 (1), 3-7..

Daley, M. 1982, Child Abuse and Delinquency: Are there connections between childhood violence and later deviant behaviour? International Sociological Abstrac Harold, G. E. (1990) Childhood Sexual Abuse: long-term effect on psychological and sexual functioning, Journal of Child Abuse and Neglect, Vol. 14, 503-515.

Foster, G. and Williamson, J. (2000) A Review of Current Literature on the Impact of HIV/AIDS on Children in Sub-Saharan Africa in AIDS, 2000, 14, Supplement 3.

Harold, P. and Martin, D. 1979. Child Abuse and Development, Journal of Child Abuse and Neglect, Vol. 3, 415-421, 3788.

Kaliyati, J. et al HIV/AIDS and Child Labour in Zimbabwe: A Rapid Assessment, 2002, Paper No. 2, ILO-IPEC, Geneva.

Kirunga, C. and Ntozi, J. Socio-economic Determinants of HIV Serostatus of Rakai District, Uganda, Health Transition Review, 1997, Vol. 7, pp. 175-188.

M. Njoroge, E. Ngugi and A. Waweru "AIDS Orphans Multi Prolonged Programme in Kenya": A Case Study, XII International Conference on AIDS, 1998, Abstract No. 60116.

Mturi, J. and Nzimande, HIV/AIDS and Child Labour in South Africa: A Rapid Assessment, The case of Kwazulu-Natal, Paper No. 4, ILO-IPEC.

Mukoyogo, M. C. and Williams, G. (1991) AIDS Orphan: A Community Perspective from Tanzania, Strategies for Hope No. 5, Action Aid, London.

Mushingeh, A. C. et al, HIV/AIDS and Child Labour in Zambia: A rapid assessment on the case of the Lusaka, Copperbelt and Eastern provinces, ILO, IPEC, XI, August, 2002, p. 35, Paper No. 5, Geneva, Switzerland.

Njoroge, M., Ngugi, E. and Waweru, A., AIDS Orphans Multi Prolonged Programme in Kenya, A Case Study: XII International Conference on AIDS, 1998, Abstract No. 60116.

Oates, R. Kim, F. and Peacock, A. (1985) Self-Esteem of Abused Children, Child Abuse and Neglect, 9 (2), 159-63.

Sekar, Helen, R., Child Labour in Hazardous Industries: The Case of Slaughter House and Allied Occupations, V.V. Giri National Labour Institute, NLI Research Studies, 2004, Series No. 047.

Sekar, Helen, R., Child Labour in Urban Informal Sector: A Study of Rag pickers in Noida, NLI Research Studies, 2004, Series No. 055, VVGNLI, NOIDA.

Semkiwa, H.H., et al, HIV/AIDS and Child Labour in the United Republic of Tanzania: A Rapid Assessment: A Case Study of Dares Salaam and Arusha, 2003, Paper No. 3, ILO/IPEC, Geneva.

Sengendo, J. and Nambi, J., The Psychological Effect of Orphanhood: A Study of Orphans in Rakai District, Health Transition Review, 1997, 7, supp. : 105-124.

Taylor, J. and Stewart, S., Sexual and Domestic Violence Help Recovery and Action in Zimbabwe, Eastern and Southern African Regional Consultation (ESARC) on the Commercial Exploitation of Children, 17-19 April, 1996.

Third European Conference on Child Abuse and Neglect, Czechoslovakia, June 23-26, 1991. The International Journal of Child Abuse and Neglect, Vol. 17, 191-196.

UNAIDS/WHO, AIDS Epidemic Update, December, 2005.

UNAIDS, From know more to no more AIDS (2004) New Delhi, # 21.

Young People and HIV/AIDS Opportunity in Crisis, UNICEF, UNAIDS, WHO, 2002, p. 17, Geneva.

Internet Sources

Hope Never Dries Up: Facing the Challenges-Situational Assessment and Analysis of Children in Zimbabwe (2002) UNICEF, Harare.

http://www.org/compaigns/crp/promises/police.html.

http://www.nottinghamshire.gov.uk/home/social_care/childrenandfamilies/childprotection/childneglect., from child neglect project, practice guidance for all agencies produced by Nottinghameshire and Nottingham city ACPSs June 2003.

Investigating child labour, Guidelines for rapid assessment: A field manual, draft, January, 2001, www.ilo.org/public/english/standards/ipec/simpoc.

National Family Health Survey (NFHS-3) 2005-06, September, 2007.

The Impact of HIV/AIDS on Families and Communities, Economic Commission for Africa, Commission on HIV/AIDS and Governance in Africa, Index No. CHGA-B-l 1-0001 - www.uneca.org

Wood, B. and Mason, G. (1997) The Impact of HIV/AIDS on Orphaned Children in Kwazulu Natal – www.togan.co.za/cind/fullreport.htm.

www.who.int/violence_injury_prevention/violence/global_campaign/en/chap3.pdf

5

Children's Role in Household Livelihood in a Forest Based Tribal Community

Rajiv Pandey and Vinod Chandra

The strategic role of children for development has been consistently stressed by academics and policy makers. Their contribution in rural and poverty stricken communities is also taken as the most effective long term strategy for poverty relief and economic development. However, in forest dependent communities, the children contribution is very important for family welfare. This is partly because of the demand of family; partly because of the shortage of efficient educational resources, partly as a result of administrative inertia and because of the lack of social awareness to the essentiality of education as a basic right for children. The study explores the contribution and status of the children of a forest dependent tribal community known as Jaunsary of Dehradun, Uttrakhand. The study proposes that for the long term growth of the region and for forest conservation, the policy makers should try to regulate this youth power and streamline them through proper policy, which should not deal only the economic issues of the region rather it, should include the right choice and entitlement of these youth.

The household requirements for livelihood are availability of adequate food and other essential subsistence goods, cash for purchase of outside goods and services, savings and social security. Other than these, disaster management potential, concern about reducing critical risk factors, and local social, cultural and spiritual considerations are also integral part of human livelihood. In broader view, a livelihood comprises the capabilities, assets (including both material and social resources) and activities required for a means of living. Forest supports many of these to the forest dwellers in various forms. The forest utilization by the adjoining inhabitants also governs due to unavailability of basic amenities and facilities to them. These complex arenas of life, makes their livelihood critical hence the role of each and every family members becomes essential for survival. The contributions of members of the family towards their welfare are in the form of expenditure savings or earning income or both. The common belief is that adult members are generally contributing to household economy by their wages while young people and children help their families by saving the expenditure. Both adult's extra earning for their family's economic well-being and youth and children's savings in their expenditure result to the poor quality of life within the family. Mainly the cost of the health of the family members and education of children and young people suffer the most. This is more worst when the family issue become more worsens, if the community is living in remote and hilly location due to typically linked with the topographical issues and lack of technological interventions.

However, the significant contributions of children are generally overlooked by the policy planners in the developmental aspects. To evaluate the extent of involvement and role towards the family welfare in general and their quality of life in particular, the present study was conducted based on the field exploration for a forest dependent community of a hilly region, Jaunsar Bawar.

The Jaunsar Bawar and Jaunsaries

The spatial focus of the study is Jaunsar Bawar of Dehradun, Uttarakhand. It lies between latitudes 30^{0}-31′ N and 31^{0}-3′-30″ N and longitudes 77^{0}-45′ E and 78^{0}-7′-20″ E. It is entirely composed of the succession of peculiarly rough and precipitous hills and mountains. The total geographic area is 1002.07 square km, constituting 32.5 per cent area of Dehradun district (Pant and Samal, 1998). It is roughly oval in shape with its major axis lying North - South. This area contains forests on 64 per cent of its land.

Demographic profile of Jaunsaries: A Statistical look

The community of the Jausar Bawar is known as Jaunsaries. They are integral part of the region since generations. Settlements on the region consist of smallholder communities of 8 to more than twenty families interspersed between smaller properties in cluster form with a density of 88 persons per square kilometer as per 1996 survey (Pandey, 2007). Population of the area was 114593 in 2001, out of which, 59466 were males and 55127. The proportion of Schedule Caste population is 29 per cent. The literacy rates vary from 20 to 39 per cent in Kalsi and 13 to 27 per cent in Chakrata block.

The total agriculture land is 36,647 acres. Out of it, only 10 per cent land i.e. 3,818 acre is irrigated and 32,829 acre is unirrigated. Wastelands occupy another 43 per cent and out of it, cultivable wasteland proportion is approximately 34 per cents. However, these lands are largely unsuitable for productive purposes due to hilly tracts and lack of irrigation facilities (Joshi, 1995). This situation is not changed with the pace of recent economic development. Their agricultural fields are not suitable for cultivation due to the hilly tracts and rocks. These have been made conducive upto some extent for agriculture by the manual work of the people. Smallholder households on the region employ diversified economic strategies due to resource crunch and limited opportunity for income generation. Farming in Jaunsar is of a subsistence nature and mainly depends on rains. Other occupations are labour, value addition work on forest products, salaried job mostly as a guard, peon, driver, etc. The employment opportunity is almost negligible. Hence the livelihood options revolve around the exploitation of natural resources in general and agriculture in particular. The extractions from forest and cultivation of agriculture crop are practiced jointly by the villagers due to the situation of fields at the forest fringes. Hence, the entire socio-economic structure of the Jaunsari community revolves around the principle of 'joint living and joint agriculture' (Sishaudhia, 1981, 1993). The forest resource utilization is mainly for consumption goods. They get shelter, home and raw materials for house buildings, food, dress material, cultural equipments, spiritual life or pleasure together with psychological contentment from forests. Their way of life is strongly associated to the forests from birth to death (Pandey, 2007). Livestock rearing in Jaunsar is essential primarily for drought power and farmyard manure. The milk and milk products are secondary. The livestock includes mainly buffaloes, cows, goats, sheep and mules.

Methodology

For the present study, the study region, was classified into four zones on the basis of altitude i.e. forest types. This decision was based on the premises that forest utilisation decisions are affected more by available tree species and that the variations can best be captured in and among such strata. At first stage, two zones one from each block, the low and high hill zones; Kalsi Tehsil for low hills and

Chakrata Tehsil for high hills; were selected at random. At second level, villages were identified within the selected tehsils. Information pertaining to the time devoted in hours and minutes per day for various household chores and forest based parameters on randomly selected day was collected from 302 randomly selected households in thirty four randomly selected villages in the selected tehsils. In this area, the number of families residing in a village varies from 8 to more than 20. Therefore, 5-12 households were randomly selected for the study from each selected village. Larger sample size could not be considered due to the homogeneous livelihood pattern within a village. Villages were selected by random cluster sampling procedure, keeping in view of homogeneous group of the sampling population. The main part of the field research for this study was conducted in stages during the summer of 2003 through the spring of 2005.

Classification of household activities: The Jaunsary household activities were classified on the basis of their livelihood patterns in the following manner:

(A) *Housework* (performed within the homestead): These activities included (i) fetching water, (ii) cooking, (iii) cleaning and washing, (iv) home gardening, (v) care for children, (vi) care for sick and older members of the family, (vii) drying paddy, seed, etc. (viii) pounding and husking, (ix) construction and repair work (fence, shed), and (x) weaving and knitting.

(B) *Extended housework (Community work):* (i) leisure (free and time for enjoy) and personal care, (ii) marketing, (iii) community work, and (iv) social, and cultural activities.

(C) *Activities performed outside the homestead* or *Productive work*: e (i) crop farming and agricultural work, (ii)

feeding domestic animals, (iii) collection of firewood, (iv) hunting and trapping, (v) grazing, (vi) labour work for construction of road, channel and quarrying, etc (vii) professional job, and (viii) collection of fodder, leaf and twigs.

Data for all the above-mentioned activities were collected for all children of the family. The absolute differences in average time spent by male and female of this age class in different categories of activities, viz, (i) Housework, (ii) Community work, and (iii) Productive work, have been also worked out. Since a widespread gender bias severely affects the social, economic and political situation of the community, measurement of gender disparity by using simple composite indices has been tried for this study based on the methodology of HDR (1995). The absolute differences in average time spent by males and females in different categories of activities, viz, (i) Housework, (ii) Community work, and (iii) Productive work, have been taken and combined to arrive at a composite index of gender disparity. The gender disparity was calculated in the following manner:

$$\textit{Gender disparity index}\ (\text{GDI}) = \frac{Actual.x_i. - Minimum.x_i}{Maximum.x_i - Minimum.x_i}$$

where 'x' represent the absolute difference of the amount of time spent by men and women in different household work.

Result and Discussion

Jaunsaries, who are in general away from market mechanism and follow the "production and consumption" economy, follow the extended family system with large size with an average of 10 members (Table 1) that consists of a head of household, his/her spouse, brothers, their wives and offspring. Traditionally, the eldest among the male members of the senior generation heads the family. He enjoys the patriarchal authority in the family and is known as *Sayana*.

He has the sole authority over the family property, but in order that he does not misuse his right, often he requires and receives advice from his brothers. The wife or wives as well as children are common to all brothers, as they were following polyandry (Sishaudhia, 1981). However, this practice is disappearing now-a-days with the penetration of awareness, infrastructure and education (Pant and Samal, 1998). On average basis, there is one member of the age below five and between 5 to 15 years of age from male and female in all families. Some families are landless in both low and high hills, however, some are having land upto 80 *bighas* with an average of 17 *bighas* for low hills and 26 *bighas* for high hills.

Table 1: Some descriptive statistics of quality of life in Jaunsaries

Parameters	*Zone*					
	Low hills			*High hills*		
	Mean ± SE	*Min.*	*Max.*	*Mean ± SE*	*Min.*	*Max.*
Family size	9.51 ± 0.23	4	20	9.74 ± 0.10	4	27
Number of children upto 5 years age	1.28 ± 0.1	0	3	1.02 ± 0.10	0	5
Number of male children of 5-15 years age	1.25 ± 0.10	0	5	2.25 ± 0.10	0	8
Number of female children of 5-15 years age	1.30 ± 0.10	0	5	1.46 ± 0.10	0	7
Number of male between 15-25 years age	0.83 ± 0.10	0	8	.76 ± 0.10	0	7
Number of female between 15-25 years age	0.80 ± 0.05	0	6	0.71 ± 0.04	0	5
Age of head of household	44.54 ± 1.32	26	72	47.77 ± 1.37	28	82
Total land holding (In Bighas)	17.04 ± 1.66	0.00	70.00	25.74 ± 3.10	0.00	80.00

The poor infrastructure and rugged topography compelled the Jaunsaries to adopt more than one profession for their survival strategy yet, agriculture is the main activity for seventy three per cent households. Sixteen per cent of households are primarily involved in labour works. Only three per cent earn from salary and only two per cent are getting income from forest or by value addition to the forest products. However, while probing the role of forest, all are of the opinion that they are using various products and raw materials from forest. The contributions of all family members particularly children are common for the activities related to forest and cultivation.

The indepth study reveals that there was at least one child for 60 per cent families (Table 2). However in 10 per cent families, there were at least three children upto age five. The child below age 5 demands special care therefore engagement of family labour is essential, which reduces total labour force of the family. During survey, it was revealed that this care is primarily the responsibility of either the elders or the children upto 15 years of age.

Table 2: Household proportion with children upto five years of age

Zone	*Number of children upto five years of age*				
	None	*1*	*2*	*3*	*> 3*
Low-hills	35.6	18.4	30.1	14.1	1.8
High-hills	42.4	23.8	23.8	8.6	1.3
All sample	38.9	21.0	27.1	11.5	1.6

Eighty five per cent of families support more than one male and female child between 5 to 15 years of age (Table 3) and 75 per cent for the members of 15 to 25 years of age. These make an important workforce and contribute mainly towards less labour-intensive jobs, thus presenting the elders in the house with more working time to do other labour intensive jobs or make them free for leisure. They are contributing towards many activities related to cultivation including composting. The extent of it varies with respect to their age and their belongings. The contribution of them towards family is in the forms of expenditure savings rather than earnings in general.

Table 3: Household proportion for members upto 25 years of age

Zone	Number of male children					Number of female children				
	0	1	2	3	> 3	0	1	2	3	> 3
Members between 5 to 15 years of age										
Low-hills	14.1	52.8	27.0	5.5	0.6	11.7	57.1	22.7	6.1	2.5
High-hills	14.6	48.3	34.4	2.6	0	11.9	42.4	34.4	9.9	1.3
All sample	14.3	50.6	30.6	4.1	0.3	11.8	50.5	28.3	8.0	1.9
Members between 15 to 25 years of age										
Low-hills	33.7	52.1	12.3	0.6	1.2	33.7	54.0	10.4	1.8	0
High-hills	37.7	49.7	10.6	1.3	0.7	38.4	47.0	13.9	0.7	0
All sample	35.7	51.0	11.5	1.0	1.0	36.0	50.6	12.1	1.3	0

The proportion of families with children in labour profession in the region is less than 50 per cent. The proportion of families having one male child as labour in the age group 5 - 15 years is 26 per cent. The female children are not participating in labour profession in the region. The children participation as a labour is only for the economically weak families.

Table 4: Household proportion with children below 15 years of age engaged as labourer

Zone	No. of Male children 5 - 15 years				No. of Female children 5 - 15 years	
	0	1	2	3	0	1
Low-hills	61.5	26.2	11.7	0.6	100	0
High-hills	50.3	26.5	21.2	2.0	98.0	2.0
All samples	55.9	26.3	16.5	1.3	99.0	1.0

Children educational status has also been explored during the survey. It was observed that although, people are aware regarding the education still some socio-economic and geographic constraints compel them to withdrawal of their kids from school (Table 5). From the table it is apparent that there are very few families, in which, the children are totally engaged in domestic activities and not attending school. The non-attendance of schools by them was mainly due to lack of their interest in education or involvement in some intermittent economic activities. However, the proportion of children attending school and doing domestic duties as well is nearly fifty per cent. These domestic duties include mainly forest and livestock rearing for male children and household affaires too for female children.

Table 5: Household proportion for 5 -15 years age children position

Zone	*Number of Male children*					*Number of Female children*				
	0	*1*	*2*	*3*	*> 3*	*0*	*1*	*2*	*3*	*>3*
Children, who are not attending school and performing domestic duties										
Low-hills	73.6	14.1	12.3	0	0	68.7	14.1	16.0	1.2	0
High-hills	70.9	19.2	3.3	6.6	0	66.9	26.5	6.0	0.7	0
All sample	72.3	10.0	8.0	3.2	0	67.8	20.1	11.1	1.0	0
Children, who are attending school and performing domestic duties										
Low-hills	41.7	30.1	26.4	1.8	0	31.3	35.6	31.9	1.2	0
High-hills	31.8	49.0	12.6	4.0	2.6	33.1	38.4	27.2	1.3	0
All sample	36.9	39.2	19.7	2.9	1.3	32.2	36.9	29.6	1.3	0
Children, who are attending school and not performing domestic duties										
Low-hills	77.9	17.8	4.3	0	0	94.5	5.5	0	0	0
High-hills	65.6	19.9	14.6	0	0	92.1	7.9	0	0	0
All sample	72.0	18.8	9.2	0	0	93.3	6.7	0	0	0

For productive work, male and female children, were devoting 2.7 and 2.8 hours per day, respectively (Table 6). Over 70 per cent of female children and 63 per cent of male children were engaged in productive activities in different ways. The more time on productive activities particularly cultivation and forest collection was also due to unawareness of scientific knowledge and unavailability of suitable tools for these activities. The male children devoted maximum of 11 hours and female children upto 9 hours in productive work (Table 6). From this, it is apparent that children made a substantial economic contribution to the household in terms of savings against their services. This also provided other family members with opportunities to pursue alternate or other activities for household welfare.

Table 6: Participation of children in household activities

Members	*Household Activities*					
	Participation (%)			*Mean ± SE*		
	HA	*PA*	*CA*	*HA (h/d)*	*PA (h/d)*	*CA (h/w)*
Male Children	72.1	63.3	80.3	3.41± 0.16	2.75 ± 0.17	11.23 ± 0.79
Female Children	89.1	70.6	63.6	5.34 ± 0.20	2.83± 0.17	13.39 ± 0.82

h/d – Hours per day; h/w – Hours per week

The result of the gender disparity measure in housework activities is shown in table 7. The index reflects that for cooking, cleaning, washing and sewing, there was a high gender disparity value favouring females for all the age classes. The community work had sharp disparity and favours menfolk (Table 7). The crop farming and agriculture were gender sensitive activities and favoured males of all age classes. However grazing activities favoured males in the 15 to 25 years age class while other forest related activities were not gender sensitive in this community for this age class. This showed that children between the age classes of 15 to 25 years were equally useful for forest related extraction work irrespective of their sexes. The situation was similar for 5 to 15 years of age class except fodder collection, which favoured male. Fuel wood and leaf twig collection activities were non-sensitive as far as gender was concerned but there was marked disparity between the age classes (Table 7).

In summary, it can be concluded that female contribute significantly in productive activities. This contribution was mainly in terms of money saving either by reducing the labour cost or by the collection of raw materials for household needs.

Table 7: Gender disparity index and time devoted for different activities

Activities	*Age class 15 to 25 years*				*Age class 5 to 15 years*			
	Time spent		*AD*	*GDI*	*Time spent*		*AD*	*GDI*
	Female	*Male*			*Female*	*Male*		
Housework								
Fetching water	0.29	0.06	0.23	0.38	0.21	0.08	0.13	1.00
Cooking	0.58	0.03	0.55	1.00	0.07	0.00	0.07	0.54
Cleaning	0.29	0.06	0.23	0.38	0.11	0.00	0.11	0.85
Washing	0.38	0.03	0.35	0.62	0.06	0.00	0.06	0.46
Care for children	0.22	0.09	0.13	0.19	0.15	0.09	0.06	0.46
Care for sick and elders	0.07	0.04	0.03	0.00	0.00	0.00	0.00	0.00
Drying crop seeds	0.15	0.05	0.10	0.13	0.06	0.08	0.02	0.15
Pounding and Husking	0.09	0.12	0.03	0.00	0.09	0.04	0.05	0.38
Sewing	0.18	0.06	0.12	0.17	0.00	0.00	0.00	0.00
Construction and repairing	0.08	0.12	0.04	0.02	0.00	0.00	0.00	0.00
Productive work								
Livestock	0.25	0.21	0.04	0.03	0.17	0.13	0.04	0.21
Crop farming and agriculture	0.89	1.17	0.28	0.36	0.38	0.43	0.05	0.26
Grazing	0.46	1.21	0.75	1.00	0.63	0.82	0.19	1.00
Collection fodder	0.66	0.59	0.07	0.07	0.27	0.13	0.14	0.74
Collection fuel	0.30	0.41	0.11	0.12	0.22	0.19	0.03	0.16
Collection leaf twig	0.21	0.30	0.09	0.10	0.22	0.14	0.08	0.42
Hunting	0.03	0.05	0.02	0.00	0.00	0.00	0.00	0.00
Service	0.02	0.06	0.04	0.03	0.02	0.07	0.05	0.26
Labor work	0.00	0.14	0.14	0.16	0.00	0.00	0.00	0.00
Labor for road construction	0.00	0.31	0.31	0.40	0.00	0.00	0.00	0.00
Other labor	0.06	0.15	0.09	0.10	0.00	0.00	0.00	0.00
Community Work								
Marketing	0.16	0.60	0.44	1.00	0.00	0.04	0.04	0.15
Entertainment	0.26	0.37	0.11	0.18	0.34	0.46	0.12	0.55
Leisure and personal care	0.52	0.64	0.12	0.20	0.74	0.95	0.21	1.00
Community work	0.05	0.09	0.04	0.00	0.21	0.22	0.01	0.00

AD - Absolute difference, GDI - Gender Disparity Index

The above explorations clearly reveal that the children are an important agent for household welfare particularly for production functions. Although they all are engaged at the cost of their own development, which in turn reduce their quality of life and deprive them from the learning of many intrinsic and extrinsic qualities. This in totality will be critical for long term growth of the region. Therefore at this junction, the policy makers should try to regulate this youth power and streamline them through proper policy, which should not deal only the economic issues of the region rather it, should include the right choice and entitlement of these youth. This will ultimately reduce the pressure on the forest and help to conserve the natural resources.

REFERENCES

Human Development Report. 1995. United Nations Development Programme. Oxford University Press, Delhi.

Joshi, K. R. 1995. Jaunsar Bawar – A brief introduction. Society for Motivational Training and Rural Action (SAMTA), Chakrata, Dehradun.

Pandey, R. 2007. Contribution of forestry - Role in socio-economic of Jaunsaries and development of index. Unpublished thesis in FRI University, Dehradun.

Pant, R. and Samal, P.K. 1998. Role of culture in sustainable living and factors for its disintegration. *ENVIS Bulletin* 7(1).

Sishaudhia, V.K. 1993. Polyandry in a CIS-Himalayan community. Polyandry in India, Dehradun.

Sishaudhia, V.K. 1981. Demographic structure of a tribal village: a preliminary study. *Vanyajati*: XXIX(3).

6

Genesis of 'Nowhere' Children: A Study of Rural Households in North Bengal

Sudip Chakraborty

'Nowhere' children are those who are neither in school nor in labour force. D.P. Choudhury (1996) has coined this term to refer to the missing children. They are missed out in the workers' statistics as well as from school statistics. The specific study to look for their whereabouts and to locate the reasons for being nowhere is very scarce for two reasons. The first one is from the point of severity of deprivation. They are apparently less deprived than their counterparts in other categories like child labourers including bonded labourers, street children, commercial sex workers and children victims of physical and psychological abuse and violence at home or outside home. They fail to draw media attention, not an issue of public outcry and therefore not prioritised in the immediate public action. Secondly, the issue of nowhere children is covered under the broader study of out of school children, particularly on drop out at the elementary level of education. The research on schooling of children has gained momentum in the wake of the call for Universal Education for all as a step towards achieving Millennium Development Goal. The recent enactment to the Indian Constitution to make education free and compulsory to all children and Supreme Court of India upholding child right to education as a fundamental right are two major developments in the recent history. The launch of Sarva Siksha Abhiyan(SSA) to provide elementary education for all children in response to global commitment as well as to discharge the constitutional duty has invoked renewed interest in the study on children schooling. The research studies on child schooling (Dreze and Kingdon 1999, Duraisamy 2000, Grootaert and Patrinos 1995, Leclerq 2001) look into the determinants of child schooling. Their revelations about the explanatory variables are mostly common. Parental education, particularly of mothers' education has been found to be a major determinant. Economic well-being of the households, credit constrains, access to schooling, sibling rivalry, gender, parental perception about the value of education are factors that largely explain the children' school participation.

Specific study on school discontinuation of children (Weber 1989, Rumberger 2001) has classified the causal factors in three distinct categories. Family related factors that include family income, caste, parental education and family structure. School related reasons comprises of regularity of attendance, academic attainment, interest in school and school facilities. Personal reasons include disciplinary problems, attitudinal problems and circumstances like marriage. Ramchandran and Saihjee (2002) in a study of District Primary Education Programme has observed that "general households characteristics like income, caste, occupation and educational level of parents continue to determine access, attendance, completion, and learning achievement. The study by Sengupta and Guha (2002) focussed exclusively on girl children to study the determinants of their schooling. The determinant variables, liker the earlier study were household income, parental education and parental occupation. Caste and religion were also influencing factor in girls' schooling. Even though in another study (Vaid 2004) the influence of caste was found to be weak in explaining school participation.

The fresh look into the determinants and dimension of nowhere children is warranted for three reasons. One, the study of the determinants of dropouts of children can partially explain the incidence of nowhere. One of the prominent reasons, found in many studies (Choudhury 2006) for discontinuation of schooling is the remunerative work undertaken by children to support family. Nowhere children, as per the definition, do not undertake any work that may hinder their schooling. They are out of school not to participate in the labour market. Then what might be the reasons? Does the schooling system push them? Or the households pull them? A serious research focussing exclusively on nowhere children can locate the factors. The second reason for the importance of such study is its implication for national economic development. Denial of access to quality education to a large section of children impedes the process of human capital formation. Returns to education have found to be higher for primary school leavers (World Bank 1980, Tilak 1987, Todaro 1997 and Meir). The positive association between female education and decline in fertility, infant and child mortality has been well established (World Bank 1997). Education is key to development, vehicle of empowerment and a potent instrument of bringing an end to social injustice, exploitation and exclusion. "Education improves their health, skills, knowledge and capability for productive work. For society as a whole, education enriches the political and cultural life of the community and strengthens the community's ability to exploit technology for social and economic advancement. Because the benefits are so broad and pervasive, the development of education is key concern everywhere. The low human capital formation leads to perpetuation of poverty in developing countries. On the other plane, deprivation of schooling for children is denial of child rights as per article 28 of the UNCRC.

Debate over definition: who are 'nowhere'?

Like child labourers, the category of nowhere children is always shrouded by disputes among social scientists and NGOs and international donor agencies. Two schools of thought have emerged in the discourse specifically on what exactly constitute nowhere children: the restrictive definition and broader definition. The same difference of perception pervades the discourse of child labour. It relates to the perception of work by children in particular and childhood in general. This is also reflected in the difference of understanding of childhood as a universal concept and childhood in cultural specific context. The proponents of restrictive definition stand by one delineated by Stein and Davis (1940). They assert, " Any work by children that interfere with in the full physical development, the opportunities for a desirable minimum of education, of their needed recreation. Lieten (2000) observes" the concept of child labour in my opinion should be restricted to the sphere of production and service that interfere with normative development of child. The advocates of restrictive definition invokes article 32 of the United Nations Convention of the Rights of the Children which states that rights of the child to be protected from economic exploitation.

Proponents of broader definition vehemently contest this underestimation. Weiner (1996) argues that most of the 90 million children not in school are working children. Shanta Sinha (2000) upholds this argument by claiming that " any child not in school is immediately drawn in to supplementing family labour on full time basis". She argues that any child out of school has to be treated as child labourer. Thus the conflict of perception leads to conflict of statistics. The estimate ranges from 14 million to 114 million depending on who is doing the estimate (Roy 1999). The immediate corollary of such debate and resultant conflict of estimate has a bearing on the estimate of nowhere children. A swollen estimate of child labour, if there is, thus lessens the number of nowhere children and vice versa.

Crisis in statistical figure

The magnitude of child labourers as per census 2001 does not match with the data on out of school children released by the department of Education of the central government. Census definition of work is restrictive and is in conformity with the concept of economic exploitation as conceived by UNCRC. Child main worker as per the definition is a fulltime remunerative work or any economic activity that prevents the child from attending school. In the case of Andhra Pradesh, for example, census data recorded 0.943 million child worker aged 5 to 14 years while Education Department recorded only 0.642 million children out of school there. Thus 0.301 million full time child labourers in Andhra pradesh are officially enrolled as children currently in school. This is serious case of over estimation of current students and under estimation of out of school children and providing a basis to allow under estimation of child labourers. The estimate of child labourers further goes up to 1.36 million if marginal workers are added to the main workers as per latest census report. The possibility of higher magnitude of out of school children cannot be ruled out in Andhra Pradesh. The same is the case for both Madhya Pradesh and Rajasthan. The census data recorded 1.26 million child labourers for the former and 1.06 million for the latter. However, the Education Department data recorded 1.06 million out of school children for the former and 0.742 million out of school children for the latter. Hence school register on which the data of the Education Department is based does not seem to be reliable estimate on schooling participation of children.

Table 1: Child Workers in two census period and out of school children

State	Child Workers 1991	Child Workers 2002	% Workers 1991	% Workers 2001	Change 1991 – 2001	Out of School Children *
1	2	3	4	5	6	7
Andhra Pradesh	1661940	1363339	9.98	7.7	-2.28	2477695
Arunachal Pradesh	12,395	18482	5.65	6.06	0.41	3239
Assam	327598	351416	5.46	5.07	-0.39	78882
Bihar	942,245	1117500	3.99	4.68	0.69	8453648
Chattisgarh	N.A	364572	N.A	6.96	6.96	N.A
Delhi	27351	41899	1.27	1.35	0.08	**1122443**
Goa	4656	4138	1.95	1.82	-0.13	98178
Gujarat	523585	485530	5.26	4.28	-0.98	0
Haryana	109,691	253491	2.55	4.78	2.23	1136131
Himachal Pradesh	56438	107774	4.55	8.14	3.59	123290
Jammu & Kashmir	N.A	175630	N.A	6.62	6.62	331417
Jharkhand	N.A	407200	N.A	5.47	5.47	N.A
Karnataka	976247	822665	8.81	6.91	-1.90	93505

State	Child Workers 1991	Child Workers 2002	% Workers 1991	% Workers 2001	Change 1991 – 2001	Out of School Children *
Kerela	34800	26156	0.58	0.47	-0.11	375103
Madhya Pradesh	1352563	1065259	8.08	6.71	-1.37	1489236
Maharastra	1068418	764075	5.73	3.54	-2.19	0
Orissa	452394	377594	5.87	4.37	-1.50	642000
Punjab	142,868	177268	3.04	3.23	0.19	1123234
Rajasthan	774199	1262570	6.46	8.25	1.79	212715
Sikkim	5598	16457	5.18	12.04	6.86	00
Tamilnadu	578,889	418801	4.83	3.61	-1.22	347065
Tripura	16478	21756	2.29	2.79	0.50	71365
Uttar Pradesh	1410086	1927997	3.81	4.04	0.23	15940996
Uttranchal	N.A	70183	N.A	3.24	3.24	N.A
West Bengal	711691	857087	4.16	4.5	0.34	2134655

Census 1991 and 2001, Out of school children

Source: Rajya Sabha Unstarred question No. 1908 dated 10.3.2003

Table 1 presents the magnitude and proportion of child labourers in two census years: 1991 and 2001. It captures the growth of child labour during the inter-census decade. Column 6 presents the change in the incidence of child labour in each state. Child labourers are engaged in economic activities, for production of goods and services that derail their school attendance. Therefore child labourers and current students are mutually exclusive categories. Column 7 gives an account of the out of school children in respective states as furnished by the Government during a parliamentary debate on 10th march, 2003. Serious anomalies are detected if column 3 and column 7 are perused side by side. The magnitude of out of school children may exceed the magnitude the number of child workers and the logical conclusion is that the rest of the out of school children are nowhere children. By this estimate Andhra Pradesh has 815755, Bihar has 7336148, Delhi has 1080544, Madhya pradesh has 423977 nowhere children. Most glaring under reporting or misreporting have been observed in the estimate of many states like Arunachal Pradesh, Assam, Karnataka, Tamil Nadu where magnitude of out of school children in each of the states, as per census report, were less than the magnitude of child workers. One possibility of such a mismatch of account might be the over reporting in the school register. A child once enrolled in school register is counted as regular student at any point of time. Regularity of attendance is not taken in to account. It may so happen that child once enrolled earlier might have left school to undertake work. By this way a child who is a child worker in a census estimate may be a current student as per education statistics. The resultant effect is the over estimation of currently attending students and the under estimation of out of school children. This inaccuracy in education statistics results in inexactness of the estimate of nowhere children

Realistic statistics and pertinent question

NSSO collects detailed information about activity status of people aged 5 years onwards in different rounds. We can have information about activity status of children aged 5 years to 14 years from these survey reports. The activities of the respondents are divided between usual principal occupation and subsidiary occupation on the basis of major time criterion. Non-economic activities have been captured in the 55th round of Employment and unemployment survey.

Table 2 Proportion of Children (5 to 14 years) engaged in Work, school and Neither work nor in School (1999-2000)

Activity	*All Children*	*Boys*	*Girls*
Work	5.16	3.29	7.24
School	67.92	71.25	64.22
Idle	19.87	18.24	21.69
Work and school	0.83	0.81	0.85
Work and Idle	0.47	0.45	0.49
School and Idle	5.75	5.95	5.51

Source: National Sample Survey, Employment and Unemployment, 55th Round

Around 5 per cent of the children were found to be child labourers as per principal status criterion. Idle children, neither in school nor in work, constituted around 20 per cent of all children. The further sub categorisation of the three distinct categories of work, school and idle and permutation among them raises question and shrouds actual status of the children particularly in rural area. For example, the combination of work and school presupposes schooling as a subsidiary engagement of children. Full time formal schooling can hardly be a subsidiary engagement for them. Combining work and school may derail school attendance and regularity and may result in dropping out very soon. Likewise school and idle category of children raises similar question about the validity of such categorisation.

The study design, field work and research question

The present study is an attempt to look in to the issue of nowhere children in a rural setting. The fieldwork was carried out during 2004 in the district of Jalpaiguri in northern part of West Bengal popularly known as North Bengal. Three blocks (Panchayat samiti) namely Jalpaiguri sadar, Mal and Rajganj were selected out of 13 blocks of the district purposively due to easy accessibility on the one hand and representative characters of the blocks, representing three distinct parts of the districts, on the other. From these three blocks, two *Gram Panchayats* (GP) from each of the three blocks were randomly selected. Thus we have 6 GPs in the second stage. From each of these GPs at least one village was selected at random at the third stage. The villages thus selected were scattered through out the district. All the households having children from 6 to 14 years were taken up for the survey. The number of 'children' households stood at 1440 in total. The size of children that came out was 2392 at the end. Pre-tested questionnaire was used to record all information required for the enquiry from the head of the household in the presence of children. The information was categorised in three broad heads: children, parent and households characteristics. Child characteristics include age, gender, work and schooling and household chores. Parental features include father and mother's education, occupation, VEC membership, perception of benefits of education. Household characteristics include household poverty, caste, spending on private tuition. For the present study child labour is conceived as per convention no 138 of the ILO which states "any economic activity of underage children" that thwarts the process of normal development. Economic exploitation of any kind, in the family or outside that derails educational attainment, affects leisure play and over all well-being of the child is child labour. Light work including household chores that does not interfere with schooling and other childhood attainment is not child labour. Therefore nowhere children are those who are neither child labourers as defined above or current student. Thus the objective of the present study is to locate the factors that cause a child to belong to the category of nowhere children in a typical rural setting.

Findings of the Survey

Distribution of all children by age group and gender is presented in table 3. The cross tabulation of children status with their gender and age cohort brings forth an interesting revelation about the relationship among those variables. School participation rate declines with increase successive age cohort. Around 85 per cent of the children in the lowest age category, that is, in 6 –8 years age, attend school as compared to 63 per cent in the upper most age category. Gender disparity in school participation has also been observed: 75 per cent of the girls attend school where as the attendance for the boys is higher at 81 per cent. Incidence of child labour, like the schooling deprivation, goes up with higher age group. In other words, it establishes that as a child grows up, the probability of his or her getting out of school and joining labour force rises. Contrastingly, the incidence of 'nowhere' does not follow the same path. The younger children are rather more likely to be nowhere than their seniors. The study reveals that 'nowhere' constitutes 13 per cent for the lowest age group while it comes down to 9 per cent for the highest age group among children. The most prominent reason for the predominance of relatively younger in the nowhere group is the belated enrolment in primary schools. Many parents have been found to be sluggish in enrolling their kids when they are six years old.

Table 3: Distribution of students, Child Labour and 'nowhere' children (6 to 14 years) by gender and age group. (N = 2392)

Six Villages Combined

Students, Labour & nowhere Age Group in Years	*Students*		*Child Labour*		*No Where*		*Total*		*Total Children*
	M	*F*	*M*	*F*	*M*	*F*	*M*	*F*	
6-8	353	297	6	7	37	62	396	366	762
9-11	345	353	17	23	20	31	382	407	789
12-14	278	258	122	101	15	67	415	426	841
Total gender wise	976	908	145	131	72	160	1193	1199	2392
Total	1884 (78.77%)		276 (11.53%)		232 (9.70%)		2392 (100)		

Computed from Field data

Household poverty has been found to be a potent factor in deciding a child place in one of these three distinct categories. School participation goes up with gradual increase in economic well-being of the their families. Likewise child labour rate decreases with upward movement in the economic status. Incidence of nowhere is positively related to economic status. Poverty substantially explains the incidence of nowhere children in the study villages.

Table 4: Percentage of Distribution of Student, Child labour and no where children by economic status and age group (6 to 14 Years) (N=2392)

	Student	*Child Labour*	*No Where*	*Total Children*
6-8 Years				
Very Poor	79.71	1.93	18.35	208
Poor	84.19	1.80	13.99	450
Middle	98.96	1.03	0	97
Rich	100	0	0	7
9-11 Years				
Very Poor	83.49	3.39	13.10	206
Poor	88.36	6.68	4.95	464
Middle	97.34	1.76	0.88	113
Rich	100	00	00	6
12-14Years				
Very Poor	40.98	43.71	15.30	183
Poor	64.05	25.90	10.04	498
Middle	88.07	9.27	2.64	151
Rich	100	00	00	9
6-14 Years				
Very poor	69.17	15.24	15.57	597
Poor	78.61	11.89	9.56	1412
Middle	93.90	4.70	1.38	361
Rich	100	00	00	22

Note : The economics classification of all households in the order of 'very poor' 'poor', 'middle' and 'rich' has been performed on the basis of annual income, land, house quality, no. of livestock, assets such, T.V sets, cycle, electricity connection, radio, water source, no. of dependants in the family etc.

Explanatory Exercises: The selection of causal variables

Binary regression analysis was performed to identify the causal factors at the household, parental and children level that explain the incidence of nowhere children in the study villages. However the data for the logistic regression was collected from three villages taking in to consideration sizable presence of nowhere children to ensure proportionate response for both 'yes' (1) and 'no' (0). Therefore, for regression purpose, altogether 1089 children from 687 households were covered. The dependent variable 'nowhere" is binary in nature and the explanatory variables are combinations of binary as well as of quantitative nature. The dependent variable takes the value of 1 if a particular child is nowhere and 0 otherwise which means that the latter may be either a current student or in labour force. The explanatory variables are defined as under (1) Sex (1 if the child is a boy, 0 girl), (2) caste (1 if SC/ST, 0 otherwise), (3) Famisiz (No. of family members), (4). fathedu (Fathers' schooling in years (5) Mothedu (Mothers' schooling in years) (6) Poverty (1 if poor and 0 non-poor). The four economic classes have been clubbed in to two classes: poor and non- poor. "Poor" class consists of 'poor' and 'very poor' categories and non-poor class consists of 'middle' and 'rural rich' categories (see table (7) Pritui (1 if the family spends on private tuition 0 otherwise) (8) Second (1 if there is one secondary / middle school within one kilometre of the child' house 0 otherwise) (9) Benefit (1 if the parents perceives positive value for education 0 otherwise) (10) Houchor (1 if the child undertakes household chores for long hours 0 otherwise) (11) Dropout (1 if the child is drop out 0 never enrolled) (12) VEC (1 if either parents is member of VEC, 0 otherwise) (13) MTA (1 if the mother is MTA member 0 otherwise) (14) Casual (1 if family survives on casual income, 0 for permanent income) (15) Land (1 if the family is landed 0 otherwise)

The binomial logistic regression model expresses a qualitative dependent variable as a function of several explanatory variables, both qualitative as well as quantitative (Hamilton 1992). If p is the probability of being nowhere for a particular child, then

$$P = [\ 1 + e^{\{-\beta X\}}\ ]^{-1}$$

$$Log_e\ [Pi\ /\ \{1 - Pi\}] = \beta X = \sum_{=0}^{k} \beta_j X_{ij}$$

Where β is a vector of coefficients and X is a vector of covariates that affects the probability of being nowhere. Thus the general logistic model can further be expressed as above.

A closure perusal of table 5 reveals the effects of each explanatory variable on the outcome of the event, i.e. the factors responsible for placing a particular child in nowhere category. The signs of the regression co-efficient indicate the direction of the effect on the dependent variable. The exponential b or the odds ratio is the value by which the odds of an event change when the explanatory variable increases by one unit. The variable 'sex' has negative coefficient, which indicates that boys as compared to girls are 0.79 times less likely to be nowhere. The NSSO 55th round report as well as my field data compiled and presented in Table 3 confirms the female dominance in the category of nowhere children. On getting out of school. Boys in larger proportion undertake remunerative outside home while girls remain at home and assist mother for sometime in household chores. The social norm sometimes disallows girls to go out of home to earn for the family in the rural area. Children belonging to scheduled caste and scheduled tribes families are three times more likely to be nowhere than the children of upper caste families. Caste based discrimination in school participation of children in India is still a pervasive problem particularly in rural area. Larger family size increases the probability of being nowhere. The study finds that a unit increase in family size increases the odds of being nowhere by 1.64 times. My finding is in conformity with other studies (Knodel and Wongsith 1991, Anh 1998) that establish that family size decreases the probability of school continuation. Parental education as measured by years of their schooling experience has been found to a potent factor in deciding the incidence nowhere children. An increase in one unit in father's education reduces the odds of a child getting nowhere by 0.86 times. Similar is the case for mother's education. A unit increase in mother's schooling in years reduces the odds of being nowhere by 0.98 times. Educated parents sometimes appear as role model for their children. Children having parents with more schooling experience are more likely to continue schooling (Psacharopoulos and Arrigade 1989).

Table 5 Binary Logistic Analysis

Explanatory variables	*Estimates of Coefficients*	*Std. Error*	*Wald statistics*	*Odds ratio*
Sex (Ref. Girls)	- 230	.287	.335	0.7945
Caste(ref. Non-sc/st	1.131	.193	.000	3.0983
Famisiz	0.497	.113	.000	1.6436
fathedu	-.145	.025	.235	0.8650
Mothedu	-.012	.019	.387	0.9890
Poverty (Ref.non-poor	.603	.296	.020	1.8274
Pritui (Ref. Non-private	-.853	.315	.000	0.4261
Seconda (Ref. Not available)	-.350	.319	.357	0.7047
Benefit (Ref. Non-benefit)	-2.041	.269	.043	0.1299
Houchor (Ref. Nonpartcipating)	.458	.387	.812	1.5808
Dropout (Ref. Never enrolled	1.345	.341	.083	3.8376
VEC (Ref. Non-VEC	-1.453	.249	.847	0.2339
MTA (Ref. Non MTA	-.731	.456	.856	0.4814
Casual (Ref. Perma-nent	.739	.643	.010	2.0936
Land (Ref. Nonlanded)	-.127	.151	.025	0.8807

- 2 Log likelihood - 154.234
Measures of over all predictability- 0.75
N (No of cases)- 1089
Degree of Freedom-1

Children belonging to poor families are 1.8 times more likely to be nowhere as compared relatively rich families in the study area. Poverty as conceived in this study is not measured by only income parameter. I have classified all the children households in to four economic categories: very poor, poor, middle and rich. Households are categorized and scaled taking in to consideration, along with income, other attributes (Table 4) and households assets that indicate standing of well-being of a household. There are number of studies (Levy 1985, Burgohani 1997, Singh and Santiago 1997) to confirm that poverty places child from schooling. Private tuition has been found to be another factor in children's school continuation. Children taking supplementary private tuition are less likely to drop out and join the breed of nowhere. The study reveals that families spending on private tuition for their children are 0.42 times less likely to discontinue schooling as compared to families spending nothing on that. This particular finding of this study confirms the revelation in the Pratichi Report 2002 on the state of primary education in West Bengal. Pratichi Foundation established by, Noble laureate professor Amartya Sen, conducted the study. The report highlighted the deficiency in learning competency of children in government primary schools and the role of private tutoring in differentiating learning achievement. It came to light that children who did not receive private tuition could not write and read properly even after four years of schooling. Students who are lagging behind in the class could not get individual care apparently for overcrowding and lack of facilities. The likelihood of discontinuation goes up manifold when a student faces difficulties in coping up with the day-to-day classroom transaction and learning process. Availability of middle school or secondary school within a radius of one kilometre of the child's residence has found to be a factor influencing the outcome. The study finds that children who can avail secondary school within their neighbourhood are 0.70 times less likely to be nowhere as compared children who can not.

Parental perception about the benefit of education is also a factor that determine the probability of getting nowhere for a child. Parents who are convinced of the positive return on education are 0.12 times less likely withdraw their children from school and there reduces the probability of getting nowhere. Children undertaking household chores for long hours, three to four hours, in a day, are 1.58 times more likely to be nowhere as compared to children who don't do at all and even if they do, they do it for small hours in a day. Drop out children are 3.83 times more likely to be nowhere than never enrolled children. With the launch of DPEP in this district since 1998, there has been a constant drive to enrol all children in the neighbourhood primary schools. The establishment of SSK (Sishu Siksha Kendra) and MSK (Madhyamik Siksha Kendra) under Sarba Siksha Abhiyan (SSA) has bolstered the school enrolment drive for all children. There fore, in the wake of those initiations, out of school children are mostly dropouts rather than never enrolled. Membership of the Village Education Committee (VEC) and involvement in school affairs in the village by parents, mostly by fathers, reduces the probability of getting nowhere of their children. This study confirms that children whose father are members of VEC are 0.23 timers less likely to be nowhere than the children whose father or guardian are not members of VEC. Like wise children whose mothers are members of MTA (Mothers Teachers Association) are 0.48 times less likely to be nowhere than the children whose mothers are not members. Children whose households survives on casual income like casual wage are 2.09 times more likely to be nowhere than the children whose household have any permanent source of income. Children belonging to a landed family are 0.88 times less likely to be nowhere than children of non-landed families.

Conclusion

The present study uncovers a grey area of child deprivation in rural India. Category of 'nowhere' among children is a less focussed area in the discourse on children's well-being from both rights perspective as well from the view point of sound economic reasoning. Both push and pull factor work in tandem to generate and sustain the incidence. School related factors pushes away children form their portal. Overcrowding, inadequacy of teachers, unattractive course content, failure in coping up in class room transaction and lack of easy access to secondary schools are inhibiting factors from 'push' side. Pull factors work at household level. Poverty, landlessness, parental illiteracy, child's engagement in household chores for long hours, household inability to provide supplementary private coaching, lack of interest and non-involvement of parents in schooling affairs are factors that work at household level. Policy implications that come up after locating the factors are two-pronged. On the one hand, the education delivery system in the rural area should be overhauled. Adequate number of teachers with a teacher pupil ratio of 1:4 should be provided in the primary schools. Course content should be joyful to fascinate the first generation learners. Availability of middle or secondary school within walking distance to minimise the transport cost should be ensured. Free textbooks, uniforms and provision of stipend for all categories of poor children without limiting the provision for SC and ST students only can substantially ensure school continuation. Poverty eradication programme in the rural area through formation of self-help groups, implementation of National Employment Guarantee programme, sensitisation programme for greater involvement in the VEC and MTA can significantly reduce the proportion of nowhere children.

REFERENCES

Anh Truong Si, John Knodel and David Lam (1998), 'Family Size and Children's Education in Vietnam', Demography, 35, pp. 57–70 .

Buragohani, T. (1997), "Differentials in literacy rate by social group" Margin, vol. 29.

Chaudhuri, D.P (1996), A Dynamic Profile of Child Labour in India 1951- 1991, New Delhi, ILO.

Choudhury, Amit (2006), "Revisiting Dropouts, Old Issues, Fresh Perspective", Economic and Political Weekly, December 23, 2006, pp. 5257-5263.

Dreze, J. and Kingdon, G.G (1999), *"School participation in Rural India"*, Delhi School of Economics and Oxford University Press (Mimeo).

Duraisamy, M. (2000), 'Child Schooling and Child Work in India' Paper prepared for NCAER, New Delhi under it's "Programme of Research in Human Development (mimeo)".

Grootaert, C. and Kanbur, R. (1995), "Child Labour: An Economic Perspective" International Labour Review, Vol 134, No. 2 pp 187 203.

Hamilton Lawrence C. (1992), Regression with Graphics: A Second Course in Applied Statistics, California.

Knodel, John and M. Wongsith (1991), 'Family Size and Children's Education in Thailand: Evidence from a National Sample' Demography, 28 pp. 119-31.

Leclereq, Francois (2001), 'Household Structure and School Participation: Is there Sibling Rivalry in Rural North India " (mimeo), University of Paris, France.

Levy, V (1985) "Cropping Pattern, Mechanisation, Child Labour and Fertility Behaviour in Rural Egypt' Economic Development and Cultural Change Vol. 33, No. 4, pp. 777-791.

Lieten Kristoffel (2000), 'Child labour: Questions on magnitude' in Child labour, Policy options, Aksant, Amsterdam 2000.

Meir, Ute (1999), 'End of Term Evaluation of the WFP Country Programme in Pakistan" Technical Report, Education Sector, UNESCO, Paris.

Psacharopoulos, George and A.M. Arriagada (1989), 'The determinants of Early age Human Capital Formation: Evidence from Brazil', Economic Development and Cultural Change, 37 (4), pp 683–708.

Ramchandran, V. and A. Saihjee (2002), 'The New Segregation: Reflections of on Gender and Equity in Primary Education 'Economic and Political Weekly, 37 (17), April 27, pp. 1600-13.

Ray R. (1999) "How Child Labour and Child Schooling Interact with Adult Labour", Washington DC, the World Bank, Policy Research Working paper 2116.

Rumberger, R. (1983) : 'Droping Out of High Schools: The Influence of Race, Sex and Family Background", American Educational Research Journal, 20, 2, pp. 199–220.

Sengupta, P. and J. Guha (2002), " Enrolment, Drop out and Grade Completion of Girl Children in West Bengal" Economic and Political Weekly, 37(17), April 27 pp. 1621–1637 .

Sinha, Shantha (2000), 'Child labour and Education' in 'The Gender gap in Basic education' Sage publication, New Delhi, 2000.

Singh, R.D. and Santiago, M. (1997), "Farm earnings, Educational attainments and Role of public policy, some evidence from Mexico, World Development, Vol 29, No. 3.

Stein, E. and J Davies Eds. (1940), Labour problems in America, New York: Farraer and Richer.

Tilak, J.B.G. (1987): The Economics of inequality of education in India. Sage Publication, New Delhi.

Todaro, M.T. (1997), 'Economic Development', 6th Edition, London and New York Longman.

Vaid, D. (2004), "Gendered Inequality in Educational Transaction' Economic and Political Weekly 34, No. 35, pp. 2947 29 38.

Weiner, Myron (1991), "The child and the state in India: Child labour and education policy in comparative perspective, Princeton University Press.

Weber, J M (1989), 'Identifying Potential Drop outs: A compilations and Evaluation of Selected Procedures", Centre on Education and Training for Employment, Columbus, Ohio.

World Bank (1980), World Development Report 1980 New York, Oxford University Press.

World Bank (1996), 'India Primary Education Achievement and Challenges, Washington DC, World Bank.

Darker Side of Abused Children

7

Attitudes towards and perceptions of child sexual abuse in Indian culture

Simrit Kaur

'Sexual abusers come from every economic, cultural, racial, educational, religious and geographical background. They are doctors, policemen, prostitutes, secretaries, artists, bisexuals and homosexuals. They are happily married and four times divorced' (Forward and Buck, 1978, p. 29).

The above statement suggests the universal nature of the child sexual abuse. Irrespective of race or creed, child abuse does exist in one form or the other. But the meaning it takes and the connotations it carries changes to a considerable extent, depending on the social and the cultural milieu in which it is defined. Child abuse can be seen as a socially defined construct and not an absolute unchanging phenomenon. What is considered abusive in a society alters over time. Literature reveals that children have been abused from time immemorial in all cultures but some of what we now see as abuse was not so defined in the past.

This chapter dwells upon the findings of the study undertaken as part of my doctorate (1997-2001) in England. The primary aim of the study was to explore the attitudes and perceptions of social workers and local women about child sexual abuse in Indian communities of Leicester and Delhi. The intention was to contribute to the knowledge and understanding of child sexual abuse, which was a very recent area of investigation in India, with very little research base. The work in Leicester afforded a comparative context. It is hoped that this knowledge and understanding may be used to promote more effective strategies and policies to reduce child sexual abuse and to intervene more effectively.

It is acknowledged that there are various theoretical approaches to understanding and intervention in child sexual abuse, but for the purpose of this study sociological approach was adopted, in particular a socialist feminist analysis of child sexual abuse. The nature of a given society, its underlying ideologies and principles, are central to developing an understanding of child sexual abuse. Definitions of, and responses to, victims of child sexual abuse, are in part a product of public attitudes within the society in question. The abuse itself is not a culture specific phenomenon; but it is shaped, defined and reacted to differently in different cultures. An understanding of this helps to build culturally sensitive policies to combat such abuse (Kevorkian, 1999). Nevertheless, individual differences between people cannot be ignored, who, though products of the same society manifest different perceptions and attitudes. Understanding individual differences and the uniqueness of cases are equally important, especially in social work practice.

For the purpose of the study Renvoize's definition of child sexual abuse was followed:

'Child sexual abuse is any type of sexual exploitation of a child or adolescent by any older person or adult for the stimulation and/ or gratification of that person, which is not necessarily confined to

physical contact and which may range from exhibitionism or involvement with pornography to full intercourse or child prostitution; where the developmentally immature victim lacks the authority or power to prevent her/ himself being coerced into activities to which she/he is unable to give informed consent, which she/he does not properly comprehend but which- either at the time or later -the victim considers sexually abusive'(Renvoize, 1993 p. 36).

The above definition puts together points from many other definitions of child sexual abuse. It seems very clear in suggesting the acts that can constitute sexual abuse, at the same time putting enough emphasis on 'power' and 'lack of consent', which arises from the inability of children to comprehend the nature of act, given their lack of knowledge and developmental immaturity. It gives a holistic picture of what constitutes child sexual abuse.

Qualitative methods of data collection were used: individual in-depth interviews with social workers in Delhi and Leicester; group interviews and discussions with a group of local Indian women in Leicester; and action research with local women in a resettlement colony in Delhi, which had majority of the community members from low socio- economic group.

'THE BIG PICTURE'

(a) Gender discrimination

The feeling that was most passionately expressed by the respondents from all the data sources was that of gender discrimination and strong patriarchal values in Indian society. Be it the social workers and the local Indian women in Leicester, or the social workers and local women in India, all spoke strongly about the gender bias in the Indian society. For both groups of women in Leicester and in Delhi, the low status of women and girl children were expressed in relation to fear of disclosure of child sexual abuse. Social workers in general, especially in India, expressed an urgent need to empower girls and women in Indian society, the lack of which, they felt, not only rendered child sexual abuse an 'invisible crime' but also a secret, shrouded with shame and stigma, making intervention almost impossibility.

The group of mothers both in Leicester and Delhi placed much emphasis upon the *'shame and stigma'* that a family would suffer in disclosure of sexual abuse, which would not only affect the family honour but also ruin future marriage prospects for the girl. Interestingly, whenever the groups of women in Leicester or Delhi spoke about child sexual abuse, it was pertaining girl children and hence the social implications of disclosure, awareness about sexual abuse of boys was starkly lacking. Also lacking was the realisation that sexually abusive acts are emotionally and psychologically damaging. This is further considered, later in the chapter.

(b) Poverty

There is much research which indicates that poverty in itself does not lead to child sexual abuse (Finkelhor, 1986). This study highlights some aspects associated with poverty in India, in particular, in an urban poor community of Delhi and its implications on child sexual abuse. The women in Leicester, when contrasting India and England, felt themselves free of the gross aspects of poverty. Social workers in Delhi did not consider that poverty caused child sexual abuse but some believed that it added a different dimension to the way the problem is understood and dealt with. Many a times the main dilemma is how to intervene in cases where poverty is overriding and survival needs predominate. Much effort goes to support the family. A kind of contract between the worker and the client is built, based on monetary help. They cooperate but drop out when monetary help is no longer available. Counselling is not fully understood. Many a times they believe that they need services more than surveillance and counselling. The experience with the women of the community in Delhi highlighted clearly how people who were incessantly struggling to make their both ends meet viewed child sexual abuse. Sexual abuse for them, at that stage, was the abuse taking place in the public toilets, which were the only toilets in that community. The concern was regarding young girls and their daughters being abused by men of the community in these toilets. Poverty and the resultant lack of facilities was in a way precipitating child sexual abuse. Handling this situation was paramount, as this was the most visible form of sexual abuse to the women in the community at that point.

Also, it is reported often that young girls in India are being sold for monetary gain. Young girls and boys are forced into the sex industry, poverty being a prime causal factor. At a tender age these children become the sole bread winners of their poverty stricken families. However, even in this sorry state of affairs, it is important to acknowledge that in the same village, some parents will hand over their child to a pimp in exchange of money while many will go without food or a roof over their heads rather than sell their beloved child. We also know that in spite of the adverse outcomes associated with poverty, such as under-nutrition, inadequate prenatal health care, unsafe living conditions, inadequate educational opportunities, being poor in itself does not necessarily cause sexual abuse of children or has adverse developmental problems.

'THE MIDDLE LEVEL'

(a) Inadequate systems and gaps in Provision

This study clearly brings out the inadequacy and insensitivity of the State and judicial responses to child sexual abuse in India. At that time, there was no discussion even on a comprehensive law against child sexual abuse. The need to define and legislate further against child sexual abuse was felt deeply by social workers. The negligible role played by the state in addressing the issue of child sexual abuse was highlighted. It was felt that only a few voluntary organisations, some feminists and social workers were proactive and the state, till then had not provided them with basic resources to deal with the problem. The need for the state to co-operate and co-ordinate with the voluntary sector was felt urgent. Even networking between voluntary organisations was lacking, which inhibited the sharing of experience and information.

Due to the dearth of alternative care institutions in the country, such as residential or foster care, there was little hope for rehabilitation of the victim outside the parameters of the home. So, even if the conditions in the home were harmful for the child, there was no other option available for them. The concern was also that the institutions that do exist were in deplorable condition and might lead to further abuse of the victim. In this context, the social workers in Leicester did not feel so much pressure, as there were resources and guidelines available. But their worry was of different nature. They felt that with the procedures and guidelines in England, they found themselves in a difficult position to intervene in Indian families whose values did not accord with their approach to intervention. The need is to develop more culturally sensitive policies and guidelines.

It was widely suggested that India should have a parallel system of family law, comparable to that in England, as well as criminal proceedings. Such a system, which is not only concerned with establishing the guilt of certain behaviour, but seeks to ensure that the child is protected and that his or her best interests are paramount. Proving guilt is always difficult, the more so when the abuse is other acts than rape. Gaining convictions in the criminal courts requires high standards of proof and strict adherence to rules of evidence. Long delays and lengths of court proceedings, and investigations, can lead to secondary victimisation. These are the factors which mitigate against effective child protection when the criminal justice system is the only recourse. What is required is a system of laws and procedures, which can at least provide safe environment for the children who are at risk and who are in need for protection.

(b) Resources and 'Complementary Care'

Handling cases of child sexual abuse is a complicated matter of law, policy and practice. Many factors, such as the nature of abuse, the resources of the family, and the alternatives available, need to be taken into consideration before a rational decision can be made (Finkelhor, 1986). The issue of resources, which include infrastructure, services and skilled personnel, is obviously central to the development of any child protection system, to deal with any increase in reporting and to provide support for children and their families. At present India lacks all these resources. There is a dearth of skilled and trained professionals and lack of good quality alternative care facilities. This must be remedied, if we aim to provide a safe environment for the children who are found to be unsafe in their own houses. Temporary 'Emergency Protection Orders' for example, are beneficial, if there are adequate resources and quality care provisions for children brought into care. Of course having such provision is only the beginning. For example, in the West where resources are available and systems and procedures are developed, social workers and other professionals still find themselves in a dilemma whether to recommend that children should enter the care system, even when home circumstances strongly indicate it. This is in part because of their doubts about the quality of the 'career in care' which so many children experience and its impact on the development of the child (Stevenson, 1999), as well as a recognition of the intrinsic value of family life.

(c) Sensitising the Professionals

In India the whole system needs to be geared to the problem of child sexual abuse. The state, the judiciary, police, government officials, doctors and the rest has been relatively indifferent to the problem until now. Social change begins with raised awareness, but it must also be embodied in practice and reflected in legal and economic realities as well as in interpersonal values (Bagley and King, 1990). The framing of new law and the development of procedures would be merely a bandage on the problem as, without fundamental improvement in the resources made available and in the motivation of professionals to intervene more effectively and develop more effective preventive strategies.

DILEMMAS AND OPPORTUNITIES FOR SOCIAL WORKERS.

Social workers, in both Leicester and Delhi, expressed their innermost dilemmas in dealing with cases of child sexual abuse in Indian society. For Indian social workers, the major concern was how to intervene in cases of child sexual abuse. How to deal with the family? How much to do and how much not to do? Some social workers felt morally responsible for putting the child into problematic situations, in cases where disclosure was encouraged. In one such case, the social worker felt immense guilt and pain; one of her clients, a victim of intra-familial child sexual abuse, was killed by her mother, because she refused to change her statement to help the father come out of the prison. The social worker believed that if she had not taken a proactive approach in supporting the victim and encouraging her, she could have been at least, saved from murder. The level of discomfort and frustration among social workers was very high.

Due to lack of training and guidance in dealing with such cases, social workers found it complex and ambiguous work. It even has an impact on their emotional well being.

In Leicester too, the social workers found themselves in a difficult situation, having to work within English procedural guidelines with Indian families. They felt that the family values and expectations were so different that it became difficult to intervene as a 'professional'; their role was not understood and usually undermined. 'When minority cultural patterns do not mesh with professional practice and institutional structures which have been generated in another cultural setting. It is easy to lose sight of the real problem' (Ballard, 1979, p. 149).

Social workers struggle between the diverse cultural demands, different expectations regarding their role and their own value systems. 'Social workers like anyone else, are children of their time, and of social milieu in which they happen to have been born. The judgements which they make and the decisions which they take are never value free, although it is important that they become more aware of their assumptions' (Stevenson, 1989, p. 167). In the present circumstances, as discussed above, there lies a danger of expecting social workers and social services department to resolve problems that are well beyond their realm and area of responsibility.

Social work is recognised as a profession which seeks social change by addressing the problem of individuals, their environment, and the interface between the two (Bagley and King, 1990). Social workers have different roles to play, from social and political change, to community development and to individual case work and child advocacy. All are relevant to the reduction of child sexual abuse.

THE NEED TO RAISE AWARENESS OF THE CONCEPT OF EMOTIONAL DAMAGE AND ITS IMPACT ON CHILD DEVELOPMENT

From the findings of the study, it is clear that the lack of disclosure and reluctance by family and society to intervene in these cases is partly due to the lack of understanding of the emotional damage that abuse can have and its relationship to child development. It was evident that the women in both Leicester and Delhi saw the damage done to the (girl) child by sexual abuse only in terms of the 'loss of family honour' and her being labelled as 'damaged goods'. All this, they believed, would further affect her marriage prospects as her reputation would be ruined once society got to know about the abuse. The realisation that such abuse can be detrimental for the child's emotional and psychological well-being was sadly missing. This insensitivity does not provide a basis to work towards emotionally rehabilitating the victim. Concern was largely about the social implications, 'only if people find out it is bad...otherwise it is okay'. The social workers in India in fact discussed the resistance of the family to the whole concept of 'counselling'. Because the concept of emotional damage was lacking, parents thought that by putting a lid on such cases the problem would go away. It is true that one has to pay a heavy price for speaking out about sexual abuse in Indian society, and mostly this price is paid by the victim; thus there will be parents who, at no cost, will let out the family secret. But by keeping the secret and denying the child's right to help, they are compounding the problem to an incalculable extent.

THE SILENCE NEEDS TO BE BROKEN

'The enforcement of silence has been and remains the most potent weapon of abusers, both individually and collectively. Breaking the silence has likewise been seen as the most vital step towards bringing about change and a safer environment' (Nelson, 2000, p. 394)

All the social workers and even the women in Leicester felt strongly that the existence of child sexual abuse had to be accepted and acknowledged in Indian society. They felt that it has been long ignored and evaded and that society cannot turn a blind eye towards it anymore. It was felt, however, that the question of speaking out and seeking support in Indian context posed major dilemmas. It seems to be a no win situation; disclosure of the incident extracts a heavy social price and silence deprives the victim of her right to voice her feelings, pain and trauma, which in itself impede her recovery. This dilemma carries with it the recognition that the indifference of society in itself to child sexual abuse causes pain and humiliation to the individual. It is in effect a denial of childrens' human rights. Although this is true for any child, of either gender, the position of girl children is particularly problematic because of the widespread discrimination against females, child and adult.

'Silence' enables sexual abuse to continue unabated and protects the offenders. Abused children grow up in a world fraught with uncertainty, inconsistency, lies, violation, pain and abandonment. Abandonment does not necessarily mean leaving a child on its own. It is also a kind of emotional abandonment, leaving a frightened young child alone to deal with the inner turmoil inflicted by the abuse (Faulkner, 1996). Advising a victim not to divulge a criminal act implies that his/her emotions and psychological state of mind are unimportant (Kevorkian, 1999). Early identification of sexual abuse victims appears crucial for reduction of suffering, enhancement of psychological development and healthier adult functioning (Finkelhor *et al.*1990; Bagley, 1992).

Children have to be empowered, to enable them to express their fears, thoughts and pain (Bagley, 1996). This is possible only when there are people who are ready to listen, share and understand their pain. Somehow, somewhere, the conspiracy of silence around child sexual abuse in Indian homes has to be shattered (Virani, 2000).

Thus we have to recognise our responsibility to help to break the silence but also to provide the support needed when it happens. The task is a mammoth one and the responsibility onerous.

CONCLUDING THOUGHTS

In this chapter I have discussed the problems and the dilemmas which arise in any attempt to intervene more effectively in child sexual abuse within the Indian context. I have shown the different levels and ways in which these problems manifest themselves. It is important to stress that these different levels and factors interact with each other. Progress will not be made simply by a 'top down' strategy but by a battle on all fronts; success in one sphere will improve the chances of success in another. However, it is hard to avoid the conclusion that 'the big picture', in terms of gross poverty, social inequality and gender discrimination, are prerequisites for radical improvement. Meanwhile social workers have a continuing, painful but invaluable role in improving the lot of some children and some families. Perhaps it is 'makeshift', but the essence of the work remains focussed on the need and pain of individuals and groups in particular circumstances. Such unobtrusive work, in aggregate, helps to 'break the silence' and contributes to larger scale understanding of the extent and nature of harm done by child sexual abuse.

Note: This chapter was written before the enactment of 'The Protection of Children from Sexual Offences Act (POCSO Act) 2012'. This Act was formulated to effectively address sexual abuse and sexual exploitation of children. Many of the issues highlighted in the findings of my study, such as lack of redressal mechanism, role of professionals, judicial processes, and alternative care for children requiring protection have been addressed in the POSCO Act, 2012. However, its implementation remains a huge challenge.

REFERENCES

Bagley, C. and King, K. (1990), Child Sexual Abuse: The Search for Healing, London: Routledge.

Bagley, C. and Thurston, W.E. (1996), Understanding and preventing child sexual abuse, England: Ashgate Publishing Limited

Ballard, R. (1979), Ethnic Minority and Social Services in Khan, V.S. Minority families in Britain, London: Macmillan, pp. 147-165.

Faulkner, N. (1996), Pandora's Box: The Secrecy of Child Sexual Abuse, Retrieved from http://www.prevent-abuse-now.com/pandora.htm

Finkelhor, H. (1986), Sourcebook on Child sexual Abuse, New York: The Free Press.

Finkelhor, D. (1990), New Ideas in Child Sexual Abuse Prevention in Oates R.K. (ed), Understanding and Managing Child Sexual Abuse, Sydney: Harcourt Brace-Jovanovich

Forward, S. and Buck, C. (1978), Betrayal of Innocence: Incest and its Devastation, England: Peliean Harmondsworth.

Kevorkian, N.S. (1999), Towards A Cultural Definition of Rape: Dilemmas in Dealing with Rape Victims in Palestine, Women's Studies International Forum, Vol. 22, No. 2, pp. 157-173.

Nelson, S. (2000), Confronting Sexual Abuse: Challenges for the Future in Itzin, C. (2000), Home Truths About Child Sexual Abuse, London: Routledge, pp. 387-403.

Renvoize, J. (1993), Innocence Destroyed: A Study of Child Sexual Abuse, London: Routledge

Stevenson, O. (1989), Taken From Home *in* Shardlow, S. (ed.) Values of Change in Social Work, London: Routledge, pp. 155-179.

Stevenson, O. (ed.) (1999), Child Welfare in the UK; Blackwell.

Virani, P. (2000), Bitter Chocolate: Child Sexual Abuse in India, New Delhi: Penguin Books.

8

Children as Victims of Family Violence In India

Aparajita Chowdhury and Reeta Choudhury

"Children need to be safe and secure at Home to develop a positive sense of Self, necessary to their growing into Healthy, Productive, caring Adults....................."

(National Association for the Education of Young Children, 1996).

The biggest challenge in the 21st Century is the reduction of juvenile crime, violence and victimization of children. Worldwide, more violence occurs today at homes than elsewhere in society, which is one of the major factors of juvenile delinquency and crimes of all types. In several homes, heinous violence is let loose freely on the defenseless—especially the children, putting a huge strain on a nation's economical, social and legal services. The devastating impact of family violence is legendry and in terms of human suffering, no other social evil can excel it. The indelible scars inflicted in the human minds of victims (children) may lead to life long anguish and sorrow. Thus the psychological fallout of family violence is alarming and children are the biggest victim of this situation worldwide.

Family violence is a major problem in each and every society. Children are being exposed to family violence at an alarming rate—either as direct victims or as witness to it. As many as 275 million children worldwide are exposed to violence in the HOME. These data are quite vocal in indicating the situation at every home. This range is a conservative estimate based on the limitations of the available data. In actually, millions more children may be affected by violence in the home. Children are often exposed to such violence within family and sometime caught in the crossfire and became victims of violence, both directly and indirectly. There is also increasing evidence that physical, sexual, verbal and emotional abuse of children is more likely to occur in a home where one adult is violent towards the other than in non-violent homes.

India is home to almost 19 per cent of the world's children. More than one third of the country's population, around 440 million, is below 18 years. According to one assumption 40 per cent of these children are in need of care and protection, which indicates the extent of the problem. "India has the world's largest number of sexually abused children; with a child below 16 years raped every 155th minute, a child below 10 every 13th hour and one in every 10 children sexually abused at any point of time. Physical and psychological punishments takes place in the name of disciplining children and are culturally accepted"—Government of India Child Abuse Study Report (2007).

Theoretical Framework

A *system approach* of understanding family violence and child victimization encompasses not just the child, but all the interlocking layers that link the child, and society. It offers a useful theoretical framework for conceptualizing the effects of violence on children. A *developmental approach* emphasizes the emergence of trust and empathy as crucial sensitivities. Erick Erickson (1963) held that the development of trust is the initial step in forming healthy relationships. Trust develops early and is primarily contingent on the infants' relationship with his/her parents or care giver. If this psychosocial stage of trust building is successfully resolved, the infant will learn to trust others, which will then help with later relationship building. Mistrust, in contrast, can result from a single trauma or from chronic environmental stress. If parents are emotionally unavailable, for instance, or are inconsistent in their behaviours, continuously negative, or abusive, the infant or child may fail to develop basic trust (Egeland and Erickson, 1987). *Social learning theory* also indicates that children who are exposed to domestic violence are at much higher risk of becoming both perpetrators and victims of violence (Bell, 1995). Imitation and modeling appears to play significant roles in this process. In case of family violence, children are victims of the toxic family environment, and negative parental behaviours. Thus, learn and accept the violence situation as "normal" phenomena in family life.

Family Violence in India

Globally, violence within family is universal across culture, religion, clan and ethnicity. Despite their widespread prevalence, family violence in India, however is not customarily acknowledged and has remained invisible. It is such problem thought unworthy for any immediate attention, especially in the context of legal or political attention (Vindhya, 2003). The social construction of the divide between public and private underlines the hidden nature of family violence against children in India. Rather, it is considered as disciplining and essential for maintaining the rule of authority within the family, especially for children and adolescents.

Family violence is an abuse of the intimate, trusting and safe relationship that a family should provide. It can be between couples, parent-child, siblings, parent and grand-parents, parents and other family members. Family violence occurs in many forms; the most prominent are domestic violence, child abuse, and elder abuse. Family violence affects many persons at some point in their life and constitutes the majority of violent acts in our society. Family violence is an everyday occurrence in Indian family life irrespective of class, community, status, society and religious affiliation. It is a private affair with a few or no bystanders and no real time or opportunity to help the victim (may be women or children or adolescent or aged). The accused is often the only witness to the violence. The family in India, once considered a fortress of safety and security for women, children, adolescents and aged; and a place of peace and solace, has turned out to be breeding ground of violence (Ahmed-Ghosh, 2004). It is an irony, as Martin (1978) observes, "... family, the most intimate association to which the majority of people belong, is an unrivalled source of strength and comfort. But its very closeness can also intensify the worst of human relations. Love may be corrupted to envious possession and discipline to cruelty. And above all the private focus of hopes and fears may foster dual standards of private and public behaviour".

The pervasiveness of family violence problems in India has not been fully documented. It is one of the least reported of all crimes relative to actual frequency of occurrence (Chawla, 2004). Except for police records that are loosely maintained and a few privately conducted investigations, no nationally represented study provides data concerning the incidence of family violence in India (Ahmed-Ghosh, 2004; Chawla, 2004). Despite the absence of any uniform national investigation into the problem, there is enough evidence to show that family violence does occur in India, and that marital violence in particular is widespread though largely hidden (Chawla, 2004; Fernandez, 1997). Family violence may be triggered by such factors as patriarchy, marital discord, poverty, unemployment, job insecurity, economic strain due to chronic ill health, alcoholism, drug abuse, caste, religion and social class conflicts. These conditions can create enormous stress, tension and frustration within the family which may erupt in to episodes of violence.

Key Expressions of Family Violence in India: There are several key expressions of violence in Indian families, such as:

- *Marital Violence:* Marital Violence is just beginning to be recognised as an important social problem (Patnaik, 2007). According to Chawla (2004), "we are living in a violent society, where millions of women are victims of marital violence". The psychological, emotional and relational consequences of all these manifestations of violent behaviour can be devastating for all the family members, but especially the children are greatly affected.
- *Violence against Children and Adolescents:* Another form of family violence is abuse of children and adolescents in varieties of ways. Bassa's (1978) analysis based on his clinical experience suggests that Indian children are taught to have a naïve and helpless trust in elders which gives the Indian behaviour "a peculiar, charming, childlike quality, liable to exploitation by authority figures both inside and outside family". Physical and psychological abuse to children and adolescents in Indian families are common, as the parents often consider such behaviour as an effective way of teaching and controlling children and adolescents. Violence against children and adolescents today manifests itself in a variety of ways, including physical and psychological battering, physical and emotional neglect, sexual abuse (especially young girls),

abandonment and selling of children for profit (Chowdhury, Pattnaik and Patro, 1994).

- *Violence against the Aged:* Elder abuse in India is described as the newest and most hidden form of violence in the family (Jamuna, 2003; and Chowdhury, 2007). Older parents are being assaulted and injured by their children and other relatives, often those who are their primary care providers. Family loyalty and dependency in a country like India prevent elder persons from reporting abuse. However, this has got tremendous negative impact on children, who are closer to their grandparents than their parents and very well understand the ill intention of this victimization.

Child Abuse in India –National Survey Report 2007

Nineteen per cent of the world's children live in India. According to the 2001 Census, some 440 million people in the country today are aged below eighteen years and constitute 42 per cent of India's total population i.e., four out of every ten persons. This is an enormous number of children that the country has to take care of. While articulating its vision of progress, development and equity, India has expressed its recognition of the fact that when its children are educated, healthy, happy and have access to opportunities, they are the country's greatest human resource. A study was conducted as a National study covering 13 states to examine the incidence of child abuse, especially at home and the respondents included Children (5-18 years) and Young Adults (18-24 years). It has very clearly emerged that across different kinds of abuse, it is young children, in the 5-12 year group, who are most at risk of abuse and exploitation at home. The major findings related to child abuse at home are as follows:

Physical Abuse

- Two out of every three children were physically abused.
- Out of 69 per cent children physically abused in 13 sample states, around 55 per cent were boys.
- Over 50 per cent children in all the 13 sample states were being subjected to one or the other form of physical abuse.
- Out of those children physically abused in family situations, 89 per cent were physically abused by parents.
- Most children did not report the matter to anyone.

Sexual Abuse:

- Around 53 per cent children reported having faced one or more forms of sexual abuse.
- Andhra Pradesh, Assam, Bihar and Delhi reported the highest percentage of sexual abuse among both boys and girls.
- Around 22 per cent child respondents reported facing severe forms of sexual abuse and 51 per cent other forms of sexual abuse.
- Out of the child respondents, around 6 per cent reported being sexually assaulted.
- 50 per cent abuses are persons known to the child or in a position of trust and responsibility.
- Most children did not report the matter to anyone.

Emotional Abuse and Girl Child Neglect:

- Every second child reported facing emotional abuse.
- Equal percentage of both girls and boys reported facing emotional abuse.

- In 83 per cent of the cases parents were the abusers.
- Around 48 per cent of girls wished they were boys.

The gravity of the situation demands that the issue of child abuse be placed on the national agenda. The Ministry on its part has taken measures such as the enabling legislation to establish the National and State Commissions for Protection of Rights of the Child, the Integrated Child Protection Scheme, the draft Offences against Children Bill etc. These are a few important steps to ensure protection of children of the country. But clearly, this will not be enough, the government, civil society and communities need to complement each other and work towards creating a protective environment for children. The momentum gained needs to enhance further discussion on the issue amongst all stakeholders and be translated into a movement to ensure protection of children of this country.

Child Victimization of Family Violence

Family violence is devastating social problem that impacts every segment of the population, particularly the children. Family violence was conceptualized as both domestic violence and child abuse. The construct of family violence emerged from a family events affecting the children include: (a) exposure to parental fights; (b) witnessing paternal violence towards the mother; and (c) witnessing or experiencing abuse and/or violence on the part of the children. Family violence created a toxic environment within family that leads to child victimization to a greater extent.

Child abuse and family violence often occur within the family and are linked in a number of important ways that have serious consequences for the safety of children in several ways. Firstly, family violence often directly results in physical injury and/or psychological harm to children. Secondly, even when family violence does not result in direct physical injury to the child, it can interfere with both the mother's and father's parenting to such a degree that the children may be neglected. Thirdly, while an intervention into child abuse may be initially effective, the impact of that intervention will soon be sabotaged, if family violence is also present, and if the perpetrator is not held accountable for stopping the violence and the adult victim is not protected.

Children can be injured as a direct result of family violence. Perpetrators sometimes intentionally injure children in an effort to intimidate and control their adult partners. These assaults can include physical, emotional, verbal and sexual abuse of the children. Children are also injured – either intentionally or accidentally, during attacks on their mothers or other family members. An object thrown or a weapon used against the mother may hit her child. Assaults on younger children may occur while the mother is holding the child. Injuries to older children often occur when the child attempts to intervene in violent episodes. Although many parents believe that they can hide violence from children, children living in these homes report differently. Research suggests that between 80 to 90 per cent of these children are aware of the violence (Carlson, 1984). Even if they do not see a beating, they hear the screams and see the bruises, broken bones, and the abrasions sustained by their mothers. A New Zealand study conducted by the National Collective of Independent Women's Refugees (1991) suggested that for women receiving help from refuges, 90 per cent of their children had witnessed violence; 50 per cent of the children had also been physically abused. Overseas research (Jaffe, 1990; 1992) also confirms that children are often involved directly and indirectly in family violence and that this is likely to have damaging consequences for them both immediately and in the larger term.

However, what happens in a violent families and how the children react and get affected to it both directly and indirectly are described as follows:

- **Environment of Shame** – Children are often used as weapons in parental battles. They are used by one parent in maneuvers against the other. Sometimes, a parent may compel children to be unwilling listeners to complaints about their spouse. Children from such an atmosphere may view the family as an environment of shame.
- **Insecurity Feeling** – In several violent families, the needs of the child is of little importance to their parents. The child is overtly rejected and unwanted. Such neglected children are often haunted by an extreme sense of insecurity and feels like an outsider, as both the parents are overindulged between themselves, mostly in conflict situation.
- **The Negative Fallouts on the part of the Child** – In violent homes, children may apprehend violence at any moment. Every minute is spent in fear and anxiety. A constant atmosphere of anger, uncertainty and frustration produces destructive tensions in the child. All of these may lead to negative outcomes for children and may affect their wellbeing, safety, and stability (Carlson, 2000; Edleson, 1999; Rossman, 2001). Childhood problems associated with experiencing and exposure to family violence fall into three primary categories:
    - Behavioural, social and emotional Problems: Higher level of aggression, anger, hostility, oppositional behaviour, and disobedience; fear anxiety, withdrawal, and depression; poor peer, sibling, and social relationships; and low self-esteem.
    - Cognitive and Attitudinal Problems: Lower cognitive functioning, poor school performance, lack of conflict resolution skills, limited problem solving skills, pro-violence attitudes, and belief in rigid gender stereotypes and male privilege.

Becker and McCloskey (2002), for example, examined the impact of family violence in the development of attention and conduct problems in 287 children, who were 6 to 12 years old at the start of six years prospective study.

- Long-term Problems: Higher levels of adult depression and trauma symptoms and increased tolerance for and use of violence in adult relationships.

- **Disrespect for the Parents** – Violent parental behaviour leads to mistrust and undermines the child's ability to trust adults. The child loses all his respect for the parental authority and often turns against parents. The inevitable feeling of the child is that if only the parents had not been around, life would have been better. Such children may suffer from backlog of delayed grief. The anger at the parent can spill over throughout life; long after the parent is dead, creating even more buried feelings of violence within the child.
- **Reinforce Violence** – Family violence triggers the defense mechanism in children and reinforces resistance, rebellion and revenge. It also strengthens the idea in children that it is ethical for the strong to use violence against the weak. Children of violent parents learn to hit from the same parents who teach them to love. Thus, loving and hitting become linked up in their minds and life becomes a love-hit affairs.
- **Comfortable with Chaos** – Children who are accustomed to family violence may develop a tendency to be more comfortable with chaos than with systematized environment. They may become incapable of living an organised and systematic life in later years.
- **Displaced Battlefield** – It is found that children preempt parental violence by releasing aggression well in advance. They tend to rebel violently as a course of

spontaneous survival instinct so that parental violence may be diverted or postponed at least for the moment. The crisis created by a child may help the family to get closer and provides the only opportunity for a dead and violent family to experience love. In a family where the bonds of cohesiveness are loose, the introduction of violence by the children may help to strengthen family bonds. The child provides a displaced battlefield to help minimize parental strife and increase understanding. In other words children tend to behave in a disorderly way just to silence their otherwise disorderly parents.

- **Social Isolation** – Violent parents usually discourage children from developing friendship. They do not allow other children into their home or they order them out of the home when they do visit. Because of shame and embarrassment, children of violent parents do not want to return invitation to others who have invited them to their homes. They do not want their friends to witness family arguments and discord. Friendships therefore are less likely flourish and the child may experience social isolation.
- **A Vicious Cycle** – Family violence is a vicious cycle. It is quite possible that victims of family violence can end up as worst perpetrators of domestic violence in future. It is found that a large percentage of adults who used to be very violent at homes were themselves victims of family violence. Children who have experienced family violence are four times more likely to grow up to become violent mates or parents than those who were not subjected to family violence. In another way, violent parents would have been themselves abused as children and in a crisis they can not help reverting to the way their parents have treated them. Thus, the adverse influence of family violence may set the emotional tone that shapes children the rest of their lives.

- **The Scapegoat** – In some families one particular child is singled out for ill-treatment by the mother. The most common reason for treating a particular child as a scapegoat is that this particular child may remind the mother of a despised husband or even the hated husband himself.
- **Family Violence and Delinquency** – In families where parents are excessively violent, children tend to stay out of home even late at night to avoid the unpleasant home atmosphere. Children may also resort to extreme steps like committing suicide or running away from homes. Children of abusive parents may easily fall in love with undesirable characters of the opposite sex and land up in life long difficulties. Considerable developmental work has been documented pathways from family violence experiences to serious delinquent behaviours (Mejia, Kliewer and Williams, 2006).
- **Sibling Rivalry** – In a violent family sibling rivalry lead to dominance and possession of material things among the siblings. This morbid jealousy among children and contribute to brutal assaults and enormous violence within families.

Long term Sequel of Family Violence on Children

It is increasingly being recognised that family violence has adverse effects on the physical and mental health of children. In addition, exposure to violence also can have implications for their subsequent behaviour (Jejeebhoy, 1998; CORT, 2000). Children who are living in an environment where family violence is occurring are "at-risk" to experience violence and/or abuse either directly or indirectly. Witnessing or experiencing family violence has an extreme negative impact on children that can result in emotional and psychological trauma. According to Chawla and Kang (2007), "Children in homes where domestic violence occurs are physically abused or seriously neglected at a rate 1500 times greater than the national average in the general population". Further, hearing or visualizing the abuse and/or violence against one parent by other take a huge toll on children and adolescents.

According to a study conducted by Kliewer and colleagues (2001), violence against a family member was positively correlated with depressive symptoms and anxiety in children. Exposure to violence in the family has become a major public health problem in Western world, particularly in children and adolescents who live in environments characterized by extreme danger. These toxic environments also are associated with maladaptive behaviour responses such as substance use and abuse in youths (Klevens, Bayon and Sierra, 2000; Maya *et al.* 2000). Most of the violence that children are exposed to do not come from outside their home – it occurs in their homes behind closed doors. The consequences of family violence on children are far reaching and required urgent attention and intervention.

The child and adolescent abuse literature in India indicates that their maltreatment has its own set of negative consequences or harmful developmental outcomes for children and adolescents (Chowdhury *et al.* 1994, and Chawla, 2004). For instance, abuse tends to lead to more abuse, contributes to delinquency and aggressive behaviour in children, and increases the likelihood of adult criminality. Hence, violence tends to beget violence (Patnaik, 2007). The children inherit a legacy of violence, a gift of tyranny, which they in turn will pass into their children – one generation of violence begetting another – and so on. There is considerable evidence for the intergenerational transmission of family violence. The continuance of this syndrome erodes the basic structure of the family and society.

Maltreated children also express more anger toward, and have more conflict with their family members than non-maltreated children. They exhibit more internalizing disorders (e.g., depression and various anxiety disorders) than non-abused children and are less pro-social. In addition, abused children and adolescents tend to manifest a variety of other cognitive, emotional and social difficulties, including troubled relationships with peers, impaired social cognition, lack of empathy, and poor performance. Sexually abused children and adolescents often suffer from a variety of behavioural and emotional problems. These include depression, guilt and shame, learning difficulties and higher rates of school dropout, sexual promiscuity, runaway behaviour, somatic complaints, and sudden changes in mood, to name a few (Gelles and Coute, 1990).

Parent-children violence and inter-parental violence witnessed were significant predictors of both externalizing and internalizing behaviour problems. Further, study conducted in western world stresses on the consequences of witnessing family violence on children and adolescents, in terms of physical and biological functioning, behaviour, emotions, cognitive development and social adjustment. According to Osofsky (1995), "for children, particularly those who have experienced violence exposure throughout their lives, high levels of aggression and acting out are common, accompanied by anxiety, behaviour problems, school problems, truancy, and revenge seeking".

Various researches conducted in India have proved that witnessing family violence can cause long term effects on children. Nair (1997) and Sunny (2003) reported that children who witness family violence have more physical and mental health problems and more likely to be abusive as adults. Findings of Jaya and Narasimhan's (2003) study showed that from children exposed to family violence, 7 per cent wanted to get rid of their parents and 4 per cent wanted to run away from the family because they were frightened to the inconsistent characteristics of the parents, felt low and rejected due to their parents violence. In India, according to National Crime Records Bureau reports, rape of girls below 10 years of age has increased by 16.6 per cent from 1996 to

1997. At least 600,000 to 700,000 Indian children are likely to have experienced sexual abuse, mostly by their own family members. Around 15 per cent of Indian sex workers are children, where 40 per cent of the total cases of child sexual abuse are incestuous, with the abuser being uncles and males cousins.

Consequences of family violence vary with the sex of the child and adolescent. Boys were more prone to exhibit behavioural problems than girls, especially externalizing behaviour, such as hostility and aggression (Chowdhury and Patnaik, 2007), while girls exposed to family violence demonstrate more internalizing problems such as depression and somatic complaints. Further, the duration and intensity of the family violence has impact on child and adolescent's developmental outcomes. Children witnessing traumatic events like family violence may feel helpless and see the world as unpredictable, hostile and threatening. Researches indicate that children who live in households affected by family violence may suffer extensively and are vulnerable to developing a host of short and long term physical and mental health problems.

Children are at less risk for immediate and direct exposure to family violence. However, long term effect exists, leading to future well-being and adjustments. Specially, sexually abused children are at greater risk for unintended pregnancy, depression, suicide, anxiety, feeling of vulnerability, powerlessness, sexual identity confusion, substance use and abuse. In case of physically abused children are at greater risk for anxiety, depression, extreme adjustment and acting out problems, academic problems, sleeping problems, drug use, self-destructive or reckless behaviour, suicidal ideation, suicidal actions, violence against siblings and even parents. Family violence exposure is a potentiating factor within the environment of children. Children who live with and are aware of violence in the home face many challenges and risks that can last throughout their lives and most specifically in the following manners:

- There is a increased risk of children becoming victims;
- There is significant risk of ever-increasing harm to the child's physical, emotional and social development;
- There is a strong likelihood that this will become a continuing cycle of violence for the next generation.

Kathleen et.al. were of view that, (2006), "the impact of violence on children extends beyond their social, emotional and behavioural problems to more general aspects of their health. Children exposed to violence at home had more health problems and used medications more often than children who were not exposed to this stressor". Children's responses to their experiences with family violence vary. Children may reveal any of a range of adjustment problems and psychopathology, or may emerge from their experiences relatively unscathed (Jaffe et. al. 1990). Factors that appear to affect these responses include the child's proximity to the violence, the child's temperament, the age of the child at time(s) of exposure, the severity and chronicity of violence, and the availability of adults who can emotionally protect or sustain the child. Overall, studies indicate that children who live in households affected by family violence may suffer extensively and are vulnerable to developing a host of short and long term problems.

Thus, children may come to view violence as an acceptable way, perhaps the only way to resolve conflicts and they may learn to realize the use of violence – they know nothing else. Further, this learned behaviour on the part of the children may be repeated and can become part of an intergenerational cycle of violence (Bell, 1995). What children learn from witnessing and experiencing family violence are:

- Violence is an appropriate way to resolve conflicts;
- Violence is a part of family relationships;
- The perpetrator of violence in intimate relationships often goes unpunished;
- Violence is a way to control other people.

(**Adopted from:** The Children of Domestic Violence – A Report by Massachusetts Coalition of Battered Women Service Groups and Children's Working Group, 1995).

Family Violence Affecting Parent's Behaviour

The child's vulnerability to family violence experience and exposure may be compounded by the parent's own response to violence – as witness or victim. The parent-child relationship can be deeply affected when a mother must cope with the physical and mental health aspects of having been battered (Wolfe, Jaffe, Wilson and Zak, 1985). It is obvious that the mother fear for her own safety as well as that of her children. Moreover, parents who feel that they may not be able to protect their children from violence are likely to feel anxious, frustrated and helpless (Osofsky and Fenichel, 1994). Such parents who are constantly in fear, anxiety and with feeling of insecurity may well have difficulty being emotionally and sometime even physically available and responsive to their children. It may so happen that, as a victim of domestic violence, a mother specially may become so preoccupied with safety and survival that she can not be mindful and concern of her child's needs and requirements. Further, she may become depressed and helpless to the violence around her, so that she is unable to be emphatic toward her child.

There may be some other mothers, who may become overprotective and over indulgent about their children, affecting negatively in child's natural growth and development. Still there is different type of mothers being affected by domestic violence, feel so helpless and traumatized that, they expect their children to protect them. Unfortunately, children raised by such parents and family environment may fail to develop the sense of basic trust and security that is the foundation of healthy emotional development. As domestic violence mostly affects mothers, the goal of ending violence against women has important implications for protecting children.

In case of family violence in which one parent is a victim of the violence and the other is the perpetrator, children may be even less able to turn to their parents for support and reassurance. In some cases, victim mother may use more punitive child-rearing strategies or exhibit aggression toward their children (Jouriles et. al., 1987). Moreover, battering fathers may be less available to their children, less likely to engage in rational discussions with their children, and less affectionate than fathers who are not violent (Holden et. al., 1998).

Failure of Family to Protect the Child's Right within Family

Traditionally in India, the responsibility of care and protection of children has been with families and communities. A strong knit patriarchal family that is meant to look after its children well has seldom had the realization that children are individuals with their own rights. While the Constitution of India guarantees many fundamental rights to the children, the approach to ensure the fulfillment of these rights was more needs based rather than rights based. The transition to the rights based approach in the Government and civil society is still evolving.

Under the Convention, a child "means every human being below the age of eighteen years, unless the law applicable to the child, majority is attained earlier" (Article-1). In all actions concerning children, the best interests of the child shall be a primary consideration (Article – 3, Para 1). The adoption of the Convention on the Rights of the Child (CRC) in 1989 confirmed that children too are holders of human rights. The CRC claims, on the one hand, children's right to individuality and to have their views on all matters which affect them taken seriously; and on the other, in the light of their developmental state and vulnerability, rights to special care and protection. The CRC makes clear that wherever possible children should be raised within their family; and where the family is unable to care for and protect them adequately, an alternative family-type environment should be provided. Therefore the CRC uncompromisingly asserts that the family is the primary site for children's healthy, loving and safe upbringing. However, this role must be fully underpinned and supported by the State, including by stepping over the family threshold to intervene when necessary, in the best interests of the child.

The range of rights contained in the Convention is broad and far reaching especially with regards to family's commitment towards Children. While all most every country has adopted the Convention, including India, respect for all these rights obviously raises serious issues. In reality these rights on the part of the children are not being protected within the family, due to very many reasons, like:

- Lack of knowledge, awareness and understanding on the part of parents, regarding child growth and development – need for enriching and violent free family environment.
- Parental ignorance and attitude about the Rights of Children.
- Parental own personal bias and upbringing.
- Family history of violence.
- Parental knowledge, understanding and awareness regarding family life and its importance for future well-being of all the family members – Family life Skills.

Findings of the Sample Study

Family violence against children is an area that has not been adequately addressed in the existing Indian literature, policies and programmes. To address this gap in knowledge, a small sample study was undertaken that aim to understand forms of violence as perceived by children, the actual reported experiences of violence against children and their mothers. These data were collected as part of a Master's Studies project work carried out in Berhampur town of Orissa state in India. Investigator interviewed one hundred children

(Boys = 50; Girls = 50) aged 08 to 12 from middle and lower middle class families using semi-structured questionnaire. During these interviews, the children were asked about quarrels and fights among their parents and about violence within family that they may have experienced directly.

Forms of Family Violence - During the free-listing exercise, researcher asked children to list different forms of violence they experience within families. On average 37.6 per cent boys and 48 per cent girls mentioned experiencing violence within family (Table-1). Both boys and girls indicated that verbal abuse is more (86 per cent) followed by psychological abuse (69.5 per cent). Among the verbal abuse, scolding for every act and behaviour, arguments, asking for explanations and using bad language is very common, as stated by children. Psychologically, they were abused through constant criticism, demeaning in front of others, neglecting, comparing with other siblings or peers too often. Boys reported more physical abuse than the girls, being slapped or beaten, having objects thrown at them, tying hands and legs for longer hours to restrict movements, locking inside a room without food and water, etc. Children did mentioned sexual harassment during the individual in-depth interview.

Table 1: Forms of Family Violence Experienced by Children (in per cent)

	Forms of Family Violence	*Boys*	*Girls*	*Total*
1.	Physical	32	26	29
2.	Psychological	56	83	69.5
3.	Verbal	85	87	86
4.	Financial	08	16	12
5.	Sexual	07	28	17.5
6.	Total (average)	37.6	48	42.8

Patterns of Violence - About 33.5 per cent of children reported violence (including physical and verbal abuse) by their fathers against their mothers. A greater proportion of girls (48 per cent) than boys (19 per cent) reported having witnessed their fathers beating their mothers. Though it is not clear what accounts for the difference, one possibility is that girls were more expressive and boys were more introverts to express their family internal matters (against their fathers) openly (Table 2). In case of experiencing violence by fathers, about 36.5 per cent children were of the view that their father beats them (Boys – 46 per cent and Girls – 27 per cent) at home for slightest mistake and even some time without any reasons. It is interesting to note that about 25.5 per cent children (Boys – 22 per cent and Girls – 29 per cent) were of the view that their mothers and they were beaten by their fathers at several occasions.

Table 2: Children's Experience of Violence by Fathers against Mother and Self (in per cent)

Patterns of Violence	*Boys*	*Girls*	*Total*
Beats mother alone	19	48	33.5
Beats the child alone	46	27	36.5
Beats both mother and child	22	29	25.5
Total (average)	25	34.6	29.75

Frequency of Violence - When asked about the frequency of verbal abuse and physical violence against their mothers, around 19 per cent boys and 24 per cent girls reported that such abuse occurred *"always"*, 70 per cent boys and 63 per cent girls said *"sometimes"* and 11 per cent boys and 13 per cent girls said *"rarely"* (Table 3). About 19 per cent boys and 36 per cent girls reported experiencing violence against them directly by their fathers "always", 24 per cent boys and 64 per cent girls "sometimes" and 57 per cent boys and 10 per cent girls experienced "rarely". Children and their mothers were also experiencing violence against them together. Around 24 per cent boys and 31 per cent girls reported it to occur always, 52 per cent boys and 67 per cent girls reported it to occur sometimes and around 24 per cent boys and only 02 per cent girls reported it to occur rarely (Table 3).

Table 3: Frequency of Family Violence Experienced by Children (in per cent)

Patterns of Violence	*Boys*			*Girls*		
	Always	*Some= times*	*Rarely*	*Always*	*Some= times*	*Rarely*
To mothers	19	70	11	24	63	13
To self	19	24	57	36	54	10
To both	24	52	24	31	67	02

Reasons Leading to Violence - While investigating the reasons of situation leading to violence against children, it was found out that, there were few typical reasons associated with boys and girls separately. Boys mentioned poor academic performance, not attending school regularly and not doing homework timely, not obeying their parents, conflicts about being forced to go to work and earn money, quarrels with friends and neighbours, taking pan or khaini, getting involved in parent's fights, gossiping were few major reasons leading to violence against them. Whereas, girls reported not complying with their gender roles, not attending to household chores, talking to boys, coming late from school or work and going out without informing parents as the main reasons for violence against them.

Coping with the Violent Situation - In spite of facing abuse against them, some (31 per cent) children freely expressed that, it is a part and parcel of their family life and nothing unusual about it. Both boys and girls mentioned that they usually stopped talking or eating, spending more time with friend or relatives, when faced with such situation. Some reported feeling like crying; being alone, even feel like running out of the house. As Parson (1994) mentioned that children witnessing or experiencing violence within family attach themselves to peer groups and gangs as substitute family and incorporate violence as method of dealing with disputes or frustration. Still few mentioned that they used to get angry with their fathers and would like to hit back, and take revenge. For example, one 12 year old girl mentioned her anger saying, "My father beats me, and my mother regularly after consuming alcohol for no reason. I feel like beating him as well and teach him a lesson".

This small study provides a glimpse into the violence witnessed and experienced by children in middle and lower-middle class families of Berhampur town. It is quite evident from this study, that family violence in terms of marital and child abuse is very much present and taken as a normal life style, without knowing the long term consequences on whole family. There is a need for a deeper understanding of the dynamics and consequences of violence, including sexual violence, which may have both short-term and long-term implications for both victims and perpetrators. In addition, an in-depth understanding of the factors that lead to violent behaviour could help point to strategies to curb such family violence and provide healthy and enriching environment for our adolescents. To achieve this, more in-depth and systematic research is needed in various settings.

Promoting Violence-Free Families

The violent HOME is a "toxic" environment in which the child's well-being and development are comprised by fear, anxiety, anger and tension, that pervades the each and every family member. Every individual require a violent free home for leading a normal life style. However, due to various factors, no more the families are considered as the "safe haven", rather a place of turmoil and breeding ground of all negative emotions among the family members. In order to promote violence free families, following measures can be taken, such as:

Empowering Child Victims: Many children are injured during an attack on their mother, either trying to protect her or because they just happened to be in the way. Teach them plan exit routes, safe places to run to, and safe people they can call in an emergency. They must know that violence is not their fault, and no one deserves to be abused. Accept and respect their conflicting feelings about their parents. The child may love the abusive parent, resent the victim for not protecting them, or feel guilty for not protecting the victim.

Coaching Boys into Men: Boys need to grow into healthy young men. Boys are swamped with influences outside of the home – from friends, the neighbourhood, television, the internet, music, the movies......everything they see around them. There are numerous conflicting and some harmful messages being given to boys about what constitutes "being a man" in a relationship. Boys need to know how to behave and interact with girls. They need to understand that to become a man, violence or control is not the way and there is no place for violence in a relationship. The very presence of father figure at home makes the boys calm and poised. Fathers need to be the role model for the boys and they should know, see and hear that no relationship should be established through any form of violence. Use every opportunity to reinforce the message that violence has no place in relationship.

Empowering Parents: Parents and caregivers are primarily responsible and accountable for the safety and security of the children in their care. Therefore, there is a need to enhance parenting skills, knowledge of the subject and sensitivity, which will help them to handle situations of child sexual abuse. Life skill education of children to enhance their knowledge and capacity to deal with abuse is essential. Further, parents need to be educated about parental skills necessary for bringing up children in both normal and abnormal situations.

Strengthening Families: Protecting children and facilitating their development is a family's most basic function. Hence, strengthening and equipping families through family life education, enhancing family's ability to become more self-sustaining, counseling to promote mutual understandings etc can be done. All these intend to create a conducive, peaceful and violent free home environment for the children.

Protecting Children from Family Violence

In sum, children's exposure and experience of family violence is influenced, not only by the strength and vulnerability of individual child, but also by the character of the family setting in which they live and the ways in which they connect to their outside family and social world. To reach these hidden victims, however, all agencies, institutions and service providers for children must increase efforts to identify children who are exposed to family violence and provide assistance to counsel them accordingly. Thus, changes in social policy, effective law enforcement, evaluation of rehabilitation programmes, family life education and training can help combat the problem to some extent. A multilevel effort to improve the capacity of families in building safety nets, social controls coupled with positive and enriching school experience and reduced opportunities for engaging in crime and other risk behaviours can prove beneficial in the long run.

What policy makers can do? Children have the RIGHT to HOME environment that is safe, secure and free of violence. Government carry a primary responsibility for ensuring that children and women are safe and secure in their homes and can take several broad steps to ensure this, such as:

- Raise awareness of the impact of family violence on children in schools, colleges, Universalities and community levels;
- Create public policies and laws that protect children;
- Enhance social services that address the impact of violence in the home on children.

- Advocacy and public education.
- Elimination of Harmful traditional practices – Child Marriages etc

Private Sector Engagements: Corporate social responsibility is a growing priority for the private sector and they have a critical role to play in addressing the issue of family violence and children. Increasingly, companies are recognizing their responsibility to address issues that impact their customers, employees, the environment and communities in which they work. The private sectors can take up few steps to protect the children from certain social fallacies, such as:

- Finance or otherwise support initiatives that seek to prevent family violence and services that support all victims of family violence, including children;
- Actively engage in partnerships with NGOs to develop public awareness and communication campaigns and fundraising initiatives;
- Increase awareness of the issue through innovative employee education, counseling and training programmes;
- Taking action against the employee/s, who acts as perpetrator of child abuse and strict punishment must be initiated.

Conclusion

Thus, family violence is highly dangerous, especially for children of all age groups. Truly, children are the "biggest victim" of this evil having long lasting effect on children as well as on the whole humanity. The costs to children and to society of children's exposure to family violence are enormous. To reach these hidden victims of family violence, however, all agencies, institutions, and service providers for children must make efforts to identify, assess them and make a treatment approach. Children who are exposed to family violence in the home are denied their rights to a safe and stable home environment. Child victims of family violence present a number of psycho-social characteristics having long lasting effects on children and are "at-risk" to repeat their experience in the next generation, either as victims or perpetrators of violence in their own intimate relationships. Thus, violence has no place in a child's life. With a clear vision and concrete action, we CAN and MUST give children a brighter and more peaceful future. Interventions that help children are usually those that help parents to increase their own safety and to increase the resources available to provide safety for their children.

Child abuse and family violence are inextricably interwoven and not only hurts and harms the child; it has far reaching effects on all of society. Promising strategies to prevent violence against children in the home and family context are many and varied, ranging from programmes with a direct impact, such as parenting training, to policies with a more indirect impact, such as those governing alcohol availability or access to family planning services. Community based interventions may be the best hope for families in our society struggling with violence in their homes. Further, knowledge of human rights is the best defense against their violation. Learning about one's rights including child rights builds respect for the rights of others and children, and points the way to more tolerant and peaceful societies. Thus, ending violence against children needs to be part of National Development Plans and development assistance frameworks, not an afterthought.

REFERENCES

Ahemed-Ghosh, H. (2004). Chattels of Society: Domestic Violence in India. *Violence against Women*. 10 (1), pp. 94-118.

Bassa, D.M. (1978). From the traditional to the modern: Some observations on changes in Indian child-rearing and parental attitudes, with special reference to identity formation. In E.J.

Anthony and Chiland (Eds.) *The Child in His Family*, Vol. 5, New York: John Wiley, pp. 333-343.

Becker, K.B. and McCloskey, L.A. (2002). Attention and conduct problems in children exposed to family violence. *American Journal of Orthopsychiatry*, 72, pp. 83-91.

Bell, C. (1995). Exposure to violence distress children and may lead to their becoming violent. Psychiatric News, pp. 6-8.

Carlson, B.E. (1984). Children's observations of interparental violence. In A.R. Roberts (Eds.), Battered Women and their Families. New York: Springer, pp. 147-167.

Carlson, B.E. (2001). Children exposed to intimate partner violence: Research findings and implications for intervention. Trauma, Violence, and Abuse, 1(4), pp. 321-340.

Carson, D.K. and Chowdhury, A. (2000). Family Therapy in India: A New Profession in an Ancient Land? In: *Contemporary Family Therapy*, 22 (4), pp. 387-406.

Carson, D.K., Carson, C.K. and Chowdhury, A. (2007). *Indian Families at the Crossroads: Preparing Families for the New Millennium*, New Delhi: Gyan Publishing House.

Carson, D.K., Chowdhury, A., Perry, C.K. and Pati, C. (1999). Family characteristics and adolescents' competence in India: Investigation of Youth in Southern Orissa. In *Journal of Youth and Adolescence*, Vol. 28, No. 2, pp. 211-233.

Centre for Operations Research and Training (CORT) (2000). Baseline Survey for Action for Slum Dwellers Reproductive Health Project (Monograph), Baroda.

Chawla, A. and Kang, T. (2007). Domestic Violence: Impact on Children. *Social Welfare*, December, pp. 30-33.

Chawla, S. (2004). International perspectives on family violence and abuse: A cognitive ecological approach. In K. Malley-Morrison (Ed.), Mahwah, NJ: Lawrence Erlbaum.

Chowdhury, A. (2007). Domestic Violence against elderly Women in South Orissa: A study of incidence, patterns and perspectives. Project report prepared for National Commission for Women, New Delhi.

Chowdhury, A. and Patnaik, I. (2007). Effects of Family Life on Child Mental Health. In David K. Carson, Cecyle, K. Carson and Aparajita Chowdhury (Eds.), *Indian Families at the Crossroads*, New Delhi: Gyan Publishing House, pp. 123-145.

Chowdhury, A., Carson, D.K. and Carson, C.K. (2006). *Family Life Education in India: Perspectives, Challenges and Applications*, New Delhi: Rawat Publications.

Chowdhury, A., Pattnaik, S. and Patro, A. (1994). Psycho-social profile of abused children in India. *Early Child Development and Care*, 104, pp. 85-93.

Edleson, J.L. (1999). The overlap between child maltreatment and women battering. Violence Agianst Women, 5 (2), pp. 134-154.

Egeland, B., and Erickson, N.F., (1987). Psychologically unavailable care giving. In M.R. Brassard, R. Germain, and S.N.Hart (Eds.), Psychological Maltreatment of Children and Youth (pp. 110-120). New York: Pergamon Press.

Erickson, E. (1963). Childhood and society (2nd edition). New York: Norton.

Fernandez, M. (1997). Domestic violence by extended family members in India: Interplay of gender and generation. *Journal of Interpersonal Violence*, 12(3), pp. 433-455.

Gelles, R.J. and Coute, J.R. (1990). Domestic violence and sexual abuse of children: A Review of research in the eighties. *Journal of Marriage and the Family*. 52, pp. 1045-1058.

Government of India (2001), Census Report

Holden, G.W., Geffner, R.A., and Jouriles, E.N.(1998). Children exposed to marital violence: Theory, research, and applied issues, Washington DC: American Psychological Association.

Jaffe.P.G., Wolfe, D.A., and Willson, S. K. (1990). Children of Battered Women. Newbury Park, C.A: Sage Publications.

Jamuna, D. (2003). Issue of elder care and elder abuse in the Indian context. In: P.S. Liebig and S.I. Rajan (Eds.), *An Aging India: Perspectives, Prospects and Policies* (pp. 125-142), New York: Haworth Press.

Jaya, N. and Narasimhan, S. (2003). Violence on Children between 10-18 years in varied family contexts. *Indian Psychological Review*, 60, pp. 2-9.

Jejeebhoy, S.J. (1998). Wife Beating in Rural India: A Husband's Right? *Economic and Political Weekly* (India) 23, pp. 558-562.

Jouriles, E.N., Barling, J., and O'Leary, K.D. (1987). Predicting Child Behaviour problems in martially violent families. Journal of Abnormal Child Psychology, 15, pp. 165-73.

Kathleen, S., Michael, E.L., Guterman, E., and Abbot, C.B (2006). Effects of early and later Family violence on Children's Behaviour problems and Depression: A Longitudinal, Multi-Informant Perspective. Child Abuse and Neglect, Vol. 30, No. 3, pp. 283-306.

Klevens, J., Bayon, M. and Sierra, M. (2000). Risk factors and context of men who physically abuse in Bogota, Colombia. *Child Abuse and Neglect*, 24, pp. 323-332.

Kliewer, W., Murrelle, L., Mejia, R., Torres, D., Galvis, Y., and Angold, A. (2001). Exposure to violence against a family member and internalising symptoms in Colombian adolescents: The Protective effects of family support. *Journal of Consulting Clinical Psychology*, 69, pp. 971-982.

Martin, J.P. (1978). *Violence and the Family*. England: John Wiley and Sons.

Massachusetts Coalition of Battered Women Service Groups and Children's Working Group, (1995).The Children of Domestic Violence – A Report.

Maya, J.M., Torres de Galvis, Y., Murrelle, L., Rodriguez, M.A., Mejia, R., Gavaria, D. (2000). Use and abuse of psychoactive substances and associated factors in juvenile delinquency. Medellin, Colombia: Institute of Health Sciences-Colciencias and Inter-American Development Bank.

Mejia, R., Kliewer, W., and Williams, L. (2006). Domestic violence exposure in Colombian adolescents: Pathways to violent and pro-social behaviour. *Journal of Traumatic Stress*, 19 (2) April, pp. 257-267.

Ministry of Women and Child Development, Government of India (2007). Report on - Study on Child Abuse in India.

National Association for the Education of Young Children (1996). *Developmentally appropriate practice in early childhood programs serving children from birth through age 8 [Online].* Available http://www.naeyc.org/resources/ position_statements/daptoc.htm

National Crime Record Bureau, Government of India (1996-97). Reports on Crime during 1996-97.

National Collective of Independent Women's Refugees (1991). Treasure the Child: Children Living without Violence. Wellington.

Nair, G.R. (1997). An anatomy of child abuse. *Social Welfare*, 44, pp. 76-78.

Osofksy, J.D. (1995). Social Policy Report on Children who witness Domestic Violence: The Invisible Victims. Society for Research in Child Development, Vol. IX, Number 3.

Osofksy, J.D., and Fenichel, E. (Eds.) (1994). Hurt, healing, and hope: Caring for infants and toddlers in violent environments. Arlington, VA: Zero to three/National Centre for Clinical Infant Programme.

Patnaik, M.M. (2007). Family Violence: Impact of Family Life: In Carson and Chowdhury (Eds.), *Indian Families at the Crossroads: Preparing Families for the New Millennium.* New Delhi: Gyan Publishing House. pp. 35-50.

Rossman, B.B. (2001). Longer term effects of children's exposure to violence. In S.A. Graham-Bermann and J.L. Edelson (Eds.), Domestic violence in the lives of Children: The future of research, intervention, and social policy (pp. 35-66). Washington DC: American Psychological Association.

Sunny, C. (2003). Domestic violence against women – Report on a situational analysis in Ernakulam District, Kerala, *Social Change*, 33, pp. 26-54.

Vindhya, U. (2003). Private Crimes and Public sanction: Violence against women in the family. In Margrit Pernau, Imtiaz Ahmad, and Hrelmut Reifeld edited book on: Family and Gender:

Changing Values in Germany and India. New Delhi: Sage publication, pp. 322-348.

Wolfe, D., Jaffe, P., Wilson, S., and Zak, L. (1985). Children and battered women: The relation between child behaviour, family violence, and maternal stress. Journal of Consulting and Clinical Psychology, 53, pp. 657-665.

World Report on Violence against Children (2006). An End to Violence against Children. United Nations Organisation, New York Publications.

9

Gruesome faces of child abuse: A Problem of Socio-psychological Concern

Tushar Singh and Shivali Sharma

"The eyes with perished dreams,
A body bruised beyond repair,
A soul which is scarred,
And the faith completely lost...."

(Lines by Shivali Sharma)

"...I was born in 1928 in a different but a crooked family. My childhood was a picture of relentless horror. My mother died when I was two years old and I along with my father started living with my stern and self-righteous grand mother. My father used to beat me up practically everyday with his leather belt. At other times he locked me in his closet. He would enjoy smashing my head into the wall. All these practices were endorsed by my grand mother. At the age of six he took me in his bed. Apart from rape his sexual acts are truly unspeakable. I got married to a gentleman in 1947 and I assumed that I would be a very loving mother. I was unaware that I had a injected gene of monstrous violence. I started battering my children almost from the beginning. I screamed at my younger one while beating my elder son Patrik with a leather belt. My elder son became my chief target...."

This is the case of Patricia Bissel, who survived the violence of her childhood only to find herself abusing her own children. Patrick Bissel, her son became a brilliant and widely acclaimed ballet dancer but died a tragic death at the age of 30 due to drug overdose. This case is an appropriate example to show the impact of childhood abuse on the socio-psychological functioning of an individual.

Childhood is the most crucial phase of individual development. It is the period of physical, perceptual, sensory-motor, emotional and cognitive development. Any trauma at this stage can scar an individual's life beyond repair. Childhood is the period of craving for warmth and affection. The deficiency of care and love at this stage can result in psychological/emotional handicap of children.

Child abuse is as old as human history but the first published work dedicated to child abuse specifically appeared in France in 1857. It was published in the Medical Legal Studies of Sexual Assault by Auguste Ambroise Tardier, who was a noted French pathologist and a pioneer of forensic medicine. It is a commonly occurring phenomenon with tremendous psychological and social impact to our society. It is a complicated psychological phenomenon because it takes various forms. It can be defined as the adverse treatment of children under the age of 18, by parent, caretaker, or someone living in their home (Chalk, Gibbons and Scarupa, 2002). Psychologists have defined child abuse as any action or lack of action that endangers or impairs a child's physical, emotional, psychological health and development. It can have physical, mental and sexual forms (Browne and Herbert 1999). It is the physical, psychological emotional and sexual mistreatment of children. Child abuse have been categorized in mainly four categories namely, neglect, physical abuse, emotional abuse and sexual abuse.

Neglect

Neglect, unlike abuse, is defined by the absence of specific events. A neglected child is the one who is not properly cared for. When parents or concerned adults fail to provide for various needs like physical, emotional or educational needs it is called child neglect. There are currently five identified types of neglect (Brown and Khan, 2003).

(1) **Physical neglect** involves denial of basic needs. It is defined as a failure to provide for a child's physical needs. This includes failure to provide adequate food, clothing, shelter or hygiene.

(2) **Emotional or psychological neglect** results from the failure to provide nurture, encouragement, love, security and warmth. It is defined as a failure to provide for a child's emotional needs. In extreme cases, this can lead to non-organic failure to thrive (stunted growth and physical illness/abnormalities).

(3) **Medical neglect** is failure to provide proper medical treatment for a child (e.g., immunizations, surgery, medications).

(4) **Mental health neglect** is failure to provide appropriate therapeutic procedures in cases of serious emotional or behavioral disorders. This form of neglect is not widely accepted and investigated as a form of neglect.

(5) **Educational neglect** is failure to provide the child with proper educational facilities.

A child's proper growth and development depends upon the interplay of physical, emotional and social factors. Parents and adults play a very significant role in the development of children. If the parents or care givers do not give enough time or neglect the child, the child's physical and psychological development will be stunted. Neglected children may seek bad company and develop unhealthy habits. Neglected are particularly vulnerable to drug abuse, delinquency and suicides. Neglect is as harmful or detrimental to child's well-being as other forms of abuses. According to a study on child abuse by Ministry of Women and Child Development, Government of India (2007) 48.4 per cent of girls faced childhood neglect and wished they were boys.

Physical abuse

Child physical abuse includes physical aggression directed at a child by an adult. It has been defined as any physical injury to a child or adolescent by a parent or other caregiver, which is not accidental (e.g. punching, hitting, kicking, twisting ears etc.). It is defined not by the act, but as the results of these acts (e.g., bruises, burns, broken bones). It is detected when neither the parents nor the child seems willing or able to explain the reason for a bruise, burn or fracture. Often the physically abused children try to hide the marks of abuse and offer feeble tales about them. Parent's and school teacher's use of corporal punishment is wide spread. Many national and international agencies have made laws to prevent children physical abuse.

Physical abuse affects hundreds of thousands of children every year and account for about a quarter of all child abuse reports. The study of Ministry of Women and Child Development, Government of India (2007) reported that two out of every three children were physically abused and out of 69 per cent physically abused children, 54.68 per cent were boys. This study also found that over 50 per cent children were being subjected to one or the other form of physical abuse out of 88.6 per cent was physically abused by parents. This report says that most children did not report the matter to anyone and 50.2 per cent children work seven days a week.

Though younger children sustain severe physical injuries, the rates of reported abuse do not differ by age or gender. This type of child abuse is commonly perpetrated by parents and other loved ones. There are several factors responsible for child physical abuse. According to Lynch and Cicchetti (1998) family's interactional and contextual variables (cultural and community factures) are major factors affecting physical abuse of children. It is also believed that parent's expectations, perceptions and attributions of children's behaviours; their developmental knowledge and problem solving skills and their belief about the appropriateness of using physical discipline, tolerance for stress and ability to inhibit aggression act are important determinant of child physical abuse (Wolfe, 1999; Kolko, 2002). Even religious beliefs can play an important role in physical abuse. Such beliefs, some times, directly support abusive behaviours (e.g. spare the rod spoil the child). Greven (1991) points out that encouragement for violent and physically abusive child rearing techniques can be traced to biblical passages for eg. "...withhold the correction from the child, for if the then beatest him with the rod, he shall not die. Then shall beat him with the rod, and shall deliver his soul from hell" (Proverbs 13:24 and 23: 13-14, respectively). Such passages encourage some parents to use corporal punishment to enforce their authority and to prohibit sinful behaviour. Motivated by these passage some parents and teachers believe that corporal punishment helps to deliver children from sin. Physical abuse is also culture dependent. In some countries including India, the parents and teachers have a complete license for beating their children. It is justified as a corrective action on part of the parents and it is considered to be beneficial for children. Such parents and teachers feel that they should use corporal punishment to 'strengthen up' their children but mostly they are releasing their frustrations on children. The study of Ministry of Women and Child Development, Government of India (2007) states that 65 per cent of school going children reported facing corporal punishment (i.e. two out of three children were victims of corporal punishment) and 62 per cent of the corporal punishment was reported in government and municipal school. It often goes unnoticed by parents and teachers that the punishment being rendered by them is becoming abusive. In some cultures parents usually have unrealistically high expectations from their children and any underachievement becomes simply unacceptable for these parents. Comparing the achievements of their child with the children of relatives and neighbors is also a reason for parental frustration and child abuse. In some cultures such abuse can be gender based as girls are considered to be a burden for parents who have to marry them off spending a lot of money. Girl child in such cultures are often abused as it is considered necessary for disciplining them. It is believed that pampering of any kind would spoil them and would make them unadjusting. Strict disciplinary actions are justified in the name of training them for in-laws house.

Typically such abuse occurs when parents cannot handle the daily stress of child rearing and have no support from anyone. Some parents use physical abuse as they have learnt this pattern of dealing with children from their parents.

Child Sexual Abuse

Child sexual abuse is a form of child abuse in which a child is abused for sexual gratification of an adult or older adolescence. According to Schechter and Roberge (1976)"*Sexual abuse is defined as the involvement of dependent, developmentally immature children and adolescents in sexual activities they do not truly comprehend to which they are unable to give informed consent, or that violate the social taboos of family roles*". It involves any form of sexual activity with a child or adolescent in which consent is not or cannot be provided (e.g., if there is a significant disparity in age, development, or size) (Kolko, and Brown, 2000). The sexual activity often includes physical contact (e.g., penetration, touching) and may also reflect non-contact sexual acts (e.g., exposure to pornography). Examples of sexual abuse include: fondling, penetration, exposure to adult sexuality and pornography, exhibitionism, child prostitution, and forced observation of sexual acts. In addition to direct sexual contact, perpetrators of these hideous crime abuse young children by indecently exposing their genitals to a child, ask the child to perform sexual acts, display pornography, masturbate using the child or produce children pornography by using the child. There are many types of child sexual abuse. These are:

a. **Sexual assault:** It is a term defining offenses in which an adult touches a minor for the purpose of sexual gratification such as rape, and sexual penetration with an object. Any penetrative contact with the minor, if performed for sexual gratification is termed as sexual assault.

b. **Sexual molestation:** Offenses in which an adult engages in non penetrative activities like exposure of genitals, indirect talks laden with sexuality or exposing the child to pornography is considered to sexual molestation.

c. **Sexual exploitation:** It is victimization of a minor for advancement, sexual gratification or profit (eg. Commercial sexual exploitation) is considered as sexual exploitation.

d. **Sexual Grooming:** The social contact of a potential child sexual abuser who seeks to make a minor more precocious and accepting of their sexual advances (eg. On line chat room) comes under this category.

e. **Incest:** It is sexual exploitation by a parent or close relative. This type of abuse is rarely reported.

A report from U.S. Department of Justice indicates that girls are significantly more likely than boys to be victims of sexual abuse (nearly six times) and further it indicated that males are significantly more likely to be perpetrators of sexual abuse (96 per cent of cases reported to law enforcement). The study by Ministry of Women and Child Development, Government of India (2007) stated that 53.22 per cent children of the study reported having faced one or more forms of sexual abuse and Andhra Pradesh, Assam, Bihar and Delhi reported the highest percentage of sexual abuse among both boys and girls. 21.90 per cent children of the study reported facing severe forms of sexual abuse and 50.76 per cent other forms of sexual abuse. 50 per cent of these abuses were committed by persons known to the child or in a position of trust and responsibility. Out of the total respondents, 5.69 per cent reported being sexually assaulted specially in states like Assam, Andhra Pradesh, Bihar and Delhi. Children on street, children at work and children in institutional care reported the highest incidence of sexual assault.

Sexual abuse is one of the most devastating forms of abuse. Studies reveal that the majority of these crimes are perpetrated by trusted family members. Incestuous crimes often go unreported as the victims are warned not to tell or they are not believed. Child sexual abuse is related to increased arrest rates for sex crimes and prostitution (Friedrich *et al.*, 2001; Salter *et al.*, 2003). A close relationship to the perpetrator has a more severe impact (Feiring, Taska and Lewis, 1999; Tricket *et al.*, 2001).

Commercial abuses of children

This type of abuse typically involves exploiting a child for profit and advancement. It mainly includes child labour and commercial sexual exploitation of children.

a. **Child Labour:** More and more children are entering into work force and this practice is flourishing especially in the developing countries like India. Illiteracy is one of the main reasons for the increase in child labour. In India, child bondage was exposed in 1984, only after the sordid condition of 32 bonded children was brought to public notice by Bonded Labour Liberation Front through a writ petition in the Supreme Court of India. These children were kidnapped from a village in Bihar and were bonded to a loom owner in U.P. These children were beaten up by bamboo sticks and burned with red hot iron rods. Despite of all the laws and petitions this practice is still continuing uninhibitedly. The four main factors responsible for this type of exploitation are: (a) unemployment, (b) poverty, (c) population growth and (d) illiteracy.

Children are the cheapest and most vulnerable source of human labour and they are easier to exploit due to physical and mental vulnerability. Poverty and inequity is forcing children into labour. Their income is considered essential to maintain economic level in the household. As the parents are unemployed and uneducated, they are desperate to secure income at any cost. Children are preferred as they are innocent, malleable, flexible and therefore easy to train. As children are less powerful then adults, they are physically and sexually abused by employers.

b. **Commercial Sexual Exploitation of children (CSEC):** It is one of the worst forms of child abuse and slavery. The world congress against commercial exploitation of children defines it as "a fundamental violation of children's right". It comprises sexual abuse by the adult and remuneration in cash or kind to the child or a third person or persons. The child is treated as a sexual object as well as a commercial object. The commercial sexual exploitation of children constitutes a form of coercion and violence against children and amounts to forced labour and contemporary form of slavery". Commercial sexual exploitation of children usually takes three primary forms.

    i. **Prostitution:** In this case child is made available for sexual purposes, for remuneration or any other form of consideration. The prostitution of children is closely connected to the trafficking of children for sexual purposes and child pornography.

ii. **Child pornography:** It includes the exploitative use of children in pornographic performances and materials. There are many different kinds of child pornography materials made available by various types of media. They essentially involve depicting a child or children in a manner that is intended to aid sexual arousal or gratification. Internet has tremendously increased child pornography. New technologies have enabled abusers to exchange millions of images and videos of sexual exploitation of children.

iii. **Trafficking:** Though trafficking is prevalent in all age groups, the children are most vulnerable victims of this phenomenon. It includes the recruitment, transportation or receipt of person for sexual exploitation, forced labour, slavery, servitude or removal of organs.

Emotional/Psychological Abuse of Children

Psychological or emotional abuse is any attitude or pattern of behavior that impairs a child's emotional or social development and a child's mental health or sense of self-worth. This may include constant criticism, threats, or rejection, as well as withholding love, support, or guidance. This kind of abuse is often difficult to detect. Emotional or psychological abuse is supposed to be embedded in all other types of abuse. Yelling, screaming, name calling, shaming, negative comparisons to others, and telling children they are "bad" or "no good" are some of the examples of this type of abuse. Failure to provide the affection and support necessary for the development of a child's emotional, social, physical and intellectual well-being is also another aspect of emotional abuse. Ignoring, withdrawal of attention, lack of praise, and lack of positive reinforcement to the child comes under this category. Despite of increased attention to child abuses in recent years, there is little understanding of the incidence of emotional or psychological abuse. According to the study of Ministry of Women and Child Development, Government of India (2007), every second child with equal percentage of both girls and boys reported facing emotional abuse. In 83 per cent of the cases, parents were the abusers.

Impact of Child Abuse

Abuse and neglect may interfere with a child's development in various ways. All types of childhood abuses have somewhat similar repercussions. It affects the over all perception of children and they lose the skills required for socialization process. Relationships with other people, self-esteem, physical activity, academic performance, and psychological functioning are affected by child abuse and neglect. Survivors of childhood abuse cannot develop close interpersonal relationships essential for healthy living. These abused children often become precocious and therefore are deprived of the joys and innocence of childhood. The unique experiences of childhood are bypassed by them. The abused children are presented with faulty models and therefore such children often find themselves at a loss of learning appropriate reaction patterns. This internalization of inappropriate behaviour increases the possibility of these children becoming abusers themselves in adulthood.

There is a large body of research literature to show the negative effects of childhood abuse on psychological functioning in adulthood. Not all children however, will show the same results. Some children are able to recover from or cope with chronic child abuses (which is referred to as *resilience*), majority of them are often left with various socio-psychological problems. It is important to note that even when short-term effects are not apparent, there may be long-term effects on children's well-being (Beitchman *et al.*, 1992). It results in intellectual deficits and other academic problems such as delay in acquiring language and problems in mathematics and reading tests (Eckenrode, Laird, and Doris, 1993). As students, they may have problems at school, which take the form of learning difficulties and conflicts with their colleagues (Martin and Mohr 2000). It also leads to eating disorders (e.g., bulimia, anorexia and obesity) (Chandy, Blum, and Resnick, 1996), alcohol and substance use/dependence (Chandy, Blum, and Resnick, 1996); and self-injurious behaviour and suicide (Oates, 1996).

Impact on Health

Physical health: Research literature exploring the effect of childhood abuses on survivors' physical health have found that children who are physically abused by their parents or caregivers are at high risk of serious physical injuries. They may have broken bones and teeth, bruises, scalds, burns, or cuts. Sexual abuse can result in infections, pelvic pain, urinary tract infections or pregnancy and sexually transmitted diseases. The results of research and anecdotal observations show that children who have been victims of family abuse are at increased risk of hepatitis, diabetes, heart disease, cancer, stroke and are more likely to have surgery and are at increased risk of having one or more chronic pain symptoms (Kendall-Tackett, 2002; Glaser 2000). Many adults who have been abused in childhood feel chronic pain, have asthma and hepatitis. These physical health problems are attributed to the complex interaction of the psychological, behavioural and social harms associated with abuses (Kendall-Tackett, 2002). It has been found that abused children are more likely to engage in smoking and other substance abuse and high-risk sexual behaviour which have well-documented negative health outcomes.

Psychological health: Depression and Post Traumatic Stress Disorder (PTSD; a combination of symptoms that involves reliving the trauma over and over, avoiding things that remind one of the trauma, anxiety responses in the body, behavior problems, and interpersonal deficits) have been frequently reported as common indicators of adult psychological distress that result from childhood abuses (Casey and Nurius, 2005; Paolucci, Genuis and Violato, 2001). These children often have complains of chronic pain, sleep disorders, chronic fatigue syndrome. It has been shown that those women who have been victims of child abuse show higher rates and severity of PTSD than women who have not been abused in childhood (Briere, 1992; Rodriquez, Ryan, Vande Kemp and Foy, 1997; Widom, 1999). Widom (1999) in his study found that children who have been abused in childhood are 1.75 times more likely to develop PTSD at 20 year follow-up. Researches have also shown that childhood abuse also results in depressed mood and anxiety in adulthood (Leserman, *et al.*, 1998; Bohn, 2003; Turner and Butler, 2002). Such children are permanently at a higher level of anxiety, afraid of many things, even though they are not objectively dangerous. Further, research on child maltreatment has identified a significant, positive relationship between severity of abuse and depression severity (Peters, 1988; Russell, 1986). Children who are victims of childhood abuse report more depressive symptoms than non-abused children (Beitchman *et al.*, 1992; Cerezo and Frias, 1994). They may withdraw from any kind of help and support, both emotional and financial. Not only children, but also adults, and especially young teenagers (adolescents) who have been abused or neglected may make many attempts at self-injury or even commit suicide. Their behavior indicates self-destructive and self-injuring tendencies. Such persons may also have much more serious accidents in their lives (Glaser 2000).

Impact on social resources: Social resources (such as social support and ability to get along with others) have been considered important factors for stress resistance and good mental health functioning (Seligman and Csinkzentmihalyi, 2000). These resources buffer the negative effects of stress and allow individuals to adequately integrate within the environment (Dohrenwend, 2000). It has been found that adults who have experienced childhood abuse often lack social resources and thus show poor adult mental functioning. They have been found to display relationship problems with their parents and peers. For instance, they may be anxious or ambivalent toward their parents and be more passive and withdrawn with their peers (Critteden, 1992). They often have smaller supportive networks (Gibson and Hathorne, 1996; Harmer, Sanderson, and Mertin, 1999), perceive their relationships as less supportive (Davis, Petretic-Jackson and Ting, 2001; Stroud, 1999) and report more conflictive interpersonal relationships (Browne and Finkelhor, 1986; Hammen, Henry and Daley, 2000; Hammen, 2003) when compared to non-abused children. These adults often have exploitative and victimizing relationships (Flemming et. al., 1999) and show high divorce rates (Felitti, 1991; Flemming *et al.*, 1999). Vranceanu (2007) have reported various reasons to explain this lack in social resource. First, childhood abuses distort children's cognitions regarding themselves and others, which are internalized and lead to unhealthy adult relationships. Second, since the abusers are the parents or loved ones or they are also harmed by childhood abuse, they fail to or provide limited support (Browne and Finkelhor, 1986) or become ineffectual as supporters (Elliott and Carnes, 2001) to the survivors of childhood abuse. Third, often individuals with childhood abuse grew up in dysfunctional family environments and thus they may have poor scripts for healthy adult relationships (Browne and Finkelhor, 1986). Fourth, they often develop avoidant or intrusive coping styles and thus they choose to cut themselves off from others (Teegan, 1999). Finally, childhood abuses impair their ability to read social cues, speak up for themselves and find people who will not exploit or abuse others (Kendall-Tackett, 2002).

Impact on Psychological Resources: Besides social resources, psychological resources (such as self-efficacy and self-esteem) have been considered essential for mental health functioning (Hobfoll, 2002). These resources help individuals to function effectively in the environment and to cope with stressful life events (Lefcourt, 1992). These resources allow individuals to effectively avoid or prevent stressful events and circumstances, experience and perceive life events as less problematic (Turner, Lloyd, and Roszell, 1999).

It is found that children who have been abused or neglected have lower psychological resources. These children have been shown to have low self-esteem, increased fear, guilt, self-blame (Casey and Nurius, 2005; Corby, 2000; Jumper, 1995; Sedney and Brooks, 1984; Yama *et al.*, 1993) and self-efficacy (Beck and Weishaar, 1989; Gagnon and Hersen, 2000; Seligman, 1975). Persons with childhood abuses usually lack belief in their strengths. They prefer isolation from others or have negative relationships with their schoolmates, coming into conflict as a result of their aggressive behavior (Briere and Elliot 1994). Vranceanu (2007) have listed some of the reasons for this effect. First, childhood abuses lead to dysfunctional modeling which acts as a lens through which survivors see the world as being dangerous and overestimate danger and adversity (Briere and Elliot, 1994), this lead to underestimated sense of self-efficacy and self-worth in dealing with both real and perceived danger. Second, childhood abuses results in the development of self-deprecating and self-blaming schemas (Beck and Weishaar, 1989), which can internalize and become part of adult functioning. Third, it results in a sense of pervasive helplessness (Seligman, 1975), hopelessness, powerlessness and danger (Teegen, 1999; Silk, Lee, Hill, and Lohr, 1995), which lead to a generalized perception of inefficaciousness (Gagnon and Hersen, 2000).

Consequences associated with specific types of child abuse

Besides these common symptoms of child abuses there are many specific patterns of consequences associated with specific types of child abuse.

Physical Abuse

Physical Problems: Studies have shown that physical abuse results in infections, bruises, broken bones, visual and auditory impairment, brain damage, contusions, burns, and death (Oates, 1996). Those children who are being abused by violent shaking are at risk of being suffering from 'Shaken Baby' Syndrome which is associated with a range of physical effects, including bruising, broken bones, and bleeding of the brain, which may lead to permanent, severe brain damage or death (National Institute of Neurological Disorders and Stroke, 2001).

Psychological Problems: Research evidence suggest that physically abused children are more likely to develop aggressive behaviour problems. They are also more likely to interpret the actions of their peers as hostile, and to respond inappropriately in an aggressive manner (Dodge, Bates, and Petit, 1990).

Sexual Abuse

Physical Problems: Sexual abuse can result in acute, immediate injuries such as genital trauma, and pregnancy among pubertal females. This abuse also results in continued physical problems such as genital abnormalities, and sexually transmitted diseases (Trickett, 1997).

Psychological Problems: Researches show that survivors of childhood sexual abuse often feel shame and guilt (Browne, and Finkelhor, 1986). They have also been found to be less trusting of others and have a tendency to perceive sexual or exploitative motivation in the behaviour of others (Corby, 2000). These children also exhibit unusual and inappropriate sexual behaviour (Corby, 2000) from early ages. This tendency further results in increased sexual curiosity and frequent exposure of genitals (Trickett, 1997); simulated sexual acts with siblings and friends (Mian, Marton, and LeBaron, 1996); premature sexual knowledge; and sexualized kissing of friends and parents (Oates, 1996).

Neglect

Physical Problems: It has been found that neglect can result in increased rates of physical accidents (resulting in bruises, broken bones, death), and other health problems such as nappy rash, infections, colds, malnutrition, physical defects (Smith and Fong, 2004). It is also found to be associated with delays in physical development (Oates, 1996).

Psychological Problems: It has been found that intellectual and academic neglect may result in problems in language development (Smith and Fong, 2004). These children also show poor social competence such as aggressive behaviour and engagement in fewer social activities (Parkinson and Humphreys, 1998). It is also evident that children who face neglect are more likely to become abusive parents than children who have not been neglected (Tomison, 1996). This phenomenon is called intergenerational transmission of abuse.

Combating Child Abuse: A Challenge

The Role of Parents/Community

Though the incidence of child abuse comes as a shock to the parents, any denial or disability on their part can aggravate a child's misery. When a child is trying to say something parents/caregivers should not take their statements casually as there might be a possibility of abuse. They should provide the child with a comfortable environment and listen carefully to them. They should not show impatience and give their child enough time to speak. The child should not be forced for more information. Any expression of shock will lead them to withhold information or become secretive. If the child believes that he is deserving of abuse, all efforts should be made to change his/her beliefs and cognitions. Unconditional love and support is needed in great quantities by these children. To help these children:

1. Parents and caregivers should keep a vigilant eye over children and be receptive to any warning signs.
2. All concerned adults have the responsibility for creating safe environment for children before they are actually harmed.
3. Parents should be friendly and should subtly explain undesirable actions by adults to them.
4. Parents should inquire if they find any unexplained money, toys or gifts with their children.
5. If children display adult like behaviours, resist removing clothes or play sexual games it can indicate sexual abuse.
6. Children should be told all the mobile numbers of the parents and trusted adults for emergency.
7. Parents should not wait for 100 per cent proof and act instantly at any warning signs.
8. Parents should not hide these acts and report as some other child may be targeted.
9. High risk places like toilets, abandoned places etc. should be monitored.
10. All touching between caretakers and children however slights should take place in front of others.
11. Parents and concerned adults should have proper knowledge of developmental milestones and typical behaviours.
12. Frank discussions about bad behaviour by adults should take place with children.
13. School and home should work together for teaching children self protection skills.
14. Families with low socio-economic status should be provided with social support as these families are at high risk of child abuse.

15. Individuals and community should work together to prevent child abuse and neglect.
16. Parents or caregivers should know about parenting and child developmental skills and therapies.
17. In case of any child abuse the parent or caregivers should immediately seek expert help and should consult skilled psychologists/ counselor.

Role of Psychologists:-

The role of psychologists is very important in providing immediate help and support not only to the victim but also to his/her family. This situation is very much different from other counseling/ therapy situations. Psychologists have to choose appropriate therapy for the child based on the specific type of child abuse and neglect. As this problem is related not only to the child but also to the family and community, family therapy and community intervention becomes inevitable. The therapeutic techniques which are beneficial in dealing with abused children, are given below -

(a) **Holistic Therapy:-** The intervention policy for child abuse includes a range of therapeutic approaches, e.g. psychotherapy, play therapy, cognitive therapy, and psycho-educational approaches for children/youth/ adults. The therapeutic approach of the psychologist should focus on developing self esteem, managing depression, anger, teaching social skills and providing post abuse support.

(b) **Family therapy:-** Family therapy may be used to improve overall family functioning and developing communication skills. Family therapy also includes anger management and stress management for the parents and caretakers so that they may learn to deal with anger and frustration of child rearing.

(c) **Cognitive Behavioural Therapy (CBT):-** A number of studies have proposed cognitive behavioral therapy

(CBT) as an effective therapy for children exposed to sexual and physical abuse. It has been found that compared to other forms of therapy, CBT decreases symptoms of PTSD, general anxiety, depression, behavior problems, and social skills deficits. This therapy suggests the importance of focusing directly on the traumatic event and including both children and their caregivers. CBT involves both the abused child and parent or caregiver. The goals of this therapy is to provide children with a model to understand their reactions to abuse, normalize their experiences and symptoms, teach coping skills for upsetting thoughts, feelings, and behavior, and discuss the abusive events. The specific techniques can be tailored to take into account developmental differences (e.g., age, cognitive development).

(d) **Individualized Approach:** According to this approach different strategies are needed for different families dealing with different issues. Therapists also consider the type of abuse, child's age, gender, race, family composition, and characteristics of the parents (need for parent training, substance abuse treatment, etc.) to decide about appropriate therapy.

Goals of Psychotherapy

Which ever therapy is used by the therapist, the goal is to provide child with skills needed to effectively deal with the various problems caused by abuse. The therapist role is to teach these skills not only to child but also to parents and care takers.

A. **Skills for child:** The skills for child involve:

(a) **Coping Skills Training** is aimed at providing the child with skills to cope with the diversity of abuse-related emotions.

(b) **Relaxation Training** is aimed at providing training in diaphragmatic breathing and progressive muscle relaxation. There are various techniques that children can implement in multiple settings in which symptoms arise (e.g., classroom, home, car).

(c) **Cognitive Restructuring** is used to help children to systematically identify and challenge negative or distorted thoughts that may be precursors of emotional and behavioral problems.

(d) **Anger Management Skills** aims at teaching children to recognize situations which produce anger and to implement problem solving strategies.

(e) **Personal Safety Training** involves teaching communication skills and developing a safety plan. Throughout the therapy, therapist uses role play and homework techniques to teach various skills to deal with real life situations.

B. **Skills for Parents/ caregivers:** The skills for parents involve:

(a) **Skills to deal with children:-** The first goal of therapy with parents is to provide them skills to normalize their feelings and thoughts about their child's experience.

(b) **Coping skills:-** The parents are provided relaxation training and cognitive restructuring which would help them in presenting a positive model for coping before their children.

(c) **Behavioral management:-** This is a very useful training for families who have abused children. Forehand and McMahon's (2003) have shown that behaviour management improves parenting practices with non-compliant children. The goal of behavioural management is to encourage problem solving skills through discussion, role playing, rehearsal, and live therapist feedback.

Conclusion

India is the home of nineteen per cent of the world's children population. According to the 2001 Census, some 440 million people in the country today are aged below eighteen years and constitute 42 per cent of India's total population i.e., four out of every ten persons. Children are the future and require proper attention and care. To prevent any kind of childhood abuse, the family, community, teachers and psychologists are required to work collectively and develop an environment in which children can safely grow. These agencies should not only be providing immediate help and support to abused children but should try their level best to prevent it in the first place.

REFERENCES

Beck, A. and Weishaar, M. (1989). Cognitive therapy. In R. Corsini and D. Wedding (eds.), *Current Psychotherapies* (pp. 284-320). Itaska, IL.

Beitchman, J.H., Zuchr, K.J., Hood, J.E., daCosta, G.A., Akman, D. and Cassavia, E. (1992). A review of the long-term effects of child sexual abuse. *Child Abuse and Neglect,* 16, pp. 101-118.

Bohn, D.K. (2003). Lifetime physical and sexual abuse, substance abuse, depression, and suicide attempts among native American women. *Issues in Mental Health Nursing,* 24, pp. 333-352.

Briere, J. (1992). Methodological issues in the study of sexual abuse effects. *Journal of Consulting and Clinical Psychology,* 60, pp. 196-203.

Briere, J.N., and Elliot, D.M. (1994). Immediate and long-term impacts of child sexual abuse. *The Future of Children,* 4, pp. 54-69.

Brown, E.J. and Khan, S.A. (2003). Child abuse and neglect: Definitions, consequences and treatment. *Letter of the Child Study Center,* 7(4).

Browne, K. and Herbert, M. (1999). *Zapobieganie Przemocy Wrodzinie.* Warsaw: PARPA (in Polish).

Browne and Finkelhor, (1986). Impact of child sexual abuse: A review of the research. Psychological Bulletin, 99, pp. 66-77.

Casey, E. and Nurius, P.S. (2005). Trauma exposure and sexual revictimiation risk: Comparisons across single, multiple incident, and multiple perpetrator victimizations. *Violence Against Women,* 11(4), pp. 505-530.

Cerezo, A.and Frias, D. (1994). Emotional and cognitive adjustment in abused children. *Child Abuse and Neglect,* 18 (11), pp. 923-932.

Chalk, R, Gibbons, A. and Scarupa, H. (2002). The multiple dimensions of child abuse and neglect: new insights into an old problem. *Child Trends: Research Brief,* accessed at http://www.childtrends.org/PDF/ChildAbusRB.pdf [20/1/2003]

Chandy, J.M., Blum, R.W.M. and Resnick, M.D. (1996). Gender-specific out-comes for sexually abused adolescents. *Child Abuse and Neglect,* 20, pp. 1219-1231.

Corby, B. (2000). *Child Abuse: Towards a Knowledge Base* (2nd ed), Buckingham: Open University Press.

Crittenden, P.M. (1992). Children's strategies for coping with adverse home environments: an interpretation using attachment theory. *Child Abuse and Neglect,* 16, pp. 329-343.

Davis, J.L., Petretic-Jackson, P.A. and Ting, L. (2001). Intimacy Dysfunction and Trauma Symptomatology: Long-Term Correlates of Different Types of Child Abuse. *Journal of Traumatic Stress,* 14, pp. 63-79.

Dodge, K.A., Bates, J.E. and Pettit, G.S. (1990). Mechanisms in the cycle of violence. *Science,* 250, pp. 1678-1683.

Dohrenwend, B.P. (2000). The role of adversity and stress in psychopathology: Some evidence and its implications for theory and research. *Journal of Health and Social Behavior,* 41, pp. 1-19

Eckenrode, J., Laird, M. and Doris, J. (1993). Academic performance and disciplinary problems among abused and neglected children. *Developmental Psychology,* 29, pp. 53-62.

Elliott, A.N. and Carnes, C.N. (2001). Reactions of nonoffending parents to the sexual abuse of their child: A review of the literature. *Child Maltreatment*, 6(4), pp. 314-331.

Feiring, C., Taska, L.S. and Lewis, M. (1999). Age and gender differences in children's and adolescent's adaptation to sexual abuse. *Child Abuse and Neglect*, 23, pp. 115-128.

Felitti, V. J. (1991). Long-term medical consequences of incest, rape, and molestation. *Southern Medical Journal*, 84, pp. 328-331.

Fleming, J., Mullen, P.E., Sibthorpe, B., and Bammer, G. (1999). The long-term impact of childhood sexual abuse in Australian women. *Child Abuse and Neglect*, 23, pp. 145-159.

Friedrich, W.N., Grambusch, P., Damon, L. and Hewitt, S.K. (2001). Child sexual behaviour inventory: Normative and clinical comparisions. *Child Maltreatment*, 6, pp. 37-49.

Gagnon, M. and Hersen, M. (2000). Unresolved childhood sexual abuse and older adults: Late-life vulnerabilities. *Journal of Clinical Geropsychology*, 6(3), pp. 187-198.

Gibson, R.L., Harthorne, T.S. (1996). Childhood sexual abuse and adult loneliness and network orientation. *Child Abuse and Neglect*, 20, pp. 1087-1093.

Glaser, D. (2000). Child abuse and neglect and the brain: a review. *Journal of Child Psychology and Psychiatry*, 41(1), pp. 97-116.

Greven, P. (1991). *Spare the child: The religious roots of punishment and the psychological impact of physical abuse*. New York: Knopf.

Hammen, C. (2003). Interpersonal stress and depression in women. *Journal of Affective Disorders*, 74, pp. 49-57.

Hammen, C., Henry, R. and Daley, S. (2000). Depression and sensitization to stressors among young women as a function of childhood adversity. *Journal of Consulting and Clinical Psychology*, 68, pp. 782-787.

Harmer, A.L., Sanderson, J., and Mertin, P. (1999). Influence of negative childhood experiences on psychological functioning, social support, and parenting for mothers recovering from addiction. *Child Abuse and Neglect*, 23, pp. 421-433.

Hobfoll, S.E. (2002). Alone together: Comparing communal versus individualistic resiliency: In E. Frydenberg (Ed.) *Beyond Coping: Meeting Goals, Vision, and Challenges* (pp. 63-81). Oxford, G.B.: Oxford University Press.

Jumper, S.A. (1995). A meta-analysis of the relationship of child sexual abuse to adult psychological adjustment. *Child Abuse and Neglect,* 19(6), pp. 715-728

Kendall-Tackett, K. (2002). The health effects of childhood abuse: Four pathways by which abuse can influence health. *Child Abuse and Neglect,* 26, pp. 715-729.

Kolko, D. J. (2002). Child physical abuse. In J. E. B. Myers, L. Berliner, J. Briere, C. T., Hendrix, C. Jenny, T. A., Reid (Eds.), *The APSAC handbook on child maltreatment, 2nd ed.* Thousand Oaks, CA: Sage Publications.

Kolko, D.J. and Brown, E.J. (2000). Child sexual abuse. In R.T. Ammerman and M. Hersen (Eds.) *Case Studies in Family Violence,* (2nd ed., pp. 177-207). New York: Plenum Publishing.

Lefcourt, H. (1992). Durability and impact of the locus of control construct. *Psychological Bulletin,* 112, pp. 411-414.

Leserman, J. Li, Z., Drossman, D. A. and Hu, Y.J.B. (1998). Selected symptoms associated with sexual and physical abuse history among female patients with gastrointestinal disorders: The impact on subsequent health care visits. *Psychological Medicine,* 28, pp. 417-425.

Lynch, M. and Cicchetti, D. (1998). An ecological-transactional analysis of children and contexts: The longitudinal interplay among child maltreatment, community violence, and children's symptomatology. *Development and Psychopathology,* 10 (2), pp. 235-257.

Martin, P. and Mohr, P. (2000). Incidence and correlates of post-traumatic stress disorder in Australian victims of domestic violence. *Journal of Family Violence,* 15, pp. 411-422.

McMahon, R.R. and Forehand, R.L. (2003). *Helping the Noncompliant Child.* New York: The Guilford Press.

Mian, M., Marton, P. and LeBaron, D. (1996). The effects of sexual abuse on 3- to 5-year-old girls. *Child Abuse and Neglect, 20,* pp. 731-745.

Ministry of Women and Child Development, Government of India (2007). *Study on Child Abuse: India 2007.* Study Report.

National Institute of Neurological Disorders and Stroke (2001). *NINDS Shaken Baby Syndrome* Information Page, Available at: www.ninds.nih.gov/health_and_medical/disorders/shakenbaby.htm

Oates, R.K. (1996). *The Spectrum of Child Abuse: Assessment, Treatment, and Prevention,* New York: Brunner/Mazel.

Paolucci, O., Genuis, E. and Violato, M. (2001). A meta-analysis of the published research on the effects of child sexual abuse. *Journal of Psychology,* 135(1), pp. 17-36.

Parkinson, P., and Humphreys, C. (1998). Children who witness domestic violence: the implications for child protection. *Child and Family Law Quarterly,* 10, pp. 147-159.

Peters, S. D. (1988). Child sexual abuse and later psychological problems. In G.E. Wyatt and G.J. Powell (Eds.). *The Lasting Effects of Child Sexual Abuse.* Beverly Hills: Sage Publications.

Rodriguez, N., Ryan, S.W., Vande Kemp, H. and Foy, D.W. (1997). Posttraumatic stress disorder in adult female survivors of childhood sexual abuse: A comparison study. *Journal of Consulting and Clinical Psychology,* 65, pp. 53-59.

Russell, D.E.H. (1986). *The Secret Trauma.* Basic Books: New York.

Salter, D., McMillan, D., Richards, M., Talbot, T., Hodges, J., Bentovim, A. and Hastings, R. (2003). Development of sexually abusive behaviour in sexually victimized males: A longitudinal Study, *Lancet,* 361, pp. 471-476.

Schechter, M.D. and Roberge, L. (1976). Sexual exploitation. In R.E. Helfer and C.H. Kempe (Eds.), *Child abuse and neglect* (pp. 127-142). Cambridge, MA: Ballinger.

Sedney, M.A. and Brooks, A. (1984). Factors associated with a history of childhood sexual experience in a nonclinical female population. *Journal of the American Academy of Child Psychiatry,* 23(2), pp. 215-218.

Seligman, M.E.P. (1975). *Helplessness.* San Francisco: Freeman.

Seligman. M.E.P., and Csinkzentmihalyi, M. (2000). Positive psychology. *American Psychologist, 55,* pp. 5-14.

Silk, K.R., Lee, S., Hill, E. M. and Lohr N. E. (1995). Borderline personality disorder symptoms and severity of sexual abuse. *American Journal of Psychiatry,* 152(7), pp. 1059-1064.

Smith, M.G. and Fong, R. (2004). *The Children of Neglect: When No One Cares,* New York: Brunner-Routledge.

Stroud, D. (1999). Familial support as perceived by adult victims of childhood sexual abuse. *Sexual Abuse: Journal of Research and Treatment,* 11(2), pp. 159-175.

Teegen, F. (1999). Childhood sexual abuse and long-term sequelae. In A. Maercker, M. Schutzwohl, and Z. Solomon (Eds.) *Posttraumatic stress disorder: A lifespan developmental perspective* (pp. 97-112). Seattle: Hogrefe and Huber.

Tomison, A.M. (1996). Intergenerational transmission of maltreatment. *Issues in Child Abuse Prevention,* 6, Melbourne: Australian Institute of Family Studies.

Tricket, P.K., Noll, J., Reiffnaan, A. and Putnan, F. (2001). Variants of intra-familial sexual abuse and experiences: Implications for short and long term development. *Developmental Psychopathology,* 13, pp. 1001-1019.

Trickett, P.K. (1997). Sexual and physical abuse and the development of social competence. In S. S. Luthar, J. A. Burack, D. Cicchetti and J.R. Weisz (Eds.), *Developmental Psychopathology: Perspectives on Adjustment, Risk, and Disorder,* New York: Cambridge Press.

Turner, H. and Butler, M. (2003). Direct and indirect effects of childhood adversity on depressive symptoms in young adults. *Journal of Youth and Adolescence* 32, pp. 89-103.

Turner, R.J., Lloyd, D.A. and Roszell, P. (1999). Personal resources and the social distribution of depression. *American Journal of Community Psychology* 27 (5), pp. 643-676.

Vranceanu, A.M. (2007). Sequelae od child abuse: the role of social and personal resources. Unpublished doctoral dissertation submitted to Kent State University.

Widom, C.S. (1999). Posttraumatic stress disorder in abused and neglected children grown up. *American Journal of Psychiatry,* 156, pp. 1223-1229.

Wolfe, D. (1987). *Child abuse: Implications for child development and psychopathology.* Newbury Park, CA: Sage.

Yama, M.F., Fogas, B.S., Teegarden, L.A. and Hastings, B. (1993). Childhood sexual abuse and parental alcoholism: Interactive effects in adult women. *American Journal of Orthopsychiatry,* 63(2), pp. 300-305.

10

Growing Violence Among Kids

Vishesh Kumar Gupta

The main theme of this chapter centres round the growing violence among children under the age of playing and feeding. The first part of this paper provides the background information of the issue. The second part attempts to throw light on the crux of the phenomena. The last portion discusses the remedial measures. The nature of this paper is purely theoretical. The paper, being theoretical in nature, follows the technique of data collection and analysis which is based on secondary data.

Needless to say that violence in schools is making headlines again. In recent times more and more instances of aggression and violence among children are coming to light. One or two examples are worth mentioning for making its background more meaningful. It would not be out of place to mention here the very popular incident of Euro International School of Gurgaon (Haryana). Perhaps it was the first incident of its kind in the country that brought the terror of innocuous school rivalry which took a ghastly turn, where two 8th class boys of the public school shot a class mate dead in school with the licensed revolver of one of the boys. This shocking incident occurred in the school in question in Gurgaon, soon after the class got over. Without showing any shame the accused boys said that they wanted to kill the deceased in front of everyone because he used to bully them and other students. This is not the first time something like this has happened in the country. Dozen of incidents happened in last one or two years. The occurrence of these incidents, raises a question? Why are more and more kids restoring the violence? There is a great concern about the incidents of violent behaviour among children and adolescents. This complex and troubling issue needs to be carefully understood by parents, teachers and policy makers.

There are so many questions floating in the air for seeking answer of this burning problem. Here one prominent question is whether it is violence through TV or video games. Doubtless, kids today. are exposed to it more than anybody else. Psychiatrists say that some kids resort to violence to vent their frustration and at times even depression, whereas many are of the opinion that too much exposure to violence is the reason for impressionable minds to get hooked on to it.

Media experts and social scientists too have been wrestling with this question for decades and thousands of studies have been done on it. And most of them have come to the same conclusion that the media violence is responsible for aggressive behaviour in children. Researches have found that the more violence children watch on TV, the more likely they may act in aggressive ways towards others. Also, they become less sensitive to others' pain and are less likely to help a victim of violence. It is truism that media violence affects how children view themselves their world and other people. An overdose of screen violence can have lifelong detrimental effects on the health of the kids

What makes the situation worse is that children today are viewing more violence and conflicts than ever before. As a result, they are left feeling insecure and fearful. And since media rewards and glorifies violence, kids accept aggression as the best form of conflict resolution. A study of violence on Indian TV and its impact on children commissioned by UNESCO accused 'Idiot Box' of bombarding young minds with all kinds of violent images, cutting across the channels, programmes and viewing times. In all, they identified 759 distinct acts of violence across five channels over a period of nine days. These included assaulting, slapping, punching, shooting, strangulating, burning, pushing and stabbing etc. Not only studies, but also incidents go to prove that children who watch violent episodes show likelihood of behaving aggressively. It is common observation that if the children watch WWF, there remains a half an hour wrestling competition at home. That competition is admittedly harmless, but there are occasions on which the TV is known to have led to bizarre and horrendous incidents.

There is no doubt that media is a powerful teacher and contributes greatly to the way we act and behave. In some cases, the effects are immediate and in others there is a sleeper effect where the results show up much later. It is the one side of the coin. Another side of the coin is not to neglect of the other factors which are directly responsible to the problem. Individual predisposition of the child, parental attitudes and reaction to aggression are probably equally important. In most of the cases media is only the fourth most important influence in a child's life with parents, teachers and peers being the first three. The social scientists say that the main issue is getting sidelined by blaming the media. The question is not how they did it, but why they are doing it. They point out the view that the growing "here-and-now" culture in which kids are getting used to immediate gratification, is leading to an intolerant society on the whole. Children are not taught how to handle failure, success and conflict. As a result, they resort to aggression. The media critics refuse to buy it. They insist the content of media needs to be monitored and care be taken to reduce violence if not remove it. But even if all the gore and violence is completely removed from the media, will it make a significant difference in aggressive behaviour of children? And then how do you justify the fact that studies have shown that viewing violence on TV also provides an opportunity to discharge the bent up, aggressive feelings of anger, hostility and frustration.

Basically the problem is not with the media, but the lack of media education. No one teaches the children how to assess the reality status of TV programmes. Good parenting may be perhaps the greatest defence against the negative effects of violent images of TV. It is the responsibility of the concerned persons, sensitive and careful adults to bring the children back to reality. Social scientists say that it is time that parents and teachers took a long hard look at themselves in the mirror. Most of the parents treat TV as a baby-sitter when it suits them. And when something goes wrong, they turn around and blame TV for it.

Range of Violent Behaviour

Violent behaviour in children and adolescents can include a wide range of behaviours — explosive temper tantrums, physical aggression, fighting, threats or attempts to hurt others, use of weapons, cruelty towards animals, fire setting, intentional destruction of property and vandalism. Numerous research studies have concluded that a complex interaction or combinations of factors leads to an increased risks of violent behaviour in children and adolescents. These factors include – previous aggression or violent behaviour, exposure to violence in the home or community, use of drugs or alcohol, presence of fire arms in home, single parenting, loss of support from extended family and brain damage from head injury. Children who have several risk factors and show the following behaviours like intense anger, frequent loss of temper or blowups, extreme irritability, extreme impulsiveness and becoming easily frustrated, they should be evaluated carefully. Parents and teachers should be careful not to minimize these behaviours in children.

Remedial Measures

As incidents of childhood and teenage aggression, depression and even suicide start sounding alarmingly familiar each day, we should be pressing the panic button about our children's mental health. No doubt, there is a lot of work needed in the area of children's mental health. WHO indicates that by the year 2020 childhood, neuropsychiatry disorders, internationally, will arise proportionately by over 50 per cent to become one of the five most common causes of morbidity, mortality and disability among children. But there are hardly any figures or researches in India that show mental, emotional and behavioural problems being faced by the children today. "The issue is huge, but the level of intervention is at an infantile stage". Experts agree that academic and learning-related problems need to be examined along with mental health problems of children. For this, we need to have adequate systems at all levels to provide positive mental health to kids.

Last but not the least, research studies have shown that much violent behaviour can be decreased or even prevented if the above risk factors are significantly reduced or eliminated. Most important efforts should be directed at dramatically decreasing the exposure of children and adolescents to violence in the home, community and through the media. It is clear view that violence leads to violence. Resultantly, we should be very careful about this problem.

In addition, the following strategies can lessen or prevent violent behaviour among children. These are – Prevention of child abuse, Parent training and family support programme, sex education, early intervention programmes for violent youngsters, and lastly monitoring child's viewing of violence on TV, videos, movies and sparing some time to have dialogue with the children. While all these measures surely need to be implemented without delay, what's really needed is the right amount of support for these children. We all are passing through a critical transitional phase. At this time, it is dire need of the hour to look after properly of our children. So that we could form the best society of the future. It is truth that children are the future of the society If we want to protect the society, we must invest more and more our time and healthy dialogue among the children.

REFERENCES

Ahuja, Ram 1982: Sociology of Youth subculture. Jaipur: Rawat Publications.

Bandura, A. 1973: Agression: A Social Learning Analysis. New Jeresy: Prentice Hall.

Bollon, F.G. and Bollon, S.R., 1987: Working with Violent Families. New York: Sage Publications.

Gelles and Connel, 1985: Intimate Violence in Families. Beverly Hills: Sage Publications.

Joshi, Uma, 1986: A Disgrace in our Family. New Delhi: Hindustan Times June 25, 1986.

Shard, Neel K., 1988: The Legal, Economic, and Social Status of the Indian Child. New Delhi: National Book Organisation.

Modi, Ishwar, 1997: Drugs: Addiction and prevention. Jaipur: Rawat Publications.

Joshi, P.C., 1992: Culture, Communication and Social Change. New Delhi: Vikas Publishing House.

Awasthi, Abha, 1997: Social and Cultural Diversities (edited). Jaipur: Rawat Publications.

Atal, Yogesh, 2006: Changing Indian Society. New Delhi: Rawat Publications.

Singh, Youndra, 1993: Social Change in India-Crisis and Resilience. New Delhi: Har Anand Publications.

Marshall, Gordon, 2005: Oxford dictionary of Sociology (edited). New Delhi: Oxford University Press.

Wayne, Ellwood, 2005: The Guide to Globalization. New Delhi:Rawat Publications.

11

Unmasking the Mask: Childhood Realities of Victims of Child Abuse

Sangeeta Sharma and Anshumali Sharma

In today's world children grow up in an atmosphere of violence. .Violence at home and outside, violence in the form of abuse at home or in the form of corporal punishment in school or at workplace in the form of exploitation and so on. Child abuse occurs in strata of society in all countries and still it is very difficult to be reported or to talk about, and to identify the victims of abuse, though they may be there under our nose. Everyone feels proud to say that we all have right to express, to speak, but do our children get the atmosphere where they can express and speak? At times they speak but adults do not believe them or they may not themselves be in the position to accept what is told to them. A culture of silence and shame does not allow adults to accept and discuss sexuality, abuse and exploitation at any platform more so with their children. Children are encouraged to avoid 'keep quiet', overlook, ignore such behavior of the victimizer, especially if he is a family member .A false notion of self- blame and shame is the main reason for the day to day increase in the incidents of the abuse of children.

Review of Child Abuse in India

Child sexual abuse has often been viewed as a social phenomenon linked to general attitude and practices towards children, and ways in which social relationships are organized and regulated in a particular society [Glaser and Frosh,1993] Studies show that four factors, most likely increase the occurrence of sexual abuse. These may be listed as Motivation, which includes the abuser's sexuality; absence of internal inhibitors i.e. moral values of adult; absence of external inhibitors i.e. supervision of child by others, and child's own resistance towards the adult [Finkelhor,1984] 'Family System Theory'[Furniss,1984;1991], on the other hand, postulates father- daughter incestuous relationship occurs due to dysfunctional arrangement where suffer from an emotional-sexual conflict. Child gets sexual response when child comes to a parent for emotional relief or care. According to this theory the result is either a' conflict avoidance'-the family is too insecure to cope with acknowledging the abuse, or 'conflict regulation'—the family hide the abuse from the outside world, they openly recognize the abuse leading to frequent arguments amongst the members.

An exploiter or an abuser violates child's rights and personal integrity, it also causes serious psychological as well as physical harm, it is often destructive of the whole personality of the child. The courts shoulder a great responsibility while trying such cases and 'should deal with them with utmost sensitivity' holds the Supreme Court in T. K. Gopal Alias Gopi, *v.* State of Karnataka, (2000) 6 SCC 168. [Ashok Priyadarshi, Law against abuse of children, 2007]

The Supreme Court in State of Karnataka, *v.* Krishnappa, (2000) 4 SCC 75 has expressed anguish on the Karnataka

High Court 's " lacking sensitivity" towards a child rape victim and increased the sentence of the accused and held that where a child is involved punishment can not depend on the social status of the victim or of the accused, the reduction of sentence should not be in a mechanical manner without proper application of mind, on the ground long lapse of time and the prosecutor might have got married and settled in life.

The media has played a great role in bringing into light the sexual abuse and exploitation of children, the events are such that it is beyond one's imagination and belief and has helped the society in raising voice against such crime and the government and police machinery in booking the criminals and in controlling the crime. The Supreme Court in State Of Maharastra Vs. R.J. Gandhi (1997) 8 SCC 386 has warned the media that the crime against the children should not be glorified by their reporting. Studies show that persons, who are holding trust and power vis-à-vis, have sexually exploited and abused the child and the abuse is done in different forms:

- In cases of exploitation of a child labour and domestic workers by the employer and other adults as sexual gratification.
- Further the migrants, refugees, displaced children are the worst sufferers, as there is no record regarding them.
- In some institutions, those who are supposed to provide care and protection, sexually abuse children.
- It is unfortunate that the increasing number of sexually transmitted diseased has increased the demand of child prostitutes and the children have become the victim of international flesh trade, specially at tourist centers
- In India, cultural and traditional factors leading to child marriage have led to the sexual abuse of the child, primarily the tender aged girl child.

Various investigations and studies have proved that the exploitation, which a child is facing, is in every walk of life and the worst sufferer is the girl child.

It is necessary to give equal rights to both, male and female child irrespective of their sex, so as the juvenile is brought out from the cover of neglect and injustice. Children's exploitation in every walk of life all over the world has resulted in formulation of 'Convention on the Rights of the Child' (CRC) in the year 1989. The main motive behind this Convention was not only to provide certain privileges to children but also to provide certain rights to protection and participation. They have been given special rights of protection from all forms of abuse and exploitation either in their own homes or in their public life. This is very unfortunate that after so many years of adoption of the CRC the children are still abused and exploited.

In Indian context, laws have been framed and the existing laws have been made more effective. The Supreme Court in Vishka vs. State Of Rajasthan AIR 1997 S.C.3011 held that the International Conventions and norms, consistent with the spirit of fundamental rights, can be read into those rights for interpreting them in the larger context to promote the objectives of the Constitution of India.

The Juvenile Justice (Care and Protection of Children) Act 2000, which was later amended in 2006, in its present form has been enacted to discharge the obligation of Indian Government to follow the United National Standard a conjoint reading of the sections, preamble, aims and objects of the Act leaves no manner of doubt that the legislature intended to provide protection, treatment, development and rehabilitation of neglected or delinquent juveniles and for the adjudication thereof. The Act being a piece of social legislation is meant for the protection of children who commit criminal offences and, therefore, such provisions should be liberally and meaningfully construed so as to advance the object of the Act (AIR 2005, SUPREME COURT 2731 "Pratap Singh *v.* State of Jharkhand").

A government of India commissioned survey sponsored by Women and Child Development Ministry in New Delhi has found that more than 53 per cent of children in India are subjected to sexual abuse, and the fact is that many cases are not even reported. The forms of child abuse covered by the survey are physical, sexual and emotional, as well as female child neglect, two out of every three children have been physically abused. It is usually found that parents and relatives, persons known to the child or in a position of trust and responsibility were perpetrators of child sexual abuse. According to this report, which assumes greater significance in the backdrop of the Nithari killings, the issue of children's safety, especially those in the age group of 5-12 years, has got focussed.

The survey, carried out across 13 states and with a sample size of 12,447, revealed that 53.22 per cent of children reported having faced one or more forms of sexual abuse, with Andhra Pradesh, Bihar, Assam and Delhi reporting the highest percentage of such incidents. In 50 per cent of child abuse cases, the abusers were known to the child or were in a position of trust and responsibility and most children did not report the matter to anyone.

This survey on child abuse also disclosed that nearly 65 per cent of school children reported facing corporal punishment — beatings by teachers — mostly in government schools. Of children physically abused in families, in 88.6 per cent of the cases, it was the parents who were the perpetrators. More than 50 per cent had been sexually abused in ways that ranged from severe — such as rape or fondling — to milder forms of molestation that included forcible kissing.

The survey also interviewed 2,324 young adults between the ages of 18 and 24, almost half of whom reported being physically or sexually abused as children. When it comes to emotional abuse, every second child was subjected to emotional assault and in 83 per cent of the cases, parents were the abusers.

In a survey conducted in America it was found that 53 per cent women were sexually exploited as a child, 21 per cent were made to take part in sexual acts they did not understand or like, it was also found that where women were assaulted as children, 6 per cent of assailants were 'respected adults' 13 per cent were strangers and 33 per cent were someone known to the child 47 per cent were family members (Women Support Project Survey,1989). This shows that such problems are faced by children all over irrespective whether it is a developing or a so-called developed country like America. Problems and issues seem to be same.

When the child is sexually abused not only her boundaries are violated, she loses sense of control and believes that she is not valued, her self esteem, individuality, sense of reality and world is lost immediately. The feeling of worthlessness and negativity overpowers the personality leading to self haterate. Such children do not grow up into a normal adult being, it found that approximately 40 per cent of the sexually abused children suffer consequences serious enough to need therapy in adulthood. (Browne and Finklehor, 1986). Adult women who were sexually abused in childhood score poor on mental health measure (Brayden, Ditrich, and Sherrod 1996). Studies have shown that the survivors of of child abuse face the problem of cohabitation at younger age marital disruption and divorce (Finkelhor, Hotaling, Lewis and Smith,1989)

It is reported that sexually abused women ranked personal values such as inner harmony, self respect, wisdom and health as most important to them. The non abused women, on the other hand, ranked the outer values of equality, a world of peace, national security and world of beauty as more important indicating greater psychological maturity (Bohan 1997).

There are number of cases that occur in day to day life of children living in their homes or on streets or in observation homes, government homes, schools public places etc. there seem to be no place which is completely safe for child. Own home is supposed to be the safest place, and parents and known the most trustworthy, but many a times our home becomes the most unsafe, parent and known adult most untrustworthy.

Few case-studies have been selected here to provide a clear picture how a child at home may not be as safe as we generally believe and how the people who are generally trusted can be the most untrustworthy. Life truly is very uncertain and things can be very unpredictable, these case-studies prove this.

Case-1

Nazma is 12yrs old .She is very soft spoken. She works at home like an adult woman, she cleans her house,utensils and does everything told to be done. She says 'I am always at home, I do work which seems to be unending. Sometimes I feel that I am born just to work, there is nothing else that I will be able to do or learn. I know if I don't work I will not get food. *Amma* says that to get food everyone has to work, no one can have anything just by playing or by sitting and doing nothing.' '*Abba* [father] is always out painting houses or shops he hardly speaks to me. If he is at home he is either sleeping or shouts at *Amma*, very often he beats her at night when he comes home drunken.' My younger brother Asif, is the one who speaks to me but he is out the whole day when he comes home he orders for all that he wants,as if he is much older to me. I know he orders because he earns, sometimes he remains out for the whole night no one questions him, if *Amma* asks he reply very rudly, *Abba* is not bothered about anyone.' 'I am always told that since we are muslims we should not talk too much with neighbours. I am also told to be in *parda* and remain *inside* the house all the time. I don't like it.' 'Waseem lives in the same locality, he works in the same *dhaba* where my brother works, sometimes he also comes home with Asif I like him, he is the only one who talks to me sweetly. He even tells me that I am very hard working, I like him for this.'

Nazma has a lot to say about herself like a long story longer than her own life. She narrated how she steped out of her home. 'Asif had a friend who suggested that I should also go out to earn since I do a lot of work at home. I knew no one would allow me to stepout of the house so I ran away. I wanted to earn and buy things for myself and also for Amma. Shafiq, Asif's friend, took me to station, I saw train I was very excited. He said that we will go to Allahabad,and he knows someone there who will give me a job and a place to live. We boarded the train and got down I don't know where. We went to a tea stall, had tea and buns. After sometime he took me to his friend's place, I was tired I slept when I woke up he was trying to do '*wrong things*' with me. I was very scared I said I want to go back to my home. He was very angry and said it is not easy to go back .I cried and cried for many days one he said that he will take me back on the condition that I will not disclose anything to anyone. I agreed and after two more days we came back. I did not tell anything to anyone, I was scolded by everyone even by my neighbours.

Case 2

Jyoti is a 14 years old girl. Jyoti has three elder sisters. Somehow, they are all married. She stays at home and look after her sibling brother,cooks food for other members who go out to work. Younger brother is very pampered being the only son. Jyoti was friendly to her next door neighbour who was a married woman much older to her, and had sympathy to Jyoti for all that she does for the family without a word of appreciation.

Jyoti says 'many a times I feel I am alone even when I have a family of my own. Every one is busy, no one asks me how was my day at home and keep on telling me that 'the day was very bad' why do they go out if the day is always bad. Everyone earns and does what they want, I cannot do anything I don't earn. I also want to go out to earn but I have the responsibility of my brother and of course, the house.' Lalita, her neighbour,was a regular visitor to her house in the absence of her parents during the day. One day she suggested her to to move out to earn and live her own life freely.

Jyoti narrates 'we planned and I come out in the evening living my younger brother inside the home, I knew, it was the time for *maa* (mother) to be back. Lalita's husband also accompanied us. We went to bus station and boarded the bus to some place, I could not hear the name. For about 9 to 10 hours we traveled and reached a place where Lalita said that they had relatives who would help us in getting job and a place to live. Two days passed we did not go anywhere. The third was the worst day of my life, Lalita's husband did all bad things with me, he raped me in the presence of Lalita, she did not even try to save me or tell her husband to stop, I was horrified. I was in pain. Then this became a regular feature. Many days passed, there was no one whom I could tell anything. One day they told me that 'we have to go now'. I did not ask where. Three of us boarded a train. I was made to sit in between the two. On the way I did not speak a word but they were talking I did not hear what, as if I was not alive. The train stopped Lalita had gone to washroom, her husband got down to take something. A woman sitting next to me asked me about the two traveling with me before I could say I burst out, I cried and cried but could not say a word. That was enough for the lady to understand that people with me are not good. As Lalita saw me crying, she came close to me, the lady fired many questions together to her. Lalita's husband was outside the train. From the window he called Lalita. They both ran away leaving me behind. The next station was Lucknow here with the help of Police and the Childline I reached back to my home.

Case 3

Heena, a 12 yrs old girl belonging to an orthodox muslim family lived quite a simple and almost a struggle free life with her family. She has four elder brothers, mother and father. All brothers work though they are not much educated, father is totaly illiterate but earns mother stays at home with Heena. Heena comes out of her house with her boyfriend he promised her to marry. 'My parents did not like him. They were fixing my marriage with my *mamu's* son who was not at all good, nor he earned properly, he was also drunkard. He was also many years older to me. I told my *amma* (mother) that I won't marry but she said she had no say in this matter 'I cannot go against the decisions of your *abba*' (father). Heena frankly says 'I had no other option but to run away with Aslam.' Heena continous 'even my cousins are married off very young, at the age of 11, 10, 12 and so on. I did not object to marry but not to that person I never liked him, in fact, none of our family members liked him except my father. No one had the power or the right to say anything in the matters taken up by the father.' 'I came out with Aslam, he was accompanied by three of his friends, he took me to the railway station where we sat in a train, and there was no one in the train. Aslam told that since engine has some problem only after two hours or so it will move. I believed him. As the time passed I was scared, I told Aslam that I want to go home. He did not say anything. His friends had gone to take something to eat. As they came Aslm told them 'we don't have much time she wants to go home.' I could not understand what he meant by that.' 'Just then they started misbehaving with me. I started crying, it was almost night, I could hear other trains moving with loud voice, no one would have heard me screaming and shouting. All the boys were together treating me like a ball hitting me against each other.' 'whole night I was in agony and pain, I was not in my senses. I don't know how I reached the police station,who took me there? But I was in a bad shape.'

Case 4

Khushboo was two when her mother died. For some time she lived with her father, but soon he married again. Her father's elder brother adopted her, his wife did not like this arrangement, as it was an added responsibility for her. There was already a son in the family. The entire family was uneducated, and was also conservative in their thought, so there was no question of sending their adopted daughter to school. Khushboo learnt all the household work, and started learning embroidery which their family profession. The family observerd strict *parda* system as a part of their muslim custom. Khushboo had a very timid and depressive personality as she was always subdued by her mother, who never allowed to open her mouth without a permission. Fed up with the treatment done to her she ran away from the house. She says 'I thought things will be better outside the home. There would be no one to beat me, I will do as I like. For two days I was not scared. Third day I did not know what to do and where to go. I did not have a single paisa with me. There were many children there who earned money as they begged I also tried but I could not beg the way they were begging. I was also scared of the policeman there. I even tried to be friendly with those children but they did not talk to me. A man of my father's age took me to his house saying that he need a maid for his wife who is handicap. But for two days I did not see anyone at that place. He said that his wife has gone out station for treatment with his son and will be back in two days. After this the man came closer to me. For many days I was at his house every day he raped me and no one came even after many days. He use to lock me up while he went out. One day with the help of a woman who lived nearby I was able to run away from there.'

Case 5

Simmi is 8 yrs old. Her father died when she was three and a half year. She has mother and four sisters, all elder to her. When her father died her mother married her husband's friend who was a regular visitor to their place. This step- father is an electrician who does not go to the job regularly and dominate the entire family. Mother also earns by working in houses in a nearby locality.

Both the parents are educated up to primary level. All sisters go to a school, run for under privileged children in the same locality, and are doing well. Eldest sister is in class 10, second one in class 9, third one in class 5 and she herself in class 2. They are Nepalese who generally come to India to earn. This family came to India in 2002. In this case both, father and mother are responsible for abuse. Economically they are not very poor. They wear decent clothes, eat food of their own choice and live a decent life as the people in the lower middle class family.

Sheena, the eldest of all daughters is very quiet by nature; it was the second one, Poonam, who stood against her father when she first saw him molesting the youngest of her sister. It took her about a week to understand what was being done by the father. She told it to one of her teachers taking her in confidence. The teacher took the help of Childline to confront her parents. It was found that mother silently supported the act of her second husband by not reacting against him. Elder sisters were sexually assaulted abused by the step father but did not revolt. It was only when the youngest one became the victim that the elder sisters could not anymore tolerate father's habit of molesting children in the absence of other members of the family. Simmi was too young to understand that something wrong was being done to her. When asked she said 'probably father was playing with me.' Abuse here was very much known to the family but no one dare to talk about it. Even the mother accepted it for the reasons unknown to her daughters. However, the intervention by the teacher, school and Childline did make difference to their life.

Top of Form

Strengthening Families and Communities to prevent child abuse and neglect is the most difficult, at the same time the safest way to prevent children and their childhood from violence and its ill-effects. It is necessary to develop protective factors that help reduce the risk of child maltreatment, strategies for changing how communities support families, and evidence-informed practices. Enhancing protective factors in families and tools to build awareness and develop community partnerships can go a long way in this direction. A guide for this purpose may be developed, common or universal in nature, for the professionals working with children and to be used by them religiously at every level, also addressing a global concern on how abuse and neglect severely threaten family viability, frequently leading to family separation. The guidance and support mechanisms proposed here can be adapted to mitigate risks and strengthen families in other country contexts.

The process of identifying and responding to abuse requires skilled interventions in order to prevent further harm to the child. Police, medical, psychological, and social services play the most important role to address the safety, physical and emotional needs of the affected children. Same type of care plan may not be applicable to all children since each individual child may differ from the other. However, any such plan must be in 'the best interests of the child' and protect them and their siblings from harm. There are additional risks of abuse for children in institutions like children homes, hostels and schools etc and care placements. Such closed environments are extremely susceptible to abuse since they are frequently isolated, insufficiently regulated, and lacking in adequate supervision. It is here that the role of social services becomes important to screen, supervise and monitor all child placements, including institutional, kinship, and foster care, to ensure the child's safety and well-being.

Whole community has the responsibility to protect its children. Education and community awareness for children and adults on the risks, signs of abuse, and responses is vital for children without parental care and those in high risk situations, such as during a conflict or displacement when sexual violence, exploitation, and recruitment into armed forces are prevalent.

According to a study conducted by Government of India mentioned above the world's largest number of sexually abused children are found in India. Incest is the most common form of sexual abuse in homes; at least 25 per cent of the adult population has been molested before the age of 16. The exact magnitude of the problem is difficult to ascertain as there is gross underreporting because of the stigma associated with the abuse and the insensitive machinery to deal with sexual abuse. Sexual abuse spans class, caste, creed, colour and socio-economic status. Both girls and boys are vulnerable to sexual abuse, but the sheer physical strength of boys once they reach puberty reduces their vulnerability to some extent. Disabled children and particularly mentally challenged girls are always at even greater risk of sexual abuse than other girls.

There also exists a differential definition for "boys and girls". This is clearly seen in the Juvenile Justice Act, 2000 amended in 2006, which defines a male minor as being below 16 years and a female minor as being below 18 years of age. Further, in the Indian context the age of an individual in order to be determined as a "child" is NOT uniformly defined which offers various gaps in the legal procedure which is used by the guilty to escape punishment and also it confuses a layperson to take any firm action.

There is an urgent need to clarify variety of sexual activities that are involved to constitute Child Sexual Abuse as also the age of the child. Child abuse cases are handled under various sections of the Indian Penal Code, which are laws meant for adults. A separate law for crime against children with specific sections can address problems dealing with various offences against children, including sale/ transfer, sexual assault, sexual/physical/emotional abuse, commercial sexual exploitation, child pornography, grooming for sexual purpose, incest, corporal punishment, bullying and economic exploitation. This has to be in addition to other legislations within the IPC and the Juvenile Justice Act because these laws do not separately cover persons who commit crimes against children and some other categories of children under various circumstances of abuse, exploitation and neglect. However, simply making of law could never ensure the safety of children, unless it is taken seriously and implemented sternly.

Realities of childhood are unfold and untold. Each individual child has problems-hidden and visible, many a times even the visible ones are not addressed leave aside the hidden ones. Children have their own world of truth, realities, innocence and imaginations which is necessary for them to enjoy to successfully enter the youthhood. But it is a bitter fact that in today's world not all children are fortunate enough to have a happy and healthy childhood. Each adult is responsible to help children in making their childhood a real one by protecting them from any kind of abuse.

REFERENCES

Bohan, M.J (1997). Dissertation Abstracts International: Section B: The Sciences of Engineering, 57 (7-B), p. 4694.

Brayden, R.M. Ditrich, M.G.; Ditrich, M.S. and Sherrod, K.B. (1996). Child abuse and Negelect, 19, pp. 1255-1262.

Browne, A. Finklehor, D. (1986). Impact of child sexual abuse: A review of the research. Physcological Bulletin.

Finklehor, D., Hotalling, G.T. Lewis, I.A. and Smith, C. (1989). Sexual abuse and its relationship to later sexual satisfaction, marital status, religion and attitudes.

Finkelor, D. (1984). Child Sexual Abuse. New York. Free Press.

Finkelhor, D. and Berliner, L. (1995). Research on the treatment of sexually abused children: a review and recommendations. Journal of American Academy of child and adolescent Psychiatry.

Glasser, D. (2000). Child abuse and neglect and the brain; a review. Journal of Child Psychology and Psychiatry.

Glasser, D. and Frosh, S. (1993). Child Sexual Abuse. (2nd edition) London McMillan Press Ltd.

12

Influence of *Sexism* on Children in Elementary Education

Divya Pande

It is a concern of every educationist and social scientist that persistent gender bias is rooted in the social and educational-system and is operational worldwide in varying forms. The child undergoes informal and formal education which comprises of family values, fairy tales (informal) and elementary school (formal).

This paper attempts to trace it from the perspective of stereotyped roles. The influence of family and society is vital while fairy tales are analyzed to revisualise the paradigms which shape the children's romantic expectations and to illuminate psychic ambiguities which often confound contemporary children.

Any debate on Gender equality is insignificant and a sham if we choose to ignore the fact that most families and elementary literature implicitly accept the status-quo in terms of stereotypical gender-roles.

To Freud's 'Anatomy is destiny' Simmone de Beavior says 'Women are not born, women are made'. Rightly so in the social set up gender is differentiated by allocating specific roles to the males and females. This acculturation manifests itself from the very birth of the child where blue is attributed to a male child and pink to a female.

Home is the first school and family the first unit where the child learns to interact. The family is the most elementary unit of the society and hence the social values and norms play the most vital role in sensitizing the child or promoting sexism. Thus it becomes very crucial to monitor the role of the family and society as the initial educators of the child. It is well known that when a baby is born the biological or physical construction determines the 'sex' but it is hard to accept that other than few biological differences especially that in reproductive organs girls and boys are not different.

Biological differences are created by nature so they are same all over the world while the differences in their clothes, behaviour, education etc. are all socio-cultural and hence different across the world. They constitute the gender which evolves into sexism. Nature produces males and females; society turns them into men and women, feminine and masculine.

The society upholds that man is superior; woman inferior, man powerful, woman powerless and the child absorbs this. Instead of encouraging similarities between boys and girls, society and family keeps on emphasizing the difference. All over the world one finds that gender differences or sexism is mainly meant to promote patriarchal power but it is ironical that sexism is equally harmful for boys as well. Due to sexism several rigid roles, qualities and responsibilities are imposed upon boys. They too are prisoners and victims of gender and thus one finds that sexism brings irreversible harm to the entire community.

Surrounded by a sexist environment a child imbibes the differences allotted by the society to its sex and internalizes it. Because of the sexist social definitions the differences between boys and girls go on increasing. They accept it unconditionally that girls play with dolls within the house while boys play outdoors, girls help their mothers in the kitchen while the boys socialize and go out with friends, the boys are sent to better schools so that when they grow up, they can look after the family business or get good jobs while generally education of girls is only a means to prepare them for the future role of wives and mothers.

Again in the family itself motherhood is put as the women's ultimate goal which completes her. The concept of completeness in motherhood is passed on as culture from generation to generation by women themselves. All societies glorify the mother's spiritual strength, her moral superiority and her emotional sensitivity.

The traditions in the name of religion treasured by the family and imbibed in children emphasize that woman must be pure, patient, endure all suffering, be chaste because she is responsible for keeping the honour of her family. She is supposed to be reserved, obedient and not think for herself, as her highest duty is to care for her husband, home, and children. Hence the family emerges as the sexiest institution because here women's roles are defined solely in terms of others. The traditional roles for girls are daughter, wife, daughter-in-law, mother, mother-in-law and widow. Women are forced to change their last names to that of their last names to that of their husbands obliterating their identity.

Researches across the world have clearly indicated that children brought up in sexist households tend to uphold sexiest values whereas children reared in homes which do not promote sexism in ideology or behaviour tend to grow up as liberal adults. A child who sees the father helping in the kitchen and mother doing well in her career tend to transgress the social stereotyped roles.

This acculturation of promoting stereotyped roles and traits extends itself in fairy tales which are an intrinsic part of literature for children. While nurturing, care and passivity is associated with feminine; assertiveness, activeness and rationality are the male attributes.

In the process of growing up every child goes through a ritual of fairy tales loaded with gender. There is an internalization which stays with them making their foundation gendered as they absorb cultural norms where feminine stereotypes are glorified. Studying five popular fairy tales – Show White, Cinderella, Sleeping Beauty, Rapunzel and The Little Mermaid inherent sexism is exposed which colours the impressionable minds of the children. The effects of gender bias and sexiest stereotyping on the self-esteem, relationships and behavioral expectations of children are analyzed through these fairy tales.

In these entire tales one finds a marked similarity i.e. the absence of real women. The feminine qualities are glorified and the patriarchal status quo is maintained. The suffering of women is glamorized and the binaries of feminine and masculine are projected in a stereotyped manner.

Although the fairy tales are based on pure fantasy and are intended to develop a child's imaginative faculty yet one cannot deny the fact that in the impressionable years for children the difference between the reality and imagination gets blurred. These tales leave an everlasting effect on their minds and the first lessons or relationships outside their immediate family are learnt through them. In all in these stories a distinct gender colouring is visible and pre-dominant.

In the most popular fairy tale Snow White the first striking aspect is that all the negative characters are women. A stepmother cannot be anything but cruel and she is jealous of her daughters' beauty. The immediate concern of her existence seems to be 'Mirror Mirror on the Wall, which is the fairest of them all'. And when the mirror replies Snow White she immediately orders that Snow White is killed. Beauty is associated with whiteness; Snow White is beautiful because she is white as snow. This explains the fascination of white skin in children.

Surprisingly all the noble characters are males – the wronged father of Snow White who is tortured by his wife and eventually dies, the huntsman who is hired by the stepmother for killing Snow White is a compassionate man who cannot kill her and the dwarfs look after her justifying their role as providers. The sexiest stereotype begins when we see that the dwarfs go to work while Snow White stays back at home cooks, cleans and kisses them goodbye. They are the providers and Snow White a 'damsel in distress'. While they work she 'dances around hoping for her prince to come and rescue her. Again the scheming stepmother disguises herself and offers her the poisoned apple. Snow White is a naïve girl without any common sense and she eats the apple and falls in deep sleep. To restore her to senses the requisite is deep kiss of true love and so a prince comes riding by, kisses her and she wakes up to marry her prince charming and to 'live happily ever after'. Hence women are either naïve and foolish or scheming and treacherous while males are sensible creatures who are entitled to punish wicked women and rescue the gullible ones.

Children immediately internalize the gender-stereotype and accept the appropriate roles assigned to their gender. Little girls learn to feign helplessness and boys take up the role to assert their masculinity.

Another widely read fairy tale is that of **Cinderella** who suffers at the hands of her stepmother and cruel stepsisters. They are jealous of her beauty and ill-treat her by dooming her to a life of managing all household chores. The prince announces a feast where he would take the most beautiful girl as his bride. As always, being beautiful is the sole merit of the girls' life and all the girls of his kingdom make great preparations for the feast including Cinderella's two stepsisters. The focus is on good cloths and shoes making them the most important things in a female existence. Thankfully a fairy Godmother steps in and provides Cinderella with al the requisites to enhance her beauty. There is strange time-constraint but she goes to the feast and charms the prince. Lost in her conquest she forgets all about the time and hurrying back when the clock strikes twelve she forgets her glass-slippers. Now, the agenda for the prince is to find the mystique woman whom the glass-slipper will fit and when eventually it fits Cinderella to the dismay of her sisters, prince marries her and they live happily ever after. Again one cannot fail to see how gender stereotype works in this tale as well. The concept of virtuous maiden enamoring the male is presented and the sole aim of a girls' life seems to look beautiful and find a partner to look after her.

Similarly, **Sleeping Beauty** as the name suggests is the story of a girl who is cursed by a wicked fairy (female) into deep sleep. The spell of her curse will last until there is a kiss of true love. A prince representing the male attributes of power, chivalry and heroism reaches the palace, kisses her breaking the curse and marries her to live happily ever after.

In **The Little Mermaid**, Ariel is innocent gentle fish-maiden who is cheated by the sea-witch Ursula. The stereotype of innocuous and wicked female is perpetuated again. Ariel disobeys her father who signifies patriarchal-supremacy and as a result has to face grave-consequences. She falls in love with a prince and is changed into a human for three days. During this period she has to make the prince kiss her and then she would remain a human forever. Wickedness and treachery is further presented in the female garb of Ursula when she disguises herself as a lovely girl and steals Ariel's voice to woo the prince. Her mal intentions are exposed and the prince combats her for he is an embodiment of male-power and sense of fair play. Ariel gets back her voice, marries him and lives happily ever after.

In **Rapunzel**, the concept of beauty is associated with long black hair and white skin. She is trapped in a tower by a witch i.e. a female incarnation of evil and with the help of a prince she escapes, marries him and lives happily ever after.

Now, reading these fairy tales one cannot overlook the strong gender stereotype that works in them. They all are stories highlighting love and romance and inculcate romantic ideas where sexism pre-dominates. Marriage is presented as the ultimate bliss and kisses are magical and life giving. Absence of 'real women' is significantly marked, they are either virtuous maidens or evil temptresses and wooing men is the only worthy aim in their lives. The virtuous maidens cook, clean, sing and dance waiting for their prince to arrive while the wicked ones contrive and contemplate to make other women's life miserable. These tales present life as a permanent beauty contest where subconsciously girls transfer cultural norms from them into real life which exalts passivity, dependency and self-sacrifice as female cardinal virtues. They perpetuate the patriarchal status quo and glorify the suffering of women. Generally the innocent maiden passes through some common experiences like Separation from biological mother, Stepmothers persecutions, the father's desertion, Waiting and dreaming and Final awakening and rescue by the prince.

The feminine is presented as passive, submissive, sweet, emotional, intuitive damsel in distress and the masculine as active, dominant courageous, rational, logical knight in shining armour. Virtues like sacrifice, honour and delicacy are glorified and once they get married they live happily ever after. Anne Sexton has re-examined the concept of 'Lived happily ever after' in Transformations:

'Cinderella and the Prince
Live they say, happily ever after
Like two dolls in a museum case
Never bothered by diapers or dust
Never arguing over the timing of an egg
Never telling the same story twice
Never getting Middle Ages spread
Their darling smiles pasted on for eternity.'

[Anne Sexton 1971]

The fairy-tales are perpetuating a utopia for children presenting marriage as ultimate bliss while encouraging submissiveness in young girls. In modern scenario this equation needs an honest analysis for contemporary woman not only has to combat sexism in form of deep-rooted stereotypes but also has to address many other issues which deal with gender-discrimination. Globally the agendas are significantly different for women in developed and under-developed countries. While women in developed countries are concerned with sexiest attitudes, the state of powerlessness to change their condition in life is the prime concern for women in third-world countries. Kate Millet in **Sexual Politics (rep 1998)** defines 'patriarchy as a political institution' and speaks of 'power-structured relationships' where 'relationship of dominance and subordination exists between males and females. These fairy tales glamorize the same where women characters are simultaneously idolized, patronized or punished by their male counterparts. The supremacy of males is maintained throughout. The stereotypes gloss the females' inability to act self assertively and the fantasies are transferred into real lives which exalt acquiescence to the male power and make marriage the only state towards which women should aspire. They promote romanticization of marriage and reinforce the traditional gender roles emphasizing Physical beauty.

It is important to re-examine the stereotype concepts like- The stepmother, the wicked witch, the dutiful wife, innocent maiden, life as a beauty contest, the glamour of suffering and the associated binaries of feminine and masculine. It is also important to understand that the fairy tales present women oppressed from birth, insulated from the real world who inevitably grow up helpless and ignorant. They are like the 'conduct books' which recommend the womanly virtues of meekness, charity and exaggerated self-abnegation, stressing the central importance of modesty which is a polite synonym for chastity. The helpless princes and girls are told from their infancy that they must find a man to look after them and they learn to exploit their charms failing to realize that in the quest of waiting around for prince to come they might miss out on a lot of great experiences. These tales actually highlight masculine gallantry which in actual is an attempt to keep women in their places and the most 'feminine' women is one who best fulfills the fantasies of a male.

Talking about stories that are narrated to most Indian children in their most impressionable year's one often finds a translation of the western fairy tales or stories of kings and queens narrated to them. Here also the gender stereotype works very strongly since most of the princesses are made to wait for the eventual goal of their life which happens to be the wait of the prince charming. The prince is taught the art of valour and weapons preparing them for their future roles of kings. The significance of the stories from mythology cannot be ruled out in Indian context as well. These tales are meant to imbibe a strong value system in the child focusing on Indian traditions and culture. But ironically they also transmit the same sexist approach which they uphold as reaffirming the centrality of familial structures. The story of lord Rama and Sita, Draupadi and the Pandavas and Savitri and yamaraj perpetuate the concept of purity of woman and machismo of man. Marriage remains central in the lives of women and no sacrifice is too big for them if it is done to honour the men in their lives. Children see them as role-models and try it incorporate the same values in the lives of people around them and later in their own lives. Commenting on the fascination for 'rich and glorious' past of India in Indian children's books published today Sandhya Rao and Radhika Menon in 'the little magazine (Vol IV, issue 3, 2003) comment on the repition and monotony of the Ramayans and Mahabharats, along with the Panchatantra, the Hitopadesha, the Jataka, Vikram and Betal etc, "there are hundreds of books in thousands of versions, mostly indifferent, mediocre and downright deplorable, published by innumerable small, medium and big houses in the industry." The Indian obsession with moral stories for children takes us far away from the spirit of storytelling and further away from our own cultural space. "The text and pictures are replete with racial, sexist and communal overtones, banal writing, poor and often wrong use of language, plainly chauvinistic or downright insensitive dialogue, blandly rendered narrative and decontextualised perspective."

Further analyzing the textbooks one finds a strong stereotype where women are mothers and housewives and even in developed countries like Hungary and Holland are hardly portrayed outside their home environment. The situation now needs to be analyzed while exposing the binaries of culture/nature and Gender/Sex contrasted with biological male/female.

Gender Stereotype also works strongly in textbooks at pre-primary level where children are learning to read and write simple sentences. While 'Shyam eats his food', 'Mohan goes to work' and Raghu goes to play' once finds that 'Vimla cooks the meals' and 'Rita cleans the home'. These books transmit society as culture to children and they contribute to the image children develop of their own role and that of gender in society.

In a study done by Ernst (1995) where he analyses the title of books he notes that Male names represent nearly twice as female names and the names in titles revolve around the male characters.

Rudman's study (1995) shows that while girls are shown to achieve their goals due to help of others; boys are presented doing so by demonstrating ingenuity and courage. Infact most children's books frequently portray girls as acted upon rather than active. Similarly Purcell and Stewarts study (1990) analyzing 62 textbooks shows that in the textbooks boys are still portrayed many times as being forced to deny their feelings to show their manhood.

Researchers at a 1990 conference reported that even texts designed to fit within the guidelines of gender equity showed subtle language bias, neglect of scholarship on women, omission of women as developers of history and initiators of events, and absence of women from accounts of technological developments. (Bailey, 1992)

The gender-expression in textbooks is predominately masculine like 'Every citizen has the right to express his thoughts' and 'Each individual must be able to give of his best to the society'. When SCERT Delhi incorporated the change in Class VII Civics textbook by replacing his with her the critics reacted wondering if 'generic' woman could carry the burden of weighty public roles. The all inclusive generic 'man' leads to male gender associations whereas unspecified language ex 'people' reduces (though not totally eliminates) the tendency to think of men only. The studies reviewed by Schan and Scott (1984) demonstrated that among children sexist material contributes to more sex-typed attitudes whereas for fulfillment of individuals potential, a flexible gender-role attitude is necessary and thus equitable portrayals of male and female characters with both masculine and feminine traits are needed in children's textbooks.

It is however equally significant to point out the fact that woman has been nearly invisible in the documentations so far and their contributions have been intentionally marginalized. It relates to stereotyping of gender where women are projected as having made negligible contributions in the development of society perpetuating the myth that probably they were incapable of making any contribution. This consolidifies how gender biases work from primary level and find its way to the top.

The manner in which genders are represented in children's literature impacts their attitudes and perceptions of gender- appropriate behaviour in society. Sexism in literature can be so insidious that it quietly conditions boys and girls to accept the way they see and read the world, thus reinforcing gender images (Fox, 1993). This reinforcement pre-disposes children to not question existing social relationships. At the same time, however, books containing images that conflict with gender stereotypes provide children the opportunity to re-examine their gender beliefs and assumptions.

Sexism is also reinforced through curricular and extra-curricular means like craft and sports. Painting, making pencil stands, home science etc. are offered to girls whereas technical craft i.e. making model papers aeroplanes and repairing model cars to boys. Boys are encouraged to play professional sports like cricket, football etc. while girls play hide and seek, ringa roses and musical chairs.

Thorne's research (1993) about children's behaviour in schools shows that boys and girls recognize acceptable behaviour for their gender at early ages. She noted that this is often reinforced perhaps unwittingly, by teachers and school staff. Girls are more group-oriented, whereas boys maintain their argumentative and aggressive behaviour. Boys aggressive behaviour is accepted as natural or unchangeable and are often excused with the rationale that 'Boys will be boys'. These behaviours are socially reinforced by such rationales and sexism in textbooks reiterates this which is probably socially sanctioned by the schools themselves. The label of 'sissy' is given to boys who avoid tough aggressive play, including sports and those who exhibit any weakness through affection or tenderness. This is interpreted as a possibility of them becoming 'crossovers' and hence aggressiveness is encouraged. This is an obvious manifestation of the devaluation of feminine traits.

The socialization of gender in schools assures that the girls are made aware that they are unequal to boys. Every time students are seated or lined up by gender it is affirmed that girls and boys should be treated differently. In British Columbia, standardized testing indicates that girls outperform boys at all levels of reading and writing and in Alberta testing shows that girls 'significantly outperform boys on reading and writing tests, while almost matching them in Maths and Science' (O'Neill, 2000). Infact sexism within schools demonstrated that the girls are shortchanged in the classrooms.

Teachers socialize girls towards a feminine ideal. Girls are praised for being neat, quiet and disciplined whereas boys are encouraged to think independently and speak up. This socialization of feminity begins at the elementary level where girls begin to define themselves in relation to boys. Diane Reay (2001) studied Cl. III and examined four self-sorted groups of girls within the class room. The nice girls, the girlies, the spice girls and the tomboys. Through interview she found that 'nice girls' was considered a derogatory term indicating an absence of toughness and attitude. The girlies spend their time in flirting, tomboys played sports with boys and spice girls espoused girl power and rated the boys. 'Spice girls' were not approved by the teachers and this reinforces the notion that 'girls misbehaviour is looked upon as character defect, while boy's misbehaviour is viewed as a desire to assert themselves'. (Reay, 2001)

Often in elementary schools a notion is perpetuated that boys will excel in maths, science and technology and girls in arts. Such subtle and unintended messages can create the idea among girls and boys that there are fields they cannot be successful in because of their sex. Children reflect and reinforce this attitude through their peer interactions later in life.

A DEBATE

Gender and sexism is social, created by us and hence if we want to we can change it by creating new definitions of girls and boys. A society is desired where being a girl does not mean being inferior, weak and being a boy does not mean being harsh, domineering or violent. It is important to make the children learn that girls and boys can dress, play, study the way they want and grow up as they choose. Having a girls body does not mean confinement to household work or caring for others and a boys body does not ensure fearlessness, intelligence and strength. All these qualities are learnt so it is one's upbringing that determines one's growth.

Similarly there is never only one way to tell a story and all tales could be narrated with a contemporary colour. They are highly adaptable and many alterations could be incorporated in the plot. They are still compelling and researches reveal that the identity and self-esteem of children could be affected by negative portrayals of their gender.

Through these memorable characters a choice of life could be offered to a girl that is not dependent on men. Changes should be made to stimulate the children to take women more seriously and girls could be taught to trust their judgment making their own choices in life by developing their talents and educating themselves. Eventually when there would be choices, a perpetual wait for 'prince charming' will automatically become subtle and less significant. Cinderella or Snow White can go to work, drive their cars and find Love and companionship in their stepmothers. The endings could be made more substantial where these characters could be presented as girls who are self-reliant and have a distinct self-esteem. It is time now to make Cinderella an independent, modern and sensible girl.

However it is important to give gender- neutral texts to the children from the very elementary stage because all researches have shown that the family values and education of the early years of childhood shapes the individuals ideology and personality. .In his study Rudman (1995) talks about gender-neutral books where Individuals are portrayed with distinctive personalities irrespective of their gender and their achievements are not evaluated on this basis. He emphasizes on the Occupations to be represented as gender-free, clothing as functional and females not projected as weaker as and more delicate than males.

Further it becomes also equally important that in textbooks and story books the characters are shown to act logical or emotional not according to their gender but the situations, gender-free words are selected like 'law-enforcement officer' and 'mail-carrier instead of 'policeman' and 'mailman' and Committee-head for a 'Chairman'.

However, it is important to avoid books that have strident messages on gender- equity, as children tend to reject books that preach.

Sexism also needs to be eliminated from the environment of the classrooms. Temple suggests that Questions could be raised about the characters and children thereby encouraged reversing the gender of the individuals ex – what if the sleeping beauty was a boy? Further to this there is need of alternate role models, more egalitarian gender attitude, portrayal of males and females in non- traditional roles at work, at leisure and at homes and adoption of the opposite sexes point of view about a very gendered issue (Lawrence, 1995).

Unless teachers are made aware of the sexism and gender- free socialization which they are unintentionally imparting everyday, sexism would continue. They need to be provided with the methods and resources necessary to eliminate gender-bias in their classrooms like Mandatory gender-equity resource modules to in-service teachers. According to Sadker (1994) 'Until educational sexism is eradicated, more than half of our children will be shortchanged and their gifts lost to society'.

Outside the classrooms feminist pedagogy and multi-cultural education explicates the need for social change. A non-sexist environment is to be promoted where achievements are not evaluated on basis of gender and occupations are represented as gender-free.

Ironically, the patriarchal mind is cleverly manipulating gender and sexism to justify the concept of male superiority in our education and society beyond any inquiry. It is time now to re-examine the binaries of feminine and masculine as projected in a stereotyped manner. Substituting feminine for masculine is not merely a linguistic jargon and neither has it signified the role-reversal in a power game to intimidate men but it simply means the pursuit of gender-equality which is pivotal and the only way to a sustainable, just and sensitized society.

REFERENCES

Primary Sources

·Barthdine Donald (1967), Snow White, Touchstone Books, U.K.

Cinderella (2005), Sterling Publishers.

Sleeping Beauty (2005), Sterling Publishers.

Rapunzel (2005), Sterling Publishers.

The Little Mermaid (2005), Sterling Publishers.

Secondary Sources

Best, R. (1983). We've all got soars: what boys and girls learn in elementary School, Bloomington, In: Indiana University Press.

Davidson, K. (2001) 'Masculinities' in B.Frank (ed) Sexualities and Schooling., pp 74-89, Harfax, Nova Scotia: Fernwood.

Ernst, S.B. (1995), 'Gender issues in Books for Children and Young adults', in S.Lehr (ed) Battling Dragons: Issues and Controversy in children's Literature, pp. 66-78, Portsmouth, NH Heinemann.

Gipps, C., Maccallum, B., L. Hargreaves, (2000), What makes a good primary school teacher : Expert classroom strategies, New York : Routledge Falmer.

Groden M Angela L Mark A Gooden (1999), Gender Representation in Notable children's Picture books, Indiana University Press.

Millet Kate (rep 1998) Sexual Politics, University of Illinois Press.

Orenstein, P. (1994), Schoolgirls: Young women, self-Esteem and the Confidence Gap. New York, NY. Doubleday.

Rudman, M (1995), Children's Literature: An issues Approach (3 Ed) White Plains, NY: Longman.

Sadker, D., L Sadker, M. (1994a), 'The Miseducation of boys' in E.Rassen and L.Inra (eds.) The Jossey/Bass reader on Gender in Education, pp. 182-203, San Francisco. Jossey/Bass.

Sadker, D., Sadker, M (1994 b), Failing at Fairness: How our schools Cheat Girls, Toranto, ON: Simon and Schuster.

Sexton Anne (1971) Transformations, Houghton Mifflin.

Simone, De Beauvoir (1959), The Second Sex, Picador Classics, London.

Sprinthall, N.A., Sprinthall, R.C., and Oja, S.N. (1994), Educational psychology : A developmental approach (6th ed.) New York : McGraw hill.

Thorne, B. (1993), Gender Play. New Brunshick, NJ : Rutgers University Press.

Trites, R.S. (1997), Waking Sleeping Beauty: Feminist voices in childrens novels. Iowa City : University of Iowa.

JOURNALS

Bailey, S. (1992), 'How Schools shortchange Girls' : The AAUW Report. New York, NY: Marlome and Company, pp. 25-32.

Evans C, Jones, R. Byrd, R.Campbell, R (2000), 'Gender equality training and teaching behaviour' Journal of Instructional Psychology, 27(3): pp. 173-178.

Evans Lorraine (2000), 'No Sissy Boys here. A content Analysis of the Representation of Masculinity in Elementary School. Reading Textbooks; Sex Roles', A Journal of Research, pp. 123-29

Lawrence, B. (1995), 'Teaching ideas: Getting into gender issues', English Journal, 84(3), pp. 80-82.

O'Neill; T (2000), "Boys Problems don't matter', Report/ Newsmagazine (National edition) 27(15), pp. 54-56.

Rao Sandhya, Radhika Menon (2003), "Growing pains", contemporary children's literature in India, the little magazine, Vol IV, Issue 3, pp. 34-39.

Reay, D. (2001), 'Spice Girls', 'Nice Girls', 'Girlies' and 'Tomboys' Gender Discourses, Girls Cultures and feminities in the primary classroom'. Gender and Education,13(28), pp. 153-167.

Schan, C. and Scott, K (1984), 'Impact of gender characteristics of instruction materials. An integration of the research literature.' Journal of Educational Psychology, 26, pp. 183-193.

Temple, C. (1993), 'what if Beauty had been Ugly? A Reading against the grain of gender bias in childrens Books'. Language Arts, 70(2), pp. 89-93.

Index